CREATOR AND CREATION

Nature in the Worldview
of Ancient Israel

CREATOR & CREATION

RONALD A. SIMKINS

HENDRICKSON PUBLISHERS

Copyright © 1994 by Hendrickson Publishers, Inc.
P. O. Box 3473
Peabody, Massachusetts 01961–3473
All rights reserved
Printed in the United States of America

ISBN 1–56563–042–4

Library of Congress Cataloging-in-Publication Data

Simkins, Ronald.
    Creator and creation: nature in the worldview of ancient
Israel / Ronald A. Simkins.
        p. cm.
    Includes bibliographical references and indexes.
    ISBN 1–56563–042–4 (pbk.)
    1. Nature—Biblical teaching. 2. Creation—Biblical teach-
ing. 3. Human ecology—Biblical teaching. 4. Bible. O.T.—
Criticism, interpretation, etc. I. Title.
BS1199.N34S55 1994
261.8′3628—dc20   94–21262
                                                                            CIP

For Tammy Renee Simkins

TABLE OF CONTENTS

List of Illustrations   ix

Acknowledgements   xi

Introduction: The Bible and the Environment   1

1   Ecology, Worldview, and Values Toward Nature   15

2   Creation in the Ancient Near East   41

3   Creation in the Bible   82

4   God, Humans, and the Natural World   121

5   In the Beginning: The Creation Myths   173

6   In the End: The Eschatological Myths   207

Conclusion   252

Epilogue: The Bible and the Environmental
    Crisis   256

Select Bibliography   267

Index of Modern Authors   299

Index of Scripture References   303

LIST OF ILLUSTRATIONS

Figure 1   A Model of Human-Environment Relations 20

Figure 2   A Model of Worldview Dynamics 24

Figure 3   Integration of Worldview Universals 27

Figure 4   World Domains 29

Figure 5   Solutions to the Human-Relationship-to-Nature Problem 33

Figure 6   An Ancient Near Eastern Creation Model 75

Figure 7   Domains of Israel's Worldview 118

Figure 8   The Basic Israelite Worldview 119

Figure 9   A History-Oriented Worldview 125

Figure 10   A Nature-Oriented Worldview 126

Figure 11   A Horizontal Model of Sacred Space 134

Figure 12   A Vertical Model of Sacred Space 139

Figure 13   Ingroup/Outgroup Domains 169

Figure 14   Israel's Worldview and Values Toward Nature 171

Figure 15   The Status of Humans 191

Figure 16   The Six Days of Creation 196

Figure 17   The Biblical Writers' Worldview and Values Toward Nature 254

ACKNOWLEGEMENTS

This book is the product of six years of research and inquiry into the role of the natural world in the religion and culture of ancient Israel. During this period, I have benefited from the aid and inspiration of many people. I first became interested in this topic as a graduate teaching assistant for Theodore Hiebert at Harvard University. In his Divinity School course, "Problems in Biblical Theology: Nature," he introduced me to the importance of addressing the Bible's view of the natural world and inspired me along this path. More recently, I am indebted to a number of colleagues, Bruce J. Malina, Dennis Hamm, S.J., Roger Bergman, Susan Lawler, and Mary Ann Krzemien, who through discussion of ideas or critique of individual chapters have aided in clarifying and expressing my thesis. The members of the "Old Testament and Ecology" task force of the Catholic Biblical Association have served as a congenial forum for airing my ideas and have generously offered critique at critical junctures. Patrick H. Alexander and Shirley A. Decker-Lucke, academic editors of Hendrickson Publishers, have offered invaluable suggestions for making this book more accessible to the general reader.

The writing of this book was made possible by the generous grants of release time from my teaching responsibilities by Michael Proterra, S.J., dean of the Creighton College of Arts and Sciences, and the Summer Faculty Research Fellowship

(1993) by Michael G. Lawler, dean of the Graduate School, Creighton University.

I am especially indebted to my wife, Tammy. Her constant patience and support have greatly eased the burden of this project. The dedication of this book to her does not begin to express my appreciation and gratitude.

INTRODUCTION: THE BIBLE AND THE ENVIRONMENT

A NEW FOCUS ON THE BIBLE

Chances are, any book published before 1970 on the interpretation of the Bible contains little or no information on the Bible's view of the natural world or the role of Israel's environment in shaping its religion and culture. This is not for lack of biblical references to the natural world. Indeed, the Bible is replete with such references. It begins with two creation stories in which the creation of the natural world is given as much attention as the creation of human beings. God's appearance in the Bible is repeatedly described with natural images. Numerous passages focus on the condition of the natural world, whether it will be conducive or hostile to life, and several psalms and wisdom passages extol the splendor and complexity of the natural world. The natural world was neglected in biblical interpretation because biblical scholars had understood the Bible from an exclusively history-oriented, that is, human-oriented, perspective. Yahweh, the God of the Bible, was thought to be a God of human history. Unlike all other ancient Near Eastern gods, Yahweh acted in human affairs to save Israel and to guide human history according to his plan of salvation. The religion of Israel was thus considered to be a religion of history. The numerous biblical references to the natural world were either ignored or interpreted in reference to God's activity in history. Nature was the stage for the historical drama of salvation, or nature served as God's instrument in that drama, but the natural world was not considered to be significant in its own right.

The historical focus of biblical interpretation began to change in the 1970s. At the end of the preceding decade, the emerging public concern over the environmental crisis expressed itself in an assault on the relevance of the Bible. Because biblical scholars had neglected or historicized the biblical references to the natural world, the Bible was dismissed as detrimental to a stable and healthy environment. How could a biblical interpretation that devalues nature, subordinating it to human concerns, contribute to the preservation of the environment? Some critics even accused the Bible of fostering the current environmental crisis. Biblical scholars at last began to turn their attention to the Bible's view of the natural world. Rarely, however, did these scholars abandon their historical orientation or formulate a systematic interpretation of the role of the environment in the religion and culture of ancient Israel. Their initial concern was merely to defend the Bible by correcting what they perceived to be misinterpretations of particular biblical passages.

These attacks on the Bible have had an important effect on biblical interpretation. Although the environmentally concerned critics of the Bible have often failed to characterize accurately the Bible's view of the natural world, they have succeeded, often indirectly, in unmasking the interpretive biases that have led biblical scholars to neglect the natural world and its role within the religion and culture of ancient Israel. Biblical scholars have been exclusively history-oriented in their interpretation of the Bible. Biblical scholars have too readily dismissed the natural world from being a significant factor in the development of Israel's religion and culture.

Today, over twenty years later, the situation is more positive. For an increasing number of scholars, the role of the environment must be taken into account in the interpretation of the Bible and the Israelite religion and culture from which it emerged. The frequent biblical references to the natural world, for example, are now recognized as the expression of an essential feature of the religion of Israel. No longer can these references to the natural world be ignored or historicized. No longer can the role which Israel's experience of the natural world played in the development of its religion and culture be neglected. Public awareness of the environmental crisis and the ensuing attacks on the Bible served to bring the ecology of

Israel—that is, Israel's relationship to its environment—to the forefront of biblical interpretation.

In investigating the ecology of ancient Israel,[1] three issues appear to be central: first, the impact of the Israelites on their environment; second, the influence of the environment on the development of Israelite religion and culture; and third, Israelite attitudes toward nature (Hughes 1975:3). The first issue is the most difficult to address and has consequently attracted the attention of only a few scholars (see the exceptional work by Hopkins 1985, 1987). Not only did the Israelites inhabit the land of Palestine for a mere moment of human history, Palestine was subject to numerous military campaigns and was repeatedly exploited by neighboring peoples. Moreover, the biblical literature offers little aid in assessing the Israelites' impact on their environment. The second issue has recently received treatment by a number of scholars, especially those who employ the social sciences in their research. These scholars have demonstrated, for example, how the Palestinian environment both affected the formation of the state of Israel and shaped certain features of Israelite religion (notable examples include Frick 1985; Hopkins 1985; Meyers 1988; Eilberg-Schwartz 1990; Coote and Ord 1991). The third issue has received the most attention. In response to the assault on the Bible by environmentally concerned critics, many scholars have investigated the biblical attitudes toward the natural world (Trible 1971; Barr 1972; Baker 1975; Anderson 1975, 1984a; Koch 1979; Drumbell 1985; Williamson 1985; Malchow 1987; Bergant 1991). Nevertheless, no systematic interpretation of these attitudes has been presented.[2]

---

[1] Because ecology is a complex term, some definition is needed here. In its standard biological usage, ecology refers to the interrelationship between living things and their environment, and the study of this interrelationship. When applied to human societies, variously called human ecology or cultural ecology, ecology refers to how a society affects or is affected by its physical environment—the earth with its soil, water, and vegetation; the air and the weather; other living creatures (Hughes 1975:2–3). In this context, ecology is the "study of how and why humans use Nature, how they incorporate Nature into Society, and what they do to themselves, Nature, and Society in the process" (Bennett 1976:3).

[2] Although Malchow's brief attempt to describe the Bible's view of the natural world is the most comprehensive, it is unsuccessful

In this book I will offer a systematic interpretation of the attitudes, or values, that the ancient Israelites expressed toward the natural world by analyzing the worldview of the biblical writers and the values that ensued from it. To accomplish this task, I will employ two complementary models of cross-cultural analysis—a model of worldview analysis and a model of value orientations—which will highlight the implicit worldview of the biblical texts and the values that are rooted in it. By isolating the biblical writers' values toward their environment and by placing them within the context of their worldview, this book will make a further contribution toward an ecology of ancient Israel.

Because the study of Israel's relationship to its environment has been neglected in biblical interpretation until recently, it is important to place this new focus in historical context in order to avoid some of the pitfalls of the past. Therefore, in the remainder of this introduction I will present the historical background of this study. An examination of two watershed figures in the history of modern biblical interpretation proves helpful in this regard.

HUMAN DOMINION OVER NATURE: LYNN WHITE

Lynn White is not a biblical scholar but a historian of medieval history, specializing in the development of technology. Nevertheless, in a frequently published essay entitled "The Historical Roots of Our Ecologic Crisis," White argued that modern technology and science, the means by which we exploit the natural environment, can be traced ultimately to the biblical religion. He claimed that the religion of the Bible, with its idea of linear history and perpetual progress, disenchanted the natural world. Nature was transformed from a

---

because he treats the biblical writers' views of nature in isolation. He identifies two contrasting and contradictory biblical views of nature: On the one hand, the natural world has been corrupted by human sin and can only be redeemed in the *eschaton* (prophetic literature); on the other hand, the natural world has remained good, and humans can learn from it (wisdom literature). However, without analyzing the systemic worldview in which these views of nature are rooted, he is unable to explain their relationship or how they are contradictory.

subject to be revered to an object to be used. "By destroying pagan animism, Christianity made it possible to exploit nature in a mood of indifference to the feelings of natural objects" (1967:1205). For Lynn White, the Bible's creation account most clearly and persuasively articulates Christianity's anthropocentrism. In the creation account, the first man

> named all the animals, thus establishing his dominance over them. God planned all this explicitly for man's benefit and rule: no item in the physical creation had any purpose save to serve man's purposes. And, although man's body is made of clay, he is not simply part of nature: he is made in God's image. (1205)

White concluded that, according to the biblical text, "it is God's will that man exploit nature for his proper ends" (1205).

Because, White argued, our modern science and technology grew out of the Christian attitude of humankind's transcendence and superiority over nature, more science and more technology cannot solve our environmental problems. Rather, the Christian religion that is at the root of the problem and continues to justify human misuse of nature needs to be reformulated. White himself favored the theology of Saint Francis of Assisi, for Francis "tried to depose man from his monarchy over creation and set up a democracy of all God's creatures" (1206). Nature is not simply material substance for human consumption; it is independent of humankind and was designed for the glorification of the creator. In contrast to the arrogance toward nature that White claimed characterizes orthodox Christianity, he argued that the Franciscan emphasis on the humility of the human species and the spiritual autonomy of all parts of nature points us in the right direction in order to solve our environmental crisis.

Lynn White's essay caused an immediate sensation. Although White's arguments were neither new nor complete, his treatise has been accepted, reprinted, and preached as gospel by innumerable environmental enthusiasts (Derr 1975:40–43). It has become the banner around which all those who need a convenient culprit for the crisis rally. Some Christian theologians have even taken up the charge that the biblical view of nature is responsible for the current crisis and have provided further theological rationales to justify the charge. Gordon Kaufman, for instance, argues that the biblical anthropocentrism that

White identifies as the root of the environmental crisis is
intrinsic to Christian theology (1972:349–59).

Despite the popularity and influence of White's essay,
there is no shortage of critics of its essential theses. Historians,
on the one hand, argue that modern science and technology do
not have their origin in the Christian, or biblical, worldview.
Modern science can be traced back at least to the classical
Greek culture. Moreover, Christianity and science have often
had an antagonistic relationship (Sessions 1974:73–76; Barr
1972:18–19). Biblical scholars, on the other hand, argue that
White's interpretation of the creation account and the biblical
view of nature inherent in it is distorted. He misunderstands
what the Bible means by both "dominion" and "the image
of God" and has failed to read the texts in their own historical context (Trible 1971; Barr 1972; Anderson 1975; Hiers
1984:43–45). The most damaging argument against White's
central thesis, however, is that destruction of the environment
has not been nor is now the exclusive prerogative of Christian
cultures. Environmental abuse knows no race, creed, or gender. The human species is the only common denominator.

> All over the globe and at all times in the past, men have pillaged
> nature and disturbed the ecological equilibrium, usually out of
> ignorance, but also because they have always been more con-
> cerned with immediate advantages than with long-range goals.
> Moreover, they could not foresee that they were preparing for
> ecological disasters, nor did they have a real choice of alterna-
> tives. If men are more destructive now than they were in the
> past, it is because there are more of them and because they
> have at their command more powerful means of destruction,
> not because they have been influenced by the Bible. (Dubos
> 1972:162)[3]

While it is true that Christian theology and the Bible have been
used to justify exploitation of natural resources (some of the
comments of a notorious former Secretary of the Interior, James
Watt, come to mind), Christianity is not the culprit in the
environmental crisis. The causes of the current crisis are complex and diverse.

---

[3] The invaluable study by Hughes outlines how the Greek and
Roman attitudes toward nature, in particular, had destructive consequences for their environment.

> The major factors in the emergence of antiecological attitudes and actions were not Christian axioms, but rather population pressures, the development of expansionistic capitalism in the forms of commercialism and industrialization (particularly ship-building, glassworks, iron and copper smelting), the triumph of Cartesian mechanism in science (which meant the "death" of nature, since it represented the defeat of organic assumptions, and the victory of the view that nature is "dead," inert particles moved by external forces), and the triumph of Francis Bacon's notions of dominion as mastery over nature. (Nash 1991:75)

White's conclusions cannot be accepted.

Lynn White stands as a watershed figure in the history of biblical interpretation because his attack on the biblical tradition forced scholars to examine the Bible's view of the natural world and especially its presentation of humankind's relationship to nature. By focusing on a few texts, White himself accused the Bible of fostering a despot model of humankind's role in the natural world; humans were to have authority and power over nature so that they could use it as they saw fit. Biblical scholars, in response, have argued that the Bible more accurately promotes a stewardship model for understanding the human relationship to nature; rather than exploit nature, humans are commissioned to care for the natural world. Unfortunately, biblical scholars have rarely moved beyond defending the biblical tradition from attack. Interpreting the Bible's view of the natural world is still too often dominated by White's agenda. Discussion of the relationship of humankind to nature usually is limited to those biblical passages employed by White himself. Biblical scholarship has thus failed to articulate adequately the biblical writers' attitudes toward the natural world.

CREATION SUBORDINATE TO REDEMPTION: GERHARD VON RAD

If Lynn White misinterpreted the Bible's view of the relationship between humans and the natural world, as biblical scholars have held, he can be excused, for he simply echoed the dominant position of biblical scholarship at that time. Compare, for example, Harvey Cox's popular assessment of this relationship, published only two years before White's famous essay:

Just after [God's] creation man is given the crucial responsibility of naming the animals. He is their master and commander.
It is his task to subdue the earth. Nature is neither his brother
nor his god. As such it offers him no salvation. When he looks
up to the hills, Hebrew man turns from them and asks where he
can gain strength. The answer is, Not from the hills, but from
Yahweh, who *made* heaven and earth. For the Bible, neither
man nor God is defined by his relationship to nature. This not
only frees both of them for history, it also makes nature itself
available for man's use. (1967:23)

Cox then went on to boast that the biblical disenchantment of
the natural world provided the necessary precondition for the
development of modern science and technology. From this perspective, White simply outlined the inherent dangers of such an
interpretation.

Prior to the controversy generated by White's essay,
biblical scholars largely ignored the role that the natural
world played in the Bible; instead, they emphasized God's
activity in and on behalf of human history. According to this
interpretation, the Bible is concerned exclusively with human
salvation. God acts in human history in judgment and in
deliverance in order to guide that history towards its final
consummation when God's people will be redeemed. As for
the natural world, biblical scholars considered it to be merely
the stage for the historical drama. It served as a passive instrument which God could utilize in the actualization of history's
divine plan.

This history-oriented interpretation of the Bible is widespread and rooted deeply in biblical scholarship. It can be
traced back directly as far as Hegel, who articulated in his
philosophy of history a dichotomy between history and nature
(Simkins 1991:3–10; cf. Santmire 1985), and few biblical scholars have escaped its influence. This manner of interpretation
is especially popular among scholars concerned to distinguish
the biblical religion, which is characterized as a religion of
history, from the so-called nature religions of Israel's Near
Eastern neighbors (Kaufmann 1960; Wright 1952, 1957). Of the
many prominent and influential scholars in this historical
tradition (Childs 1970:13–87; Oden 1987:1–39), Gerhard von
Rad stands out as a watershed figure in the interpretation of
the role of the natural world in the Bible.

In a seminal essay, von Rad addressed the question of how the dominant faith of the Old Testament, based on the notion of election and therefore primarily concerned with redemption, is theologically related to the belief that Yahweh is also the creator ([1936]1984). In answer to this question, von Rad stood firmly within the historical tradition: "Our main thesis was that in genuinely Yahwistic belief the doctrine of creation never attained to the stature of a relevant, independent doctrine. We found it invariably related, and indeed subordinated, to soteriological considerations" ([1936]1984:142). He based this conclusion on three observations from the biblical texts. First, neither Hosea nor Deuteronomy, books that attest to a vehement opposition against the so-called nature religion of the Canaanites, base their attack on the doctrine of creation. Instead of asserting that Yahweh is the originator and sustainer of the natural order, Hosea and the deuteronomic theologians preferred to recall Yahweh's historical acts of redemption on behalf of Israel. Second, in the passages that refer to both the doctrines of creation and redemption (Pss 33, 74, 89, 136, 148, and numerous passages in Isa 40–55), either the two doctrines stand side by side, unrelated to each other, or the belief in creation is wholly subordinate, so that "it is but a magnificent foil for the message of salvation, which thus appears the more powerful and the more worthy of confidence" ([1936]1984: 134). Finally, those passages that treat the doctrine of creation exclusively (Pss 8, 19, 104) contain conceptions and influences that are foreign to the heart of the biblical faith. According to von Rad, they most likely originated in late wisdom circles that were influenced by Egyptian thought.

In analyzing Israel's belief in creation, von Rad gave attention to its theological structure rather than to its development. He admits that the early Israelites must have had a belief in creation from the beginning, but he denies that creation ever became a theologically significant doctrine:

> Evidently a doctrine of creation was known in Canaan in extremely early times, and played a large part in the cultus in the pre-Israelite period through mythical representations of the struggle against primeval chaos. Yahwistic faith early absorbed these elements, but because of the exclusive commitment of Israel's faith to historical salvation, the doctrine of creation was never able to attain to independent existence in its own right. ([1936]1984:142)

Everywhere in the Bible, Israel's belief in creation is theologically subordinate to Israel's primary faith in redemption. Even the elaborate priestly creation account in Genesis 1, von Rad claims, does not present creation for its own sake but rather as the first stage in God's redemptive history.

Although von Rad later somewhat modified his conclusions ([1964]1984), his basic thesis that the doctrine of creation serves an ancillary function for Israel's doctrine of redemption has remained dominant in biblical scholarship. The result of his study has been the further polarization of history and nature in biblical interpretation. If Israel's faith is primarily concerned with the history of human redemption, why should scholars give attention to the role of nature in the Bible? What can it contribute toward understanding Israel's faith? Even the biblical creation faith itself is not so much about the natural world that God created but rather "an expression of confidence in the Creator's power to save, of his rulership over the tumultuous forces of history" (Anderson [1967]1987:99). Thus von Rad articulated a theological rationale that has served to justify neglect of the interrelationship between Israel and its environment.

A critique of von Rad's interpretation of the biblical doctrine of creation will be presented in a following chapter. At this point I simply want to emphasize von Rad's critical role in the history of biblical interpretation. Von Rad presupposed the long-established dichotomy between history and nature, and from this perspective he viewed history as the arena of God's activity. Consequently, even God's activity in nature—such as in creation (God creating nature), blessing (God working through the processes of nature), and theophany (God appearing in nature)—was understood to have historical purposes. The natural world itself lacked any theological import. In subsequent discussion of the relationship between humans and nature, then, biblical scholars tended only to accentuate the dissimilarity between humankind and the natural world; the God of Israel had acted in history to free humankind from the constraints of nature. No longer were humans bound to the unchanging cycles of nature, for the historical activity of God made human progress and development possible. Humans were thus free to control nature rather than simply be subject to it. It is in accord with this interpretation that Lynn White first raised the sound of alarm.

This brief historical sketch highlights the two main obstacles that any investigation focusing on the ecology of ancient Israel, and the Israelite attitudes toward nature in
particular, must face. On the one hand, this focus flies in the
face of an earlier, dominant wisdom of biblical scholarship that
gave little attention to and found no role for the natural world
in the religion and culture of ancient Israel. As a result, long-
held assumptions and conclusions of biblical interpretation
must be reformulated. On the other hand, the work that has
been done on the Bible's view of the natural world too often
has been made only as a defense against White's attack. Such
treatments have been partial and have often been driven by
contemporary concerns. No systematic interpretation of the
biblical values toward nature has yet been offered.

THE ISRAELITES' PERCEPTION OF NATURE

Before examining the values that the ancient Israelites
expressed toward the natural world and the worldview in
which they were rooted, one final issue needs to be addressed.
Because the Hebrew language has no term for the abstract
category of "nature," some biblical scholars have claimed that
Israel had no concept of nature that would correspond to
our modern idea. Israelites instead used concrete expressions,
such as "the heavens and the earth" (Gen 1:1) or "the earth . . .
and all that is in it" (Ps 24:1), to refer to the natural world. It
would therefore be inappropriate, scholars have asserted, to
apply our abstract concept of nature to the biblical texts. This
statement by von Rad is typical:

> We must not transfer uncritically our accustomed ways of
> thinking to Israel. We must, rather, face the exacting demand of
> thinking ourselves into ideas, in a 'view of life', which are
> unfamiliar to us. A beginning could already be made if we fully
> realized that Israel was not aware of this or that entity which
> we almost automatically take as objects of our search for knowl-
> edge, or at least always include in our thought processes as part
> of the given framework of that search. She did not differentiate
> between a 'life wisdom' that pertained to the social orders and
> a 'nature wisdom', because she was unable to objectify these
> spheres in the form of such abstractions. This can easily be
> shown in the case of the concept 'nature', a concept which has

become so indispensable to us but of which Israel was quite definitely unaware. Indeed, if we use the term in the interpretation of Old Testament texts, then we falsify something that was quite specific to Israel's view. (von Rad 1972b:71)

Certainly von Rad's warning that we cannot simply use our abstract concepts to interpret Israel's concrete beliefs is warranted, but did the Israelites really have a different conception of nature from our own?

In order to adequately address this issue, we must first distinguish between the various ways in which we use the term "nature." Of the numerous usages of "nature" listed in the *Shorter Oxford English Dictionary*, two definitions stand out as relevant for this discussion:

1. The creative and regulative physical power which is conceived of as operating in the physical world and as the immediate cause of all its phenomena.

2. The material world, or its collective objects or phenomena, the features and products of the earth itself, as contrasted with those of human civilization.

With regard to the first definition, the ancient Israelites would have simply labeled this power "God" (Robinson 1946:1). God was understood to be the creative and regulative force behind all phenomena in this world. The ancient Israelites had no conception of a natural force independent of God.

In relation to the second definition, however, the Israelites undoubtedly shared our recognition of the natural world as something material and non-human. The fact that they used concrete expressions rather than an abstract concept to communicate this recognition does not negate this. It is useful to examine the difference between how the Israelites experienced the natural world and how they discussed or understood their experience. Although this distinction is not always clear cut, in that experience is often affected by understanding, it serves the heuristic purpose of clarifying what is at issue in our investigation. For instance, it is inconceivable that the Israelites would have experienced a rain shower or the heat from a fire differently than we do, but it would not be surprising if they attributed a different significance to these aspects of nature. Certainly the ancient Israelites were aware of the regularities of the natural world—the falling of objects toward the earth, the behavior of animals, the courses of the sun and moon, the seasonal cycle—even though they did not formulate "natural laws" (Rogerson 1977:67–73).

Israel's experience of nature, of course, was determined by its own peculiar environment. The Israelites knew the adversity of Palestine's rugged terrain, the barrenness of Judah's desert, the vastness of the Mediterranean, and the fertility of the lowlands and valleys. They lived in a climate that oscillated between a hot dry summer and a mild wet winter. They withstood earthquakes, thunderstorms, and sirocco winds. They were surrounded by a wide range of plants and animals that were at home in the eastern Mediterranean environment. In fact, the ancient Israelites encountered the natural world in much the same way as people who live in the land of Israel today (Ben-Yoseph 1985; Lipshitz and Waisel 1980; Drori and Horowitz 1988/9).[4] Although their experience of nature was different from that of a North American in that they lived in a different environment, it was not significantly so. If the Israelites had a different conception of nature from our modern idea, undoubtedly it was in their understanding of their experience of the natural world rather than in their experience itself.

Overview

The Israelites' understanding of the natural world was shaped directly by their values toward nature and the world-view in which those values were rooted. In the following chapters, I will present an interpretation of the ancient Israelites' worldview and values toward nature. In chapter 1, I will place this investigation within the context of ecology and outline the two primary models that will facilitate this investigation: a model of worldview dynamics and a model of value orientations. Because the biblical writers did not explicitly articulate their worldview or their values toward nature that are derived from it, it is necessary to construct a model of their worldview that can account for the biblical texts as if they were predicated on this worldview. To this end, creation myths and

---

[4] For detailed studies of Israel's environment, see Baly 1974, Aharoni 1979, and Hopkins 1985.

metaphors are especially helpful for they encode the fundamental assumptions of a culture—they focus on the relationship between God, humans, and the natural world that is
essential to a worldview and illustrate the basis for values
toward nature. By examining creation metaphors in ancient
Near Eastern literature and in the Bible, I will construct in
chapters 2 and 3 a model of the basic Israelite worldview.

In chapter 4 I will outline the range of the Israelites'
values toward nature by further examining the interrelationship of the central worldview components—God, humans, and
the natural world—through the specific topics of theophany
and covenant. By taking into account the different orientations
resulting from ingroup/outgroup dynamics, we can integrate
the diverse Israelite values toward nature into a single model
of the Israelite worldview. Chapters 5 and 6 will treat the
creation myths of Genesis and their reflection in the prophetic
corpus. These chapters will complete the construction of the
model of the Israelite's worldview by analyzing the values
toward the natural world expressed in this literature.

Finally, because concern over the environmental crisis
served as a catalyst for this new focus on the role of the natural
world in the religion and culture of Israel, at the end of this
study I will consider the role that the Bible might play in the
discussion of the current crisis. Although the ancient Israelite
worldview and values toward nature are culturally specific,
they present a symbolic perception of reality that may serve
to critique our values toward and treatment of the natural
environment.

1
ECOLOGY, WORLDVIEW, AND VALUES TOWARD NATURE

In recent years a new focus has emerged in biblical interpretation on the role played by the natural world in shaping the religion, culture, and attitudes toward nature of the ancient Israelites. Earlier biblical interpretation precluded this focus. As outlined in the Introduction, scholars interpreted the Bible from an exclusively history-oriented perspective. They focused on the events of human history and God's activity in human affairs, but not on the relationship between humans and the natural world. They claimed that the natural world did not play a significant role in the development of Israelite religion and culture and that the Israelites attributed no divine qualities or importance to nature. Nature was viewed as physical material created by God for human use. Earlier biblical scholars simply did not deem the natural world to be a significant category of investigation. Consequently, readers of the Bible who are interested in ancient Israel's relationship with its environment are faced with a twofold dilemma: How can this subject be investigated, and how can the data resulting from an investigation be organized into a meaningful interpretation?

At issue in this dilemma are both the methods and the models of interpretation. Methods are the techniques applied to the biblical texts in order to extract data. The kind of data being searched for will determine the type of method applied. Methods are like tools in that each tool has a specific purpose.

If a reader is interested in isolating the literary strands of Genesis, for example, the reader will apply the methods of source criticism to the text. These methods are effective because they draw the reader's attention to discrepancies and incongruities in a literary text. They produce the desired kind of data. In contrast, the methods of narrative criticism would not be productive for this task because they draw attention to the unity of a text. These methods have a different purpose. Similarly, if a reader intends to investigate Israel's relationship with its environment, the reader should employ methods that are able to extract this kind of data. Although the natural world has been a neglected category of inquiry, many of the traditional methods of modern biblical interpretation are still useful in this task. These and some newer methods such as social science criticism will be employed where appropriate in this investigation.

Although the appropriate methods can generate data relevant for understanding Israel's relationship with its environment, methods are insufficient to produce this understanding. Data by themselves are meaningless. They are isolated "facts." The data become meaningful—they give rise to understanding—only when they are organized in relation to a meaningful frame of reference. This is the role of models. In other words, a model provides the means for assessing which data are relevant, the quality of the data, and the relationship between the data (Carney 1975:3–4).

A model is simply an organizing framework for data. It is a symbolic abstraction of reality, a simplification of real-world relationships (Barbour 1974:34–42). A model functions to select, integrate, and interpret data. First, a model is selective in that it restricts our attention to the kinds of data that are thought to be relevant. Other data are ignored and excluded from interpretation. Each model thus has a specific range of usefulness, determined by the scope of its selectivity. Like methods, different models are appropriate for different purposes. Second, a model is integrative in that it brings disparate data into relationship. It relates one datum to another and ranks the importance of the data. It establishes a configuration of data much like a conceptual map. Third, a model is interpretive in that it enables the data to make sense. The configuration of data can be explained in reference to the model, and this data can be related to other configurations. Models vary in their type and level of abstraction, but there is no meaning, understanding, or interpretation without models.

Let me return to the example of the literary strands in Genesis. Without a model of literary composition, the methods of source criticism yield only a number of literary discrepancies: that the style of Genesis 1 is different from Genesis 2, that their content is contradictory, that the name of God varies from passage to passage, that the text is needlessly repetitive. However, the relevance of these discrepancies and the relationship of the discrepancies one to another, or to literary strands, cannot be established. Only when the discrepancies are organized according to a model, such as the documentary hypothesis, can the data make sense. According to the documentary hypothesis, the data resulting from source criticism can be explained in terms of three literary strands which were written over several centuries and edited together. Alternative models, however, would interpret the same data differently, as recent challenges to the documentary hypothesis attest (Rendtorff 1993).

Although the above example illustrates the function of models, it is not meant to present an unrealistic possibility, that is, the use of methods without models. "The hard fact is that we do not have the choice of whether we will use models or not. Our choice, rather, lies in deciding whether to use them consciously or unconsciously" (Carney 1975:5). We use most models unconsciously. We have either inherited them along with our cultural perception of reality, or we have learned and embraced them as dogma, no longer recognizing them as models. These models, as long as they remain unacknowledged, restrict the scope of interpretation. They do not allow the interpreter to explore alternative perceptions of reality. Being conscious of models, on the other hand, frees the interpreter from the constraints of his or her own cultural perceptions. Through the conscious use of models, the interpreter is able to perceive the data in new ways, enabling the data to give rise to new meaning.

The dilemma for readers interested in Israel's relationship with its environment is this: The dominant models of biblical interpretation have not had as their purpose the investigation of this relationship, and so they exclude relevant data. Because the role played by the natural world in the religion and culture of Israel has long been neglected by biblical scholars, the models constructed by biblical scholars have not included nature as a significant variable. These models are history-oriented, emphasizing God's activity in human affairs. New models of interpretation are thus needed. This chapter presents three models of interpretation, each representing a different level of abstraction, each giving explicit attention to the relationship between ancient Israel and its environment.

A MODEL OF HUMAN-ENVIRONMENT RELATIONS

In order to understand ancient Israel's relationship with its physical environment, we need to construct an ecological model that can incorporate the complex interaction between human society and the natural world. The building of such a model, however, has proved to be difficult (Ellen 1982 presents a thorough discussion of the merits and failures of various approaches). Early studies of ecology argued for an environmental determinism or an environmental possibilism. Whereas adherents to the former theory claimed that a society's cultural makeup is attributable to its geography and climate—that is, culture is determined by environment—adherents to the latter theory successfully demonstrated that the environment limits but does not determine cultural development. Julian Steward offered a mediating position by arguing that human societies are adaptations to their environment. The purpose of "cultural ecology" is thus "to ascertain whether the adjustments of human societies to their environments require particular modes of behavior or whether they permit latitude for a certain range of possible behavior patterns" (Steward 1955:36; cf. Sahlins 1964).[1]

None of these approaches to ecology is adequate. Environmental determinists were only able to highlight correlations between variables of environmental configurations and human societies (such as the correlation between mean annual rainfall and population density). But they were unable to demonstrate a direct causal connection in this correlation. Because of the complexity of environmental and human systems, "simple uni-directional causal processes seldom occur in human environmental relations" (Ellen 1982:20). Possibilists, on the other hand, gave too little weight to the impact

---

[1] Steward's "cultural ecology" has been applied to the study of religions by Hultkrantz 1979. See also the critique by Bjerke 1979.

of the environment on human societies. They assumed that culture was *sui generis* and that the immediate cause of all cultural phenomena was other cultural phenomena. However, although they acknowledged that the environment limits human society, they failed to recognize that the environment thereby helps to determine the outcome of social development. Possibilism turns out to be the inverted formulation of environmental determinism. Steward's cultural ecology is similarly problematic. Although he emphasized the interaction of human societies and the environment, he assumed a causal correlation between them that could not be demonstrated. Each of these causal theories has failed because, in addition to the large number of variables in the interaction between human society and the environment, it must also incorporate the dynamics of human choice, which are not always under the control of systemic processes. As a result, recent studies in ecology have refrained from attributing causality to environmental or social configurations. Ecology can only provide a frame of reference, a model, for studying specific aspects of the human-environment interaction and for integrating those studies with one another. It cannot offer an all-encompassing theory of social formation (Ellen 1982:275–77).

Although ecology cannot offer a general theory explaining the development of Israelite religion and culture, it can provide an appropriate frame of reference for studying ancient Israel's relationship with its environment. In the Introduction I outlined three areas of investigation for understanding the ecology of Israel: the impact of the Israelites on their environment, the influence of the environment on the development of Israelite religion and culture, and Israelite attitudes toward nature. Each of these areas of investigation is sufficiently complex to require a distinct study, including the use of numerous ecological models. In this book I will specifically address the third area and will employ two complementary models for this task. Ecology can offer an overarching model that defines the interrelationship between these three areas of investigation and places each of them within its broader ecological context. Such a model is diagrammed in figure 1 (adapted from Bennett 1976:38).

This model of human-environment relations is based on two major premises. First, humans are the major agents of change in both the environment and society, and that this change is motivated by *sui generis*, uniquely human and un-predictable, forces. This premise is based on the observation that the current environmental crisis has resulted from the human capacity to exploit the environment beyond natural constraints. Humans are able to transform nature into energy at exponential rates and to produce goods of symbolic value with no biological necessity (Bennett 1976:40–49). Second, the natural world is increasingly incorporated into human affairs. Everywhere humans go on this planet, they claim the natural world as part of their domain. "Humans are constantly engaged in seizing natural phenomena, converting them into cultural objects, and reinterpreting them with cultural ideas" (Bennett 1976:4). Consider, for example, U.S. national parks. They represent our federal government's attempt to preserve selected regions of our natural heritage. They are areas of nature, but they have been wholly incorporated into our culture. They are *our* parks, icons of *our* heritage. The parks themselves are human conventions. They are defined by humans, often ignoring ecological boundaries, and are managed by humans. Humans are unable to exist in nature without altering and possessing it.

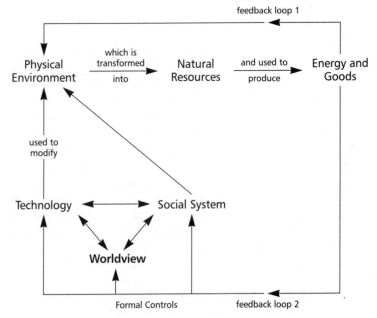

Figure 1. A Model of Human-Environment Relations

Because of the determinative role that humans play in their relationship with the environment, the ecological model of this relationship emphasizes humankind's use of the natural world. The primary component of this model is humankind's transformation of the physical environment into natural resources that can be used to produce both energy and goods. This unique capacity of humans highlights how our relationship to the environment differs from that of other species. Only humans can conceptualize elements of the physical environment as natural resources and place symbolic value on those resources according to what can be produced from them.

The other major components of the model are technology, social system, and worldview. Technology and social system function as instrumentalities. They are the means by which humans produce energy and goods. Technology, of course, refers to the tools and machines that we use to transform the physical environment into resources. But technology is not sufficient in itself to effect this transformation. "In order to produce goods the society must be mobilized in a certain manner. An adequate population base must be present, labor must be supplied, and talents must be recognized and employed" (Bennett 1976:51). As a component of this model, the social system represents primarily the population of the society, its differentiation into professions and classes, the channels of interaction among the members of the society, and the structures and vehicles of power. Finally, the worldview component in this model encompasses the dynamics of human choice. Technology and the social system do not act on the environment according to determinate patterns. They are affected by human choice, which is an unpredictable variable. Human choice in turn is influenced by value preferences which define the reasons for acting, by desires of the people involved and by the purposes that have been defined for the actions. Worldview represents the mental functioning that directs human actions.

The lines and arrows of the model on page 20 represent the interrelationships among the components and the direction of influence and causality. Some of the lines point in only one direction, indicating direct, unilateral influence. For example, technology affects the physical environment, but not vice versa. Technology, social system, and worldview, however, are joined by double-arrow lines which indicate that these components have a reciprocal relationship. A people's worldview both shapes and is shaped by its social system and technology. Similarly, the use of technology is limited by the social configuration, whereas the complexity of social system itself is dependent upon the level of technology. The two longer lines represent the major feedback loops in the system. The production of energy and goods impacts the physical environment (feedback loop 1) and influences the worldview, social system, and technology of the people (feedback loop 2). Although feedback of this type generally serves to regulate an ecosystem, in human ecosystems this feedback has been histori-cally unable to prevent human abuse and overuse of the physical environment. As a result, humans have introduced artificial means of regulation (formal controls), such as environmental protection laws, in order to preserve the environment and so protect their capacity to maintain their standard of living.

Although this generalized model of human-environment relations is inadequate for investigating the ecology of ancient Israel, other than at the most abstract level, it does underscore the systemic interrelationship between the diverse components of this ecology. In particular, it emphasizes the interrelationship between the Israelites' impact on their environment (feedback loop 1), the development of their religion and culture (feed-back loop 2), and their values toward the environment (world-view). On the one hand, the Israelites' production of energy and goods influenced the development of their religion and culture and impacted their environment. On the other hand, the Israel-ites' capacity to produce energy and goods was determined by their level of culture (social system and technology) and the condition of the physical environment. As a result, the Israel-ites' production of energy and goods might have impacted the environment in such a way (e.g., through deforestation and topsoil erosion) that they were unable to maintain their social system without the development of new technologies, which in turn might have further adversely impacted the environment. Or, their impact on the environment (e.g., through soil conser-vation) might have enabled the Israelites to produce more energy and goods and thereby further cultural development.

In the interaction between the Israelites and their envi-ronment, the Israelites' worldview would also have played a determining role. According to the model of human-environ-ment relations, their worldview would have been influenced by the social system that results from the production of energy and goods and in turn it would have influenced the use of technology on the physical environment. An integral component of the Israelites' worldview was their values toward nature. Although these values could have been ignored, ideally they would have governed the Israelites' actions toward their environment. If the Israelites valued the natural world as an exploitable resource, for example, their actions might have been directed toward increasing the production of energy and goods with little attention to their impact on the environment (unless, of course, their impact on the environment directly threatened their capacity for further production of energy and goods). If the Israelites valued nature as an unpredictable power to which they were subjugated or as a replication of their society, their actions might have been directed differently—toward maintaining their existence by adapting their society to the environment. Whatever the case, the ancient Israelites' interaction with their environment further shaped their values toward the natural world by reinforcing, modifying, or causing a reevaluation of those values. The ancient Israelites' worldview and values toward nature thus served a strategic role in defining their relationship with their environment.

A MODEL OF WORLDVIEWS

Because of the complexity of the ecology of ancient Israel, our investigation will be limited to only one component of this ecology: the ancient Israelites' worldview and their values toward the natural world which were rooted in it. However, as the model of human-environment relations illustrates, the Israelites' worldview cannot be treated in isolation, for it was interrelated with the other segments of Israel's ecology. The Israelites' worldview contributed to the formation of their social system and their production of energy and goods, but it was also dependent upon both their social and physical environments. Our investigation of the Israelites' worldview, therefore, must also take into account its ecological context.

WORLDVIEW AND THE ENVIRONMENT

As discussed above, a worldview encompasses the mental functioning that directs human actions. It is the cognitive basis for human interaction with the social and physical environments. But a worldview also represents a perception of those environments. It is a view of the world, a way of looking at reality.[2] "It consists of basic assumptions and images"—derived from the social and physical environments—"that provide a more or less coherent, though not necessarily accurate, way of thinking about the world" (Kearney 1984:45). A people's worldview shapes and is shaped by their social and physical environments. A model which highlights these worldview dynamics is diagrammed in figure 2 (Kearney 1984:120). Like the model of human-environment relations, this model emphasizes the interdependence of a worldview and its social and physical environments. Unlike that model, however, this model stresses and gives definition to the strategic role that worldview plays in this interrelationship.

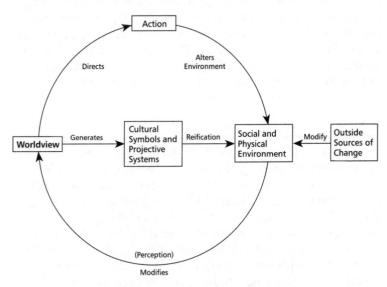

Figure 2. A Model of Worldview Dynamics

---

[2] Although the term worldview emphasizes the visual perception of the environment, all sensory contact with the environment is included.

According to this model, a worldview is a perception of the environment—both social and physical. Human existence is lived out not in a vacuum but within particular social and physical environments. The ancient Israelites, for example, lived along the eastern Mediterranean Sea, between the dominant empires of Egypt and Mesopotamia. Situated along the major east-west trade corridor, the Israelites were the recipients of both the cultural influx from and the imperialistic ambitions of their powerful neighbors. Yet their land itself was geographically less conducive to supporting life and fostering civilization than the great river valleys of Egypt and Mesopotamia. Surrounded by desert on the east and the south and by the Mediterranean Sea on the west, the narrow stretch of land inhabited by the Israelites represented a wide diversity of ecological niches that made widespread exploitation of the land difficult. Each subregion posed its own possibilities and challenges for agricultural use (Hopkins 1985:55–75). The terrain was dominated by rugged hill country, requiring extensive labor for subsistence. Moreover, the land contained few perennial water supplies, so that the Israelites were dependent upon the winter rains to supply the precipitation needed for their agriculture and vegetation to flourish. The basic social unit of the society was the nuclear family, which was replicated at all levels of the society—the clan (village), the tribe (region), the people (nation). Although some families provided for their subsistence through industries and crafts, most families maintained their existence through cultivating the land and raising sheep and goats. The ancient Israelites could not have lived within this social and physical environment without being affected by it. This total environment determined all their sensory perceptions (the Israelites' sensory perceptions would be different from those of middle-class families in the United States, for example). It structured the way they thought about themselves and their neighbors. It modified their actions and their values. It shaped the way that they perceived the world— that is, their worldview.

A people's worldview in turn impacts their environment in two ways. The first way is through the people's actions— discussed with respect to the model of human-environment relations—which have a direct effect on the environment. The second, more indirect way is through the generation of cultural symbols and projective systems that are reified as aspects of the environment. Take God, for example. What is God like? If God is absolute (the claim made by all monotheistic religions), then God is beyond comprehension. Yet we want to say something about God, so we employ metaphors such as God is a father. We create a mental image of God to which we can relate. However, when we naively assume that God really is a father—a male individual who has fathered a child—we have treated our mental image as if it were concrete. We have assumed this type of God to be an aspect of the real world, when in actuality God (the fathering-male-God) is dependent upon our perception of the world. Through this process of reification, the Israelites assumed much of the content and structure of their religion, myths, and folklore were real aspects of their environment. These reifications also modified the Israelites' perception of their environment, giving rise to new actions and reifications that further affected the environment.

The unknown variables in this model of worldview dynamics are the outside sources of change that might affect the environment. These include all aspects of change that are not a regular part of the environment, such as the invasion of enemy peoples, the exploitation of the land by foreigners, natural catastrophes, and diseases. These sources of change directly affect the environment, and, as a result, they correspondingly shape the people's worldview.

WORLDVIEW UNIVERSALS

Although discussion of the ancient Israelites' worldview occurs somewhat frequently in the scholarly literature—especially when juxtaposing the Israelites with Egyptians, Canaanites, Mesopotamians, or even with modern Westerners—no attention has been given to the cognitive categories that necessarily make up a worldview. This has been particularly problematic because of the relative nature of much of this discussion. How can the Israelites' worldview be weighed against the worldview of another people, including our own, if the fundamental categories of measurement—those cognitive categories that are present in all worldviews—are unknown? Without reference to these fundamental categories, we cannot know whether the conceptual patterns (the content of a worldview) we are relating are similar in kind or how these conceptual patterns relate to other conceptual patterns. In order to juxtapose worldviews cross-culturally, we must determine the universal cognitive categories that are essential for any worldview. Fortunately for our purposes, investigation has already begun in this area. Michael Kearney has argued persuasively, building on the earlier work of Robert Redfield, that all worldviews must necessarily include the categories of Self, Other, Classification, Relationship, Causality, Time, and Space (1984:65–107).

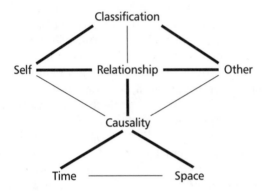

Figure 3. Integration of Worldview Universals

The particular content of these universal categories varies cross-culturally and is shaped in two ways. First, the perception of the external environment gives rise to assumptions about reality, which make up the content of the universal categories. Although they are rarely articulated or the subject of reflection, these assumptions generate the ideas, beliefs, and actions of a people. Second, the universal categories are dynamically interrelated so that they serve to bring equilibrium and consistency to diverse assumptions about reality. "This means that some assumptions and the resultant ideas, beliefs, and actions predicated on them are *logically* and *structurally* more compatible than others, and that the entire worldview will 'strive' toward maximum logical and structural consistency" (Kearney 1984:52). As illustrated in figure 3 (Kearney 1984:106)—the heavy lines indicate direct relationships, and the thin lines indirect relationships—the universal categories and the assumptions that they contain do not exist independently of one another. Assumptions in one category have logical and structural implications for the other categories. Worldview assumptions are thus shaped by the external environment and through logico-structural integration.

The distinction of the Self (the perceiver of the environment) from the Other (the environment) is fundamental to all worldviews. Yet, how the Self is understood is culturally specific. In the United States, the majority of the people define the Self in individual terms. The Self is coterminous with the body, and the individual's behavior is largely determined by personal goals, though they might overlap with societal goals. Although pervasive throughout Western culture, individualism is rare in the history of humankind (Geertz 1976:225). It is dependent upon a number of factors, including cultural complexity and affluence, which have not characterized most societies (Triandis 1990:44–45; Kearney 1984:75–77). The alternative to individualism is collectivism.[3] Collectivism is prevalent among people who share a common fate, notably in agricultural societies (Triandis 1990:70–72). In collectivist societies, including ancient Israel (Robinson 1936), the people define the Self in collective terms. A person belongs to a group, and his or her identity is embedded in the group (Malina 1989b:128–30; Malina and Neyrey 1991:72–80). In contrast to individualists, therefore, a group-oriented person's social behavior is largely determined by the goals of the group. Individual desires and values are subordinated to the desires and values of the group.

The Other entails all that is not the Self. It is the external environment. Although the Other is the complement to the Self, and thus will exhibit some of the same individualist or collectivist characteristics as the Self, it is rarely well developed. It is often designated by large domains such as the gods, nature, and society. These domains of the Other make up the Classification universal; humans have a universal tendency to name objects and to group them according to common, general characteristics. A common, though not necessarily universal, Classification is shown schematically in figure 4. Events are attributed

---

[3] The dichotomy between individualism and collectivism represents an etic model, which does not take into account cultural variations (Triandis 1990:43–44; Schwartz 1990; Triandis et al. 1993). Nevertheless, it serves as an appropriate model for distinguishing between modern Western and ancient Israelite views of the self.

to natural or supernatural causes. Animals are grouped according to whether they belong to society (pets) or nature (wild animals). In many cultures people are grouped according to whether they are male or female. The ancient Israelites classified their world according to many of these same domains, but like many collectivist cultures, their primary contrasting domains for classifying the world were ingroup and outgroup. An ingroup is simply "a group whose norms, goals, and values shape the behavior of its members," whereas an outgroup is "a group with attributes dissimilar from those of the ingroup, whose goals are unrelated or inconsistent with those of the ingroup, or a group that opposes the realization of ingroup goals" (Triandis 1990:53). The ingroup status is not restricted to humans. As a result of this type of Classification, the Israelites would have distinguished between their God and others' gods, their nature and others' nature, their society and others' society, their males and females and others' males and females.

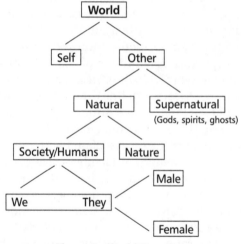

Figure 4. World Domains

Ingroup and outgroup are context specific. In the context of international relations, the ingroup for the ancient Israelites comprised all Israelites in contrast to the nations. But there were also ingroup/outgroup distinctions between the Israelites themselves. Within an inter-Israelite context, an ingroup could have been defined in terms of a family, a village, or a geographical region, a profession such as shepherd or priest, or a class such as landowner or peasant. All other Israelites would have been classified in the outgroup. Moreover, many of these classifications overlap so that each Israelite could have belonged to several ingroups. The identification of the Israelites' ingroup and outgroup will thus vary according to the specific context in which they are examined.

Whereas the Classification universal determines how the Self labels and categorizes the Other, the Relationship universal determines how the Self interacts with the Other. The assumptions contained within the Relationship universal define a person's stance toward the world and direct a person's behavior in the world. Three basic types of relationship between the Self and the Other are possible: positive, negative, and neutral. In a positive relationship the Self acts upon, or is dominant over, the Other. A negative relationship, on the other hand, is characterized by the Self's subordination to the Other. Finally, a neutral relationship is expressed as a harmony between the Self and the Other (Kearney 1984:73).

Reflecting the logico-structural integration of worldview universals, the specific assumptions of the Relationship universal are formed in relation to the Classification assumptions. The Classification universal defines the Other to which the Self relates. A person might relate differently to a male than to a female, or differently to nature than to society. The Israelites, as with all collectivist cultures, associated with ingroup members differently than to outgroup members. They emphasized a harmony with ingroup members, but either a dominance over, or a subordinacy to, outgroup members. Their relationship to nature, society, males, and females depended largely on whether these particular domains were included within the ingroup or the outgroup. Their attitudes toward their own land, for example, differed from their attitudes toward the land of their enemies. A similar difference is detected with regard to their attitudes toward society. Once this ingroup/outgroup distinction is taken into account, the Israelites' attitudes toward nature and society tended to be consistent, even replicating each other. The content of the Relationship universal is thus contingent upon the Classification universal.

The Relationship universal, which contains assumptions concerning the dynamic interaction between the Self and the Other, gives rise to the notion of causality—assumptions of "an orderly relationship between acts (causes) and desired ends (effects)" (Kearney 1984:84). The assumptions of Causality are also dependent upon the assumptions of Time and Space, which define the temporal and spatial dimensions in which the Self and the Other interact, as is shown in figure 3. Western notions of causality include both personal and natural causality. All beings—humans, but also animals and supernatural beings—are potential agents of change. Our actions in relation to the Other cause direct and indirect effects. I turn a key to open a door lock; I press the brake pedal to make my car stop; I type on a keyboard to write these sentences. Much of the change in our world we attribute to personal agents. But change is also attributed to natural causes, many of which are labeled natural laws. A thunderstorm is explained in terms of atmospheric pressure, convection, and moisture. A dead battery is explained in terms of the law of entropy. The ancient Israelites, in contrast, perceived only personal causality. All change in the world was attributed to personal agents—to either humans (and animals by personification) or the gods (Malina 1993:107–10). Natural events, for example, were manifestations of divine activity. Nature was not a causal agent, but rather the effect of divine agency.

A MODEL OF VALUE ORIENTATIONS

In this book primary attention will be given to the Relationship universal of ancient Israel's worldview. This is due chiefly to our ecological focus on the Israelites' values toward the natural world, for these values are most clearly represented by the assumptions of this universal. Nevertheless, because the dimensions of a worldview must be examined within the context of their logico-structural integration, attention will also be given to the other universals and to their effect on the Relationship universal. In order to facilitate our analysis of both the Relationship universal of the Israelites' worldview and their values toward nature, we will employ the value orientation preference model developed by Kluckhohn and

Strodtbeck. This model enables us to systematize the ancient Israelites' values and the basic assumptions in which they are rooted.

According to Kluckhohn and Strodtbeck, value orientations are principles that order and direct human actions as they relate to solving common human problems. In constructing their model for classifying value orientations, they make three assumptions derived from their empirical investigations: (1) There are a limited number of common human problems to which all people must find some solution; (2) The solutions to these problems are variable within a limited range of possible solutions; (3) All alternative solutions are present in every society, but some solutions are preferred over others ([1961]1973:10).

Of the common human problems that Kluckhohn and Strodtbeck identify, the problem that most concerns us in this book is the relationship between humans and nature.[4] This problem is analogous to the Relationship universal which defines the relationship between the Self and the Other. All cultures must find some solution to this problem, regardless of whether the solution is explicitly articulated. The range of possible solutions is defined by three alternatives: subjugation-to-nature, harmony-with-nature, and mastery-over-nature. According to the first alternative, humans feel helpless against nature. Their actions are unable to alter what nature inevitably deals them. According to the second alternative, humans identify with nature. Because there is no real separation between humans and nature, human actions inevitably affect nature, and nature determines human character. Moreover, human actions cause consequences in nature which inevitably affect humans. Humans and nature are simply extensions of one another. According to the third alternative, nature is an impersonal object that can be controlled and used by humans. Technology

---

[4] Kluckhohn and Strodtbeck identify five problems to which all humans at all times have had to find a solution. In addition to the relationship between humans and nature, these problems include the character of innate human nature (good, evil, mixture), the temporal focus of life (past, present, future), the modality of human activity (being, being-in-becoming, doing), and the modality of human relationships (collateral, lineal, individual). These problems are complementary to, and represent a different level of abstraction from, the worldview universals.

is the key to harnessing the forces of nature. These three solutions are summarized in figure 5.

Subjugation to Nature	Humans have no control over nature and are subject to the inevitable effects of nature.
Harmony with Nature	Humans are united with nature in a precarious balance so that their actions affect nature and themselves in turn.
Mastery over Nature	Nature is made up of impersonal objects and forces that humans can/should manipulate for their own purposes.

Figure 5. Solutions to the Human-Relationship-to-Nature Problem

In each culture, all of these alternative solutions are present and ranked according to preference. One solution is generally preferred, but the other solutions might be chosen under special circumstances or by subgroups within the culture (differentiated by class, profession, gender). In other words, one solution forms a group's primary, or first order, value orientation preference. If that solution, however, proves to be ineffectual or inappropriate for the particular circumstances, then the second and third order solutions serve as backup. The dominant first order preference for Westerners, for example, is the mastery-over-nature solution. Westerners will freely employ technologies to use and exploit the natural world for their own purposes. Yet because of the widespread concern over the environmental crisis, these same people often resort to their second order solution, harmony-with-nature, when they conserve water or recycle their waste. During times of natural catastrophe, such as flood or earthquake, neither of these solutions is appropriate. Falling back on the subjugation-to-nature solution, some people simply resign themselves to accept whatever nature apportions.

Because value orientations are rooted in a worldview, solutions to the human-relationship-to-nature problem reflect the integration of the Relationship and Classification universals. Within collectivist cultures like ancient Israel, a group will prefer a different solution in relation to the land of their enemies than to their own land. The land of the ingroup is treated with reverence (harmony-with-nature), whereas the land of the outgroup is treated with contempt (mastery-over-nature). In contrast, peasants, who own no land and are repeatedly exploited by the land owners, are powerless before nature. Thus they prefer the subjugation-to-nature solution. As has been shown, the value orientation preferences of the ancient Israelites chiefly depended upon the ingroup/outgroup divisions of the society and upon how the natural world was perceived in relation to the ingroup.

OUR VALUES VERSUS THEIR VALUES

Before we turn to investigate the value orientation of the Israelites, it is helpful to first focus on our twentieth-century value orientation. Without a clear understanding of our Western value orientation, we face the twin dangers of ethnocentrism and anachronism. Ethnocentrism is "the judging of all persons in the whole world in terms of one's own culture on the presumption that, since 'we' are by nature human, so if anyone else is human then they should and must be just as we are" (Malina 1986:29). Our values with regard to the environment are not necessarily the same values held by the ancient Israelites. By assuming that the people of the Bible thought and behaved like us, we run the risk of reading into the biblical texts our own agenda rather than extracting from the texts their messages. This danger is particularly acute with regard to the human-relationship-to-nature problem, for the effects of the current environmental crisis can be felt throughout the planet. Concern for the state of the environment is therefore widespread. However, if we assume that the ancient Israelites had a similar concern for their environment, we are guilty of anachronism—the judging of persons in the past according to standards only relevant to the present (Hobbs 1989:210–14). Through ethnocentrism and anachronism we impose our own concerns and standards of behavior on the people of the Bible.

One illustration of the twin dangers of ethnocentrism and anachronism is the issue of war. In the United States we have a well-defined understanding of war and the conduct of war. For the majority of Americans, war is justified only if it is defensive or responding to some prior aggression. War should be resorted to only after diplomatic solutions fail. War is fought with high-tech weapons, but has specific rules against the use of nuclear, chemical, and biological weapons. Civilian populations are not to be targeted, and prisoners should receive humane treatment. Soldiers and officers can thus be guilty of war crimes. These values are generally assumed. If we read the Bible from this perspective, we are naturally disturbed. Repeatedly, the Israelites engage in war, and often it is offensive (the wars of conquest, David's expansion of the empire). Rarely do they employ diplomacy (cf. Judg 11:12–28 for an exception). In some cases God even commands the Israelites to kill all the Canaanites in the land (Deut 20:16–18). Prisoners are often butchered, and a distinction between civilians and soldiers is never made. As interpreted ethnocentrically and anachronistically, either the Bible would be a source of embarrassment for those who are working for peace in our world, or it could even be used to justify our own militaristic actions. The Israelites, however, did not share our values with regard to war, nor did they fight wars like we do. Without first analyzing *their* values and *their* practices within their own cultural setting (the topic of another book; see the excellent treatment by Hobbs) and distinguishing them from our own, it is impossible to understand ancient Israel's view of war. Only with this analysis can Israel's view of war be compared adequately with our own view.

Readers of the Bible are never free from the dangers of ethnocentrism and anachronism. Nevertheless, by recognizing one's own value orientation, through the use of a cross-cultural model such as the model of Kluckhohn and Strodtbeck, a reader is in a better position to investigate the culturally specific value orientation preferences of the ancient Israelites. A reader who is critically self-aware is better able to distinguish between the values latent in the biblical texts and his or her own values. Therefore, take a few minutes to reflect upon and answer the following questions which were designed to make a person's value orientation explicit (adapted from Kluckhohn and Strodtbeck [1961]1973:81–89).

1. At one time a man had a large flock of sheep and goats, but eventually most of them died in different ways. Which response to this situation do you prefer?

   A. You just can't blame a man when things like this happen. There are so many things that can and do happen, and a man can do almost nothing to prevent such losses when they come. We all have to learn to take the bad with the good.

B. The sheep and goats died because the man had not lived his life right—had not done things in the right way to keep harmony between himself and the forces of nature (i.e., the ways of nature like the rain, winds, snow, etc.).

C. It was probably the man's own fault that he lost so much of his flock. He probably didn't use his head to prevent the losses. It is usually the case that people who keep up on new ways of doing things, and really set themselves to it, almost always find a way to keep out of such trouble.

2. How is God related to humankind and to the natural conditions which determine whether the crops and animals live or die?

A. It is unknown how God will use his power over all the conditions that affect the growth of the crops and animals. It is useless for people to think they can change conditions very much for very long. The best approach is to take conditions as they come and do as well as one can.

B. God and the people work together all the time; whether the conditions that make the crops and animals grow are good or bad depends upon whether people themselves do all the proper things to keep themselves in harmony with their God and with the forces of nature.

C. God does not directly use his power to control all the conditions which affect the growth of crops or animals. It is up to the people themselves to figure out the ways conditions change and to try hard to find the ways of controlling them.

3. There were three people who had fields with crops, but each had a quite different way of planting and taking care of the crops. Which one acted and believed correctly?

A. One man put in his crops. Afterwards he worked on them sufficiently but did not do more than was necessary to keep them going along. He felt that the success of his crops was dependent upon weather conditions and that nothing extra could be done to change things very much.

B. One woman put in her crops, worked hard, and also set herself to living right and moral ways. She felt that it is the way a person works and tries to keep herself in harmony with the forces of nature that has the most effect on conditions and the way crops turn out.

C. One man put in his crops and then worked on them frequently and made use of all the new scientific ideas he could find out about. He felt that by doing this he would in most years prevent many of the effects of bad conditions.

4. Which response best fits your feelings about the weather and other conditions?

A. We have never controlled the rain, wind, and other natural conditions and probably never will. There have always been good years and bad years. That is the way it is, and if we are wise we will take it as it comes and do the best we can.

B. We can ensure beneficial conditions by keeping in close touch will all the forces which make the rain, the snow, and other conditions. It is when we do the right things— live the proper way—and keep all that we have—the land, the stock, and the water—in good condition, that all goes well.

C. It is our job to find ways to overcome weather and other conditions just as we have overcome so many other things. We will one day succeed in doing this and may even overcome drought and floods.

5. Which statement best reflects your belief about whether people can do anything to make their lives longer?

A. I really do not believe that there is much human beings themselves can do to make their lives longer. It is my belief that every person has a set time to live, and when that time comes it just comes.

B. I believe there is a plan to life that works to keep all living things moving together, and if people will learn to live their whole lives in accord with that plan, then they will live longer.

C. It is already true that people like doctors and others are finding the way to add many years to the lives of most people by discovering (finding) new medicines, by studying foods, and doing other such things as exercise and vaccinations. If people will pay attention to all these new things they will almost always live longer.

If you chose "C" for most of these questions, then you are like most Westerners in giving first order preference to the mastery-over-nature solution. ("A" reflects the subjugation-to-

nature solution; "B" reflects the harmony-with-nature solution.) In fact, sociologists have recognized this preference to be
a feature of the Dominant Western Worldview. This worldview
is represented by the following four assumptions (Catton and
Dunlap 1980:17–18):

> 1. People are fundamentally different from all other creatures
> on earth, over which they have dominion.
>
> 2. People are masters of their destiny; they can choose their
> goals and learn to do whatever is necessary to achieve them.
>
> 3. The world is vast, and thus provides unlimited opportunities
> for humans.
>
> 4. The history of humanity is one of progress; for every problem
> there is a solution, and thus progress need never cease.

This dominant worldview, however, has recently been challenged by concern over the current environmental crisis. The
frequent attention that the environment receives has altered
some of these long held assumptions. As a result, sociologists
are beginning to recognize the emergence of a paradigm shift, or
a shift in value orientation preference, toward a more ecologically sensitive worldview (Catton and Dunlap 1978, 1980;
Blaikie 1992). Humans are still perceived to be exceptional, but
it is also acknowledged that we are interdependently involved
in a global ecosystem. Humans are no longer considered by
many to be exempt from ecological constraints.

Despite this recent paradigmatic shift caused by concern for
the environment, the mastery-over-nature solution to the problem concerning the relationship between humans and nature has
not been abandoned. Rather, the incongruities between this solution and the circumstances of the environmental crisis have led
many Westerners to try to incorporate their second order preference, the harmony-with-nature solution, with the mastery-
over-nature solution. This is borne out by the observation in
sociological research that although there is a high level of
environmental concern, there is also considerable confidence
that science and technology will be able to solve our ecological
problems (Blaikie 1992:154). If much of the destruction of the
environment can be traced to our misuse of technology, then
surely the *appropriate* use of technology can solve the crisis!
Faith in science and technology is so predominant in the Western

world that some sociologists do not even entertain the possibility of the subjugation-to-nature solution (Albrecht, Bultena, Hoiberg, and Nowak 1982; Geller and Lasley 1985). Are there any in the United States who would consider themselves to be powerless against nature, unable through science and technology to change their natural circumstances? Perhaps some would during times of natural catastrophe such as earthquakes, tornadoes, and floods, but these are rare occasions.

In contrast to our Western cultural preferences, mastery-over-nature was rarely ever a primary value for ancient Israelites. Nature was beyond their control; they either felt subjugated to nature or linked with it in a precarious balance.[5] An exception to this generalization, however, appears to be the king. The writer of Ecclesiastes, for instance, in assuming the role of the king, states: "I made myself gardens and parks, and planted in them all kinds of fruit trees. I made myself pools from which to water the forest of growing trees" (Eccl 2:5–6). Yet the king's mastery-over-nature preference was rooted in a different worldview than our own. In the ancient Near East, kings served as the regent of the gods. They acted on behalf of the gods, and through their actions they maintained the order and integrity of creation (Frankfort 1948). Israel's king was no different. As the king constructed parks and gardens, a common task of kings, he acted toward the natural world in the same manner as God, who planted the garden of Eden (Verheij 1991:113–15).

In the following chapters I will employ this value orientation model in order to investigate and systematize the ancient Israelites' values toward the natural world and thereby contribute toward an ecology of ancient Israel. However, unlike the contemporary cultures for which this model was

---

[5] Although the Israelites did employ a variety of technologies in order to survive in an often hostile environment (Hopkins 1987)—most notably, agricultural terracing and the hewing out of limestone cisterns—these technologies were not the means by which they could manipulate their environment beyond its natural limits. Their use of technology was not intended to overcome the ecological constraints of their environment, but rather to enable them to subsist in that environment. The use of technology in itself does not necessitate a mastery-over-nature solution to the human-relationship-to-nature problem. All cultures must include some utilitarian attitude toward nature, expressed through technologies, in order to survive in the natural world (Kay 1985:128).

designed, our investigation of the Israelites' value orientation faces two related problems. First, obviously there are no ancient Israelites around to question. We simply have no way of knowing how the Israelites would have answered the questionnaire listed above. Instead, we must reconstruct their value orientation primarily from the biblical texts (although not explicitly articulated, the ancient Israelites' values are latent in their literature) and then from diverse sources such as ethnographic data and archaeological evidence. Second, the Bible presents us with a highly selective view of Israelite culture. Most of the biblical texts, for example, originated in learned circles in and around Jerusalem. They represent the beliefs and ideology of the elite and the practitioners of normative (i.e., biblical) Yahwism. All other Israelite voices—the peasants and those practicing non-official forms of Yahwism—are presented only from the perspective of these bearers of the official tradition. The Bible cannot be used for making inclusive claims about ancient Israelites. As a result, our reconstruction by its very nature can only be a generalized abstraction from the available evidence. Nevertheless, I will argue that each of the three solutions to the human-relationship-to-nature problem is reflected in the biblical texts. The different solutions to this problem can be attributed to preferences made by different segments of Israelite society, to ingroup/outgroup relations, and to historical circumstances. Moreover, each of these solutions was rooted in a variation of a single basic worldview. This worldview will enable us to reconstruct at least the full range of the ancient Israelites' values toward the natural world.

2
CREATION IN THE ANCIENT NEAR EAST

METAPHORS, MYTHS, AND SCENARIOS

Nowhere in the Bible is the worldview of the ancient Israelites or their values toward nature explicitly laid out. This is not surprising. Ancient Israel was what Edward Hall has characterized as a high context society. In high context societies a rich common culture is assumed by all the members of the society, and the identity of individual members is defined in terms of that culture. Moreover, because the society is based upon a common culture, each individual requires an adequate understanding of that culture in order to function well within the society. Low context societies like the United States, in contrast, require little knowledge of culture in order for their members to get along, nor does culture play a determinative role in forming individual identity. According to a common axiom, the United States is not a society based on humans, i.e., culture, but on laws. A member of any other society can function well in the United States by simply adhering to minimal legal restrictions (Hall 1976:91–101).

This distinction between low and high context societies provides a helpful model for understanding the type of texts each society produces. On the one hand, low context societies tend to produce very detailed texts. Because little culture is shared among its members, texts written for low context audiences must describe in detail all the relevant cultural features that are necessary to understand the text. The texts produced by high context societies, on the other hand, frequently lack this detail. They are written by insiders for insiders, and so most aspects of culture can be assumed. All the members of the society have been socialized into shared ways of perceiving and acting. Therefore, high context audiences do not need to be instructed in the culture, because they are already intimately familiar with it (Malina 1991:19–20). Such instruction, in fact, would be considered an insult, for it would challenge an audience's identification with its own culture, thus insinuating that they were outsiders.

The Bible was produced by a high context society for high context readers. It assumes a rich culture that the biblical writers felt no need to describe. It is not surprising, then, that the Bible lacks any explicit articulation of the Israelites' worldview and values toward the natural world. Their worldview and values were simply assumed by all members of the society; they formed the presupposition of the biblical writers rather than the subject of their discourse. Consequently, we cannot expect to discover their worldview and values from a low context reading of the biblical texts.

If we hope to glean their unexpressed worldview and values from the biblical texts, then we must become acquainted with the ancient Israelite culture that is assumed by the texts. In other words, we must read the Bible from the high context perspective in which it was written. Fortunately for our purposes, the biblical texts themselves contain clues in the form of metaphor and myth that help to reveal the relevant aspects of ancient Israel's culture.

METAPHORS

A metaphor can be defined as the juxtaposition of two frames of reference—a source domain and a target domain—such that an open-ended analogy is produced (Barbour 1974:12–14).[1] The source domain is familiar and often concrete, and if communication is to be successful, both the sender and the receiver need to be able to conceptualize this domain readily.

---

[1] Literary critics typically make a distinction between metaphor and simile. Both make a comparison between two things, but the latter is considered to be more explicit and uses comparative terms such as "like" or "as." This distinction, however, is merely formal and has no functional significance. Therefore, I have lumped all comparisons together under the category of metaphor.

The target domain, on the other hand, is typically either an abstract concept from the mental or social world or an unknown element from the physical world. The target domain becomes accessible by mapping the source domain onto it (Quinn 1991:57). In other words, the familiar features and relations of the source domain are transferred to the intangible target domain.

As an example, consider the common metaphor that marriage is like a project at which both partners must work. Marriage in this context is the target domain. It is an abstract concept that is difficult to comprehend apart from concrete representations. Therefore, we apply to it a source domain that is readily understandable. We know what it is like to work on a project; we must plan out the project, gather the necessary resources, and above all put out the effort to complete the project. Similarly, a marriage does not simply happen. A couple must plan their marriage and lives together; they must secure necessary resources such as jobs and a home; and they must expend energy to ensure the success of their marriage. The metaphor of a work project thus defines and gives meaning to the otherwise intangible concept of marriage.

Also consider the common Christian metaphor of God the father. In this metaphor "father" is the source domain and "God" is the target domain. All of us know what a father is like, either from direct experience or from the report of others, and we have undoubtedly formulated an opinion about what a father should be like. However, we do not know directly what God is like. We cannot see God. We cannot touch God. We cannot conclusively identify the actions of God. The idea of God is simply an abstraction that designates the ultimate concern that forms the ground or basis of our existence (Tillich 1957:44–48). Nevertheless, by mapping the well-known source domain onto God through the use of metaphor, we are able to communicate something about what God is like, namely, that God is like a father.

From this example, several characteristics of metaphors can be delineated. First and foremost, metaphors are not literally true. In terms of our example, God is not literally a father. The two domains of the metaphor cannot be equated, for the relationship is an analogous one. That is, the two domains are similar in some respects, but dissimilar in other respects. God is like a father in that God is one who protects, disciplines, and provides for humankind. But God is not like a father in that God does not father offspring; nor are human fathers like God when they abuse their children or abandon their families.

A second characteristic of metaphors is that they are open-ended. The analogy produced by a metaphor cannot be reduced to a set of equivalent literal expressions. The correspondence between the two domains cannot be paraphrased exactly. "No limits can be set as to how far the comparison might be extended; it cannot be paraphrased because it has an unspecifiable number of potentialities for articulation" (Barbour 1974:14). Thus the metaphor of God the father, for example, cannot be replaced by an exhaustive list of statements detailing how God is like a father. Rather it invites the reader to explore the various ways in which God resembles a father without predetermining the number and nature of those similarities.

This potential for new insight that is inherent in metaphors has led some to suggest that metaphors actually reorganize thinking by providing new entailments and new inferences (Ferré 1968; Lakoff and Johnson 1980). Although metaphors can and do function in this way, this is the exception rather than the rule. This leads to the third, and for our purposes the most important, characteristic of metaphors, namely, that metaphors are culturally based (Jacobsen 1973:275). Rather than producing new understandings, metaphors are ordinarily constrained by existing cultural understandings. In other words, the selection of metaphors is a feature of culture. Metaphors are chosen to make a point that the sender of the communication already has in mind.

Let us explore this aspect of metaphors further. Metaphors function to clarify, describe, or illuminate some target domain. Although the target domain is intangible, it is not unknowable. Typically, there is already a preexistent and culturally shared understanding of reality underlying the target domain. One metaphor is then chosen over another because it more readily maps into that cultural understanding. Why is God referred to as a father and not as a tyrant? The absolute power exercised by a tyrant is indeed similar in kind to God's absolute power. Nevertheless, the Christian tradition has not found the tyrant to be a suitable metaphor for God. Why? The answer is that Christians already have a culturally shared perception of what God is like, and the metaphor of father more readily fits this understanding (Quinn 1991). Because metaphors express cultural understandings, they can thus serve as clues to the culture.

Metaphors vary in their magnitude and in their dimension. The source domain, for instance, can be limited to one word, such as "father," or it can consist of an elaborate narrative. Metaphors also can be multidimensional in that they can be composed of other metaphors. The result is often an intertwined web of metaphors that serves as the source domain for a complex extended metaphor. Such metaphors are generally in narrative form and are traditionally referred to as myths. Myth is thus closely related to metaphor.

MYTHS AND SCENARIOS

In contrast to metaphor, the definition of myth is problematic. Not only is there disagreement among specialists over the essential character of myths—for example, whether they have a formal or a functional character—but there is also little consensus over what constitutes a myth (Honko 1984; Rogerson 1984; Oden 1987:52–57). This is especially true with regard to the presence of myths in the Bible (Rogerson 1974; Oden 1987:40–52). Whether or not the stories in the Bible can be classified as myth depends in large part on how myth itself is defined. Traditionally, myth has been defined as stories about the gods or as stories about world origins. Following this definition, myth can be found in the Bible only, if at all, in the opening chapters of Genesis. But as demonstrated by recent comparative studies, these definitions are clearly too narrow to account for the numerous and diverse myths attested throughout the world (O'Flaherty 1988:25–43). The following is a more appropriate, albeit cumbersome, definition of myth:

> A myth is a story that is sacred to and shared by a group of people who find their most important meanings in it; it is a story believed to have been composed in the past about an event in the past, or, more rarely, in the future, an event that continues to have meaning in the present because it is remembered; it is a story that is part of a larger group of stories. (O'Flaherty 1988:27)

According to this definition, which is used in this book, many of the biblical stories should be included under the category of myth.

Myths play a significant role in the personal and corporate life of each culture; they serve a wide range of psycho-
logical and social functions. The myths in the Bible are no
different. Our focus, however, is not on their function within
the ancient Israelite culture but rather on their metaphorical
character. Like all myths, the biblical myths are composed of
numerous metaphors, and many of the myths even function as
extended metaphors. As a result, myths, like the metaphors
from which they are built, are culturally based. Myths are
simply narrative elaborations of culturally shared perceptions
of reality. The biblical myths, then, serve as further clues to
uncovering the culture of ancient Israel. By giving close attention to these metaphors and myths, we are able to penetrate the
high context society of ancient Israel and thus begin to discern
the worldview and values of the biblical writers.

Although metaphors and myths allow us to bridge the gap
between our low context reading practices and the high context documents of the Bible, they do not do so unambiguously.
The dangers of ethnocentrism and anachronism are ever present. For example, in our metaphor of God the father, the
modern reader of the Gospels might interpret this metaphor
from the perspective of his or her own experience of a father
rather than from the perspective of what fathers were like in
first-century Palestine. This latter perspective, of course, was
the perspective of Jesus, who most profoundly developed this
metaphor. Both perspectives might in fact inform us about
God, but only the latter perspective will disclose what the
gospel writers intended to communicate. A metaphor is only
able to communicate if both the sender and the receiver share
a similar understanding of the source domain.

Recent research into reading comprehension suggests that
people generally read and think by calling to mind a succession of mental images or scenarios (Malina 1991:12–17; Pennington and Hastie 1991). These scenarios, which have their
basis in culture, are then mapped onto a text producing a
culturally determined grid for understanding the text. Communication occurs when the author and the readers share similar
scenarios. When the readers do not share the author's scenarios,
either through misdirection by the author or the readers' unfa-
miliarity with the content of the text, misunderstanding ensues. The author of a text will often provide the readers with
hints that signal the proper scenarios. It is the responsibility of

readers to call to mind these scenarios if they want to understand what the author intends to communicate. With regard to the previous discussion concerning metaphors, these scenarios are analogous to the culturally shared understandings on which metaphors are based. Therefore, if we hope to avoid the dangers of ethnocentrism and anachronism, we must read the metaphors and myths of the Bible in light of scenarios appropriate to the culture of ancient Israel rather than to our own.

Creation myths and metaphors provide the key to ascertaining the ancient Israelites' worldview and values toward nature. These myths describe God's activity in and on behalf of the world and the product of that activity. They reveal the ancient Israelites' assumptions concerning the triangular relationship between humans, God, and the natural world—that is, the primary assumptions of the Classification and Relationship universals—by answering the most basic human questions: Who am I? How do I fit into the worlds of society and nature? How should I live? In many ancient and modern cultures, including the culture of ancient Israel, reality is perceived as a whole; everything fits together in some way. Creation myths are the vehicle by which the diverse parts of reality—the status of humankind, the structures of society and nature, and the relationship of humankind to the natural world—are integrated into the whole. In particular, creation myths proclaim a central absolute (i.e., independent) reality, such as the gods or some other primal force and describe its relation to all other, relative (i.e., dependent) realities. Around this central reality creation myths construct the basic structure of all cultural values (Sproul 1979:1–30; Lovin and Reynolds 1985:1–8).

In order to understand these myths, and the metaphors they embody, as clues to the cultural values of ancient Israel, however, we must reconstruct the culturally shared perception of reality on which these myths and metaphors are based. We must acquire the appropriate scenarios for reading these myths. From the biblical texts alone, it would be difficult, if not impossible, to reconstruct the proper scenarios or cultural understandings for adequately interpreting creation in the Bible. Too much information is assumed, and the biblical data are too fragmentary. Fortunately, we are aided by numerous creation myths from the cultures surrounding ancient Israel. These myths prove invaluable for providing the appropriate

scenarios for understanding creation in the Bible because Israel shared many of the basic cultural values of its ancient Near
Eastern neighbors. In the remainder of this chapter we will
survey the wide variety of creation myths from Mesopotamia,
Egypt, and Canaan. Through the cross-cultural comparison of
these myths, we will be able to reconstruct an ancient Near
Eastern creation model that underlies the Bible's creation metaphors and myths. This model will then be used to elucidate
the worldview of the biblical writers.

Creation myths in the ancient Near East are as diverse as
they are numerous. They range from accounts detailing the
construction of the world to those that describe the creation of
the pickax. In the following discussion I will focus on the
metaphors embedded in the myths of both world and human
creation. This is due in part to the desire to be as inclusive as
possible but also due to the fact that myths of human creation
are often inseparable from myths of world creation. Contrary
to the common assumption (see Westermann 1984:22–25), "no
good evidence exists for the view that there were two distinct
traditions of creation, one of creation of the world and the other
of creation of human beings" (Clifford and Collins 1992:8).
Nevertheless, it is convenient for strictly analytical purposes
to categorize these myths into the two groups of world and
human creation.

MESOPOTAMIA

MYTHS OF WORLD CREATION

From the first great culture of Mesopotamia, the Su-
merians, no myth of world creation has survived. However,
there are a few scattered references in other texts that allude to
this creation, especially in their introductions where Sumerian
scribes were accustomed to adding a few lines dealing with
creation. In the epic tale entitled *Gilgamesh, Enkidu, and the
Nether World*, for example, the first intelligible lines of the
introduction read as follows:

> After heaven had been moved away from earth,
> After earth had been separated from heaven,
> After the name of man had been fixed;

After An had carried off heaven,
After Enlil had carried off earth,
After (the earth) had been presented as dowry to Ereshkigal
  in the nether world . . . [2] (Kramer 1972:37)

The introduction continues by telling how Enki, the god of the sweet waters, sets out to attack Kur, but for what reason, the text does not indicate. According to this brief account, the creation of the world involves the separating of the united heaven and earth and the dividing of the respective gods of the heaven and the earth. A further detail is given in the introduction to *The Creation of the Pickax*; it is Enlil, the god of the air, who separates the heaven and the earth (Kramer 1972:39–41).

In turning our attention to the heirs of the Sumerian culture, the Babylonians and the Assyrians, the myths of world creation become more plentiful and detailed. The most elaborate of these creation myths is frequently entitled the *Babylonian Creation Epic*, or more accurately, the *Enuma Elish*, the traditional title based on the first two words of the myth. Although the myth ostensibly describes how Marduk, the chief god of Babylon, rose to prominence among the gods and established monarchy (Jacobsen 1976:167–91), it also details his construction and organization of the world and the creation of humankind. Before we examine the myth, however, a helpful distinction needs to be made between two dimensions of the world: the macrocosm and the microcosm. The macrocosm is the transcendent world of the gods that underlies and supports the microcosm. It may be eternal, or it might emerge from some preexistent state, such as water. The microcosm is best equated with the known world. This is the world of humans, animals, plants, birds, fish, but also of the sun, moon, and stars. It is the physical world that mirrors or replicates the world of the gods.

The *Enuma Elish* begins by describing the primordial state of the macrocosm, before the birth of the gods, when there existed only the two primal forces: Apsu, the fresh water; and Tiamat, the salt water.

When skies above were not yet named
Nor earth below pronounced by name,
Apsu, the first one, their begetter
And maker Tiamat, who bore them all,

---

[2] This line has been modified following Jacobsen (1970:122–23).

> Had mixed their waters together,
> But had not formed pastures, nor discovered reed-beds;
> When yet no gods were manifest,
> Nor names pronounced, nor destinies decreed,
> Then gods were born within them. (Dalley 1991:231)

From the intermingling of Apsu and Tiamat four generations of gods are born—Lahmu and Lahamu (the silt of an alluvial plain), Anshar and Kishar (the horizons of heaven and earth), Anu (the sky), and Ea (another name for Enki, the subterranean fresh water)—each more prominent than its predecessor. These younger gods then gather together to play and dance, but the clamor of their moving about disturbs the rest of their inert parents. Tiamat, the patient mother, is able to indulge their behavior, but Apsu can tolerate it no longer. Apsu thus sets plans to kill the younger gods to restore his rest. Word of Apsu's plot is relayed to the other gods, who, except for Ea, are shocked into silence. Ea, through his superior wisdom, devises a scheme to overcome Apsu. By reciting a sleeping spell Ea subdues Apsu and kills him. After taking the symbols of Apsu's authority for himself, Ea builds his dwelling on top of the Apsu, that is, the subterranean waters. Ea and his spouse Damkina then give birth to Marduk (the storm), who is majestic in form and superior to all the other gods in every way.

Although the gods have been spared the wrath of Apsu, peace does not prevail. Tiamat is continuously disturbed by the commotion of the young gods.

> Anu created the four winds and gave them birth,
> Put them in Marduk's hand, "My son, let them play!"
> He fashioned dust and made the whirlwind carry it;
> He made the flood-wave and stirred up Tiamat.
> Tiamat was stirred up, and heaved restlessly day and night.
>   (Dalley 1991:236)

Other, lesser gods are disturbed as well, and they begin to complain to Tiamat: How can Tiamat remain idle as her children, who killed Apsu her lover, intentionally disturb her rest? Their complaint works. Tiamat is incited to destroy her own children. First, she creates a group of horrible monsters, the sight of which is terrifying enough to repel all who look upon them. Then she promotes Kingu to be commander over her army and gives him the Tablet of Destinies, ensuring that his word will be law. When the younger gods discover Tiamat's plan they are terrified. Neither Ea nor Anu has the power to resist her assault. Only the incomparable Marduk is able to rival Tiamat.

Anshar, on behalf of the assembly of gods, requests that Marduk act as their champion and defeat Tiamat. Marduk agrees, but only on the condition that if he is victorious, he will rule over the other gods. With the threat of Tiamat at hand, the gods have little choice in the matter and so consent to Marduk's arrangement, hailing him as king in anticipation of his victory. Gathering together the typical weapons of a storm god, Marduk marches out to meet Tiamat with lightning before him and seven winds behind him.

> Face to face they came, Tiamat and Marduk, sage of the gods.
> They engaged in combat, they closed for battle.
> The Lord spread his net and made it encircle her,
> To her face he dispatched the *imhullu*-wind,[3] which had been behind:
> Tiamat opened her mouth to swallow it,
> And he forced in the *imhullu*-wind so that she could not close her lips.
> Fierce winds distend her belly;
> Her insides were constipated and she stretched her mouth wide.
> He shot an arrow which pierced her belly,
> Split her down the middle and slit her heart,
> Vanquished her and extinguished her life.
> He threw down her corpse and stood on top of her.
>   (Dalley 1991:253)

Upon the defeat of Tiamat, her army scatters. Marduk captures Kingu and takes from him the Tablet of Destinies. The macrocosm is secured.

At this point in the myth the actual construction of the microcosm is described. After scattering his enemies, Marduk returns to inspect the corpse of Tiamat.

> He divided the monstrous shape and created marvels from it.
> He sliced her in half like a fish for drying:
> Half of her he put up to roof the sky,
> Drew a bolt across and made a guard hold it.
> Her waters he arranged so that they could not escape.
>   (Dalley 1991:255)

---

[3] The *imhullu*-wind is a Sumerian loan-word that the text itself defines as "evil wind."

In the heavens, directly above Ea's dwelling on the Apsu, Marduk builds the temple Esharra according to the same plans as Ea's temple. He then arranges stations in the heavens for the gods to serve as the stars, moon, and sun and makes them responsible for signaling the days, months, and years. The rest of Marduk's creation focuses on the terrestrial realm. Although the tablet is damaged, the basic outline can be discerned. Marduk takes the spittle of Tiamat and forms it into clouds. He creates rain and places it under his own control. He heaps up mountains on her head and on her udder, stopping up her bodily portals. These serve as pillars to hold up the roof of the sky. He then bores through the mountains in order to release the Tigris and the Euphrates from her eyes. Finally, he stretches her tail across the sky to form the Milky Way (Pritchard 1969: 501–2; Dalley 1991:256–57). After completing the creation of the microcosm, Marduk hands over the Tablet of Destinies to his grandfather Anu, and all the gods rejoice and proclaim him "King of the gods of heaven and earth."

For his first act as king of all the gods, Marduk commands that a temple be built for him on the earth between the subterranean Apsu and his temple Esharra in heaven. In this temple Marduk will establish his cult center and display his kingship. This new temple will be called Babylon, and it will serve as a resting place for all the gods as they travel between the earth and heaven. The remaining feature of the myth that concerns us focuses on Marduk's creation of humans, but we will return to this later.

According to the *Enuma Elish*, Marduk created the world from the slain body of Tiamat. The act of creation consisted of splitting and arranging the corpse of Tiamat and controlling the flow of the waters that surge from her body. The Babylonians thus conceived of water as the primal substance of the world (cf. the similar assessment of the biblical cosmology by Frymer-Kensky 1987a:232–35). Life in this world became possible when primal water was controlled and restricted within boundaries.

A similar notion of creation is found in a Neo-Babylonian inscription discovered in the ruins of the ancient city of Sippar. After listing all that did not exist, as in the opening of the *Enuma Elish*, this text states that all the lands were a sea with a mighty spring gushing up from its midst. Then the beginning of Marduk's creation is described:

> Marduk constructed a reed frame on the face of the waters;
> He created dirt and poured it out by the reed frame.
>
> (Heidel 1951:62)

The text continues by describing the rest of the creative acts of
Marduk. Like creation in the *Enuma Elish*, this text portrays the
emergence of land out of the waters. But the similarities go much
deeper. The *Enuma Elish* and the Sippar inscription use the
same model for the creation of land. In the *Enuma Elish* land
began to emerge with the birth of Lahmu and Lahamu, the silt,
from the primal waters of Apsu and Tiamat. Not until Marduk
defeated Tiamat, and separated the land from the threatening
waters, however, did the land become secure. This myth is
rooted in Mesopotamian geography. The great Mesopotamian
rivers, the Tigris and Euphrates, emptied into an alluvial plain
in which new land was continually being formed from the silt
carried down by the rivers. The emergence of new land in the
alluvial plain became the model by which some Babylonians
described the creation of the world (Jacobsen 1976:169). This
same model underlies the Neo-Babylonian inscription from Sippar; Marduk creates the dirt that will form the alluvial plain
(Heidel 1951:61). The main difference between these two myths
is that creation in the *Enuma Elish* results from conflict against
the waters (Tiamat), whereas in the Neo-Babylonian text the
waters offer no opposition.

Biblical scholars tend to characterize the *Enuma Elish* as
the premier example of the Mesopotamian view of creation. At
the heart of the *Enuma Elish* is what has been termed the
Chaoskampf, "the struggle against chaos," or, more broadly,
the conflict myth. This myth presents the ubiquitous struggle
between order and chaos. It is essentially a drama celebrating
a warrior-god's ascendancy to kingship over his rivals by his
defeat of the chaotic forces of death and his subsequent ordering of the world into a habitation suitable for human life. It is
a cosmogonic myth that describes the creation of a new world
complete with social system, kinship organization, and cult,
though rarely does it focus on the origination of the world
per se (Clifford 1985:509–12; Knight 1985:134–37). This
Chaoskampf, which has numerous parallels in the biblical
tradition, has been employed by biblical scholars as the primary model for interpreting the biblical creation myths (Gunkel [1895] 1984). Unfortunately, however, by overemphasizing

the importance of the *Enuma Elish*, scholars have neglected other Mesopotamian creation myths that are equally vital for understanding the biblical idea of creation.

Certainly the *Enuma Elish* is the most elaborate Mesopotamian creation myth, but it is doubtful that it represents the predominant Mesopotamian view of creation. One prominent Assyriologist even characterized it as a sectarian and an aberrant combination of mythological threads that have been woven into an unparalleled composition (Lambert 1965:291). Although he perhaps depicted the myth too narrowly, he has rightly cautioned us against overemphasizing this myth in understanding the Mesopotamian view of creation. Some scholars have even argued that the *Enuma Elish* is a foreign import into Mesopotamia (Jacobsen 1968; Komoróczy 1973). The textual evidence suggests that there is no single tradition that made up the Mesopotamian view of creation.

A Mesopotamian creation myth that represents a strikingly different tradition from the *Enuma Elish* has been called the *Theogony of Dunnu*. Although the end of the text is missing, this myth is apparently about the establishment of kingship in Dunnu, which is traced back to the beginning of creation:

> At the very beginning Plow married Earth
> And they decided to establish a family and dominion.
> "We shall break up the virgin soil of the land into clods."
> In the clods of their virgin soil, they created Sea.
> The Furrows, of their own accord, begot the Cattle God.
> Together they built Dunnu forever as his refuge.
> Plow made unrestricted dominion for himself in Dunnu.
>   (Dalley 1991:279)

In the subsequent lines, the Cattle God marries his mother Earth and kills his father Plow and takes over his dominion. Then the Cattle God marries his older sister Sea who kills Earth. The Cattle God and Sea in turn give birth to a son, the Flocks God, who kills his father and marries his mother. So the generations proceed through incestuous marriage, patricide, and matricide.

According to this myth, the creation of the world resulted from both procreation and the killing of one's parents. The importance of procreation is understandable. In the *Enuma Elish*, procreation served as the means by which the macrocosm emerged out of the primordial waters. In the *Incantation against Toothache*, the creation of the microcosm is similarly described, though more abstractly:

After Anu had created heaven,
Heaven had created earth,
The earth had created the rivers,
The rivers had created the canals,
The canals had created the marsh,
And the marsh had created the worm ... (Pritchard 1969:100)

Just as a human couple is able to produce new life so also the primal gods produced by procreation, through several generations, all the vital aspects of the created world. But what is the purpose of killing one's parents? An insight from the *Enuma Elish* proves helpful. In that myth both Apsu and Tiamat are slain and are no longer active forces in the world. However, they continue to exist as inert matter, as material aspects of the creation. In the same way, each of the succeeding generations in the *Theogony of Dunnu* ceases to serve as an active agent in the world, and each generation becomes a material part of the world through its death (Jacobsen 1984: 15–16).

MYTHS OF HUMAN CREATION

Closely related to the myths of world creation are those of human creation. In fact, human creation is often placed in the context of world creation. This is true of the Sumerian myth of *Enki and Ninmah*. This myth begins by describing the structure of the world that resulted from the creation:

In days of yore, the days when heaven and earth had been
    fashioned,
in nights of yore, the nights when heaven and earth had been
    fashioned,
in years of yore, the years when the modes of being were
    determined,
when the Anunnaki gods had been born
when the goddess-mothers had been chosen for marriage,
when the goddess-mothers had been assigned to heaven or
    earth,
and when the goddess-mothers had had intercourse, had
become pregnant, and had given birth,
did the gods for whom they baked their food portions and set
    therewith their tables,
did the major gods oversee work, while the minor gods were
    shouldering the menial labor.

> The gods were dredging the rivers, were piling up their silt
>   on projecting bends—
> and the gods lugging the clay began complaining about the
>   corvée. (Jacobsen 1987b:153–54)

The creation of the world had resulted in a great disparity between the major and the minor gods. On the minor gods falls the task of maintaining the earth, particularly the work of dredging the rivers and canals. This is hard, back-breaking work, so the gods begin to complain. Fearful to approach Enki, they bring their complaint to Namma, Enki's mother and the mother who bore all the major gods. She intercedes on behalf of the minor gods and requests that Enki relieve their burden:

> My son, rise from your bed, and when you with your
>   ingenuity have searched out the required skill,
> and you have fashioned a fill-in worker for the gods, may
>   they get loose of their digging! (Jacobsen 1987b:155)

With his ingenuity and wisdom, Enki considers the problem that Namma presents him. Remembering his own conception and birth from Namma, he conceives of the idea of creating humans in the same way. Humans will be charged with the tasks of the minor gods; it will be their duty to maintain the earth by dredging the rivers and canals. Thus Enki requests that Namma create humans:

> O mother mine, since the sire who was once provided with
>   heir by you is still there, have the god's birth-chair
>   put together!
> When you have drenched even the core of the Apsu's
>   fathering clay
> Imma-en and Imma-shar [= womb-goddesses] can make the
>   fetus bigger, and when you have put limbs on it
> may Ninmah act as your birth-helper,
> and may Ninimma, Shuzidanna, Ninmada, Ninshara, Ninbara
> Ninmug, Dududuh and Ereshguna [= birth goddesses]
> assist you at your giving birth.
> O mother mine, when you have determined its mode of
>   being, may Ninmah put together the birth-chair,
> and when, without any male, you have built it up in it, may
>   you give birth to mankind! (Jacobsen 1987b:156–57)

Namma then gives birth to a human, Enki clothes it, and all the minor gods rejoice. The rest of the myth is about a contest between Enki and Ninmah over who can create the most useless human, but this need not concern us.

According to this creation myth, humans were created in order to relieve the gods from their labor. A close examination also reveals that the creations of Enki and humans are very similar. Namma, who was seen as the power in the riverbed that gives birth to fresh spring water (Enki), is identified in this myth more generally as mother earth. The "fathering clay of Apsu," the other important element in the myth, was thought to be the clay beneath the surface of the earth from which the subterranean water (Enki) was born. Therefore, just as Enki was born out of Namma from this clay, so he requests that Namma also create humans. Humans are fashioned from the fathering clay of the Apsu and are born out of the earth, out of Namma, with the help of Ninmah.

Although Ninmah plays a minor role as a divine midwife in the first part of *Enki and Ninmah*, elsewhere in Sumerian mythology, and later in Babylonian mythology, she is identified with the birth goddess par excellence. She is called by a variety of names—usually Nintur or Ninhursaga but also Mami, Aruru, and Belet-ili. These names originally represented distinct deities, but by the time the myths were composed the deities were united in the form of the great birth goddess. As the birth goddess, she was the one who shaped the fetus in the womb:

> Mother Nintur, the lady of form-giving,
> Working in a dark place, the womb;
> to give birth to kings, to tie on the rightful tiara,
> to give birth to lords, to place the crown on their heads, is in
>   her hands. (Jacobsen 1976:107)

Because this activity is analogous to the activity of artisans, the birth goddess could be identified as a potter, a bronze-caster, or a carpenter. The birth goddess was also responsible for the vital task of initiating the birth process:

> None but Ninhursaga, uniquely great, makes the innards
>   contract,
> None but Nintur, the great mother, sets birth-giving going.
>   (Jacobsen 1973:288)

She was the power in all facets of the birth process, including the actual delivery and care for the infant. Thus, she is often portrayed as a midwife, acting outside of the womb. Like her role in *Enki and Ninmah*, she aided in the birth of gods and humans.

In *Enki and Ninmah* humans are created without male assistance. This is unusual in Sumerian mythology. Typically, Enki plays a critical role in the creation of humans by supplying the necessary semen for conception. The Sumerian language makes no distinction between semen and water, encouraging a metaphorical relationship between the two. Just as water enables soil to produce, so semen enables the womb to conceive. Enki, as the god of fresh water, is therefore also the progenitor of gods and humans. An excerpt from a myth describing the creation of the plant gods thus illustrates both Enki's and Nintur's task in the birth process:

> Enki, the wise one, toward Nintur, the country's mother,
> was digging his phallus into the levee,
> plunging his phallus into the canebrake . . .
> On Ninhursaga he poured semen into the womb,
> and she conceived the semen in the womb, very semen of
>   Enki . . .
> In the month of womanhood
> like juniper oil, like juniper oil, like a prince's sweet butter,
> did Nintur mother of the country,
> like juniper oil, give birth to Ninnisiga.
>   (Jacobsen 1987b:191–92)

A different Sumerian tradition on the creation of humans claims that humans sprouted from the ground like plants. In the introductory lines to the hymn to E-engur, Enki's temple at Eridu, the text states:

> When destinies had been determined for all engendered things,
> When in the year known as "Abundance born in heaven, . . . "
> The people had broken through the ground like grass.
>   (Jacobsen 1970:112)

This idea is elaborated further in the *Creation of the Pickax*. In this myth Enlil, god of the air, separates the heaven from the earth so that humans can sprout up:

> The lord did verily produce the normal order,
> The lord whose decisions cannot be altered,
> Enlil, did verily speed to remove heaven from earth
> So that the seed from which grew the nation could sprout up
>   from the field;

did verily speed to bring the earth out from under heaven as a
   separate entity
And bound up for her the gash in the "bond of heaven and
   earth" [= Duranki]
So that the "flesh producer" [= Uzumua] could grow the
   vanguard of mankind. (Jacobsen 1970:113)

Duranki and Uzumua were sacred spots in ancient Nippur.
Duranki was the spot at which heaven and earth were attached.
When Enlil separated them, the resulting wound in the earth was
bound up so that so that Uzumua (located within Duranki?)
could grow humankind. This text seems to have developed from
the insight that seeds need to be covered by dirt in order to
sprout; otherwise they will simply bake in the sun.

Having prepared the earth for life, Enlil creates the
pickax, the indispensable tool of early agriculturalists, and
marvels over its quality. Humans, however, had not sprouted
as expected. Apparently the hard crust of the earth prevented
them from breaking through. Thus, Enlil uses his newly created pickax to free them:

[He] drove his pickax into the "flesh producer."
In the hole which he thus made was the vanguard of mankind
And while the people of his land were breaking through the
   ground toward Enlil
He eyed his black-headed ones [= Sumerians] in steadfast
   fashion. (Jacobsen 1970:114)

Although this tradition of human creation and the tradition of *Enki and Ninmah*, along with related myths, share the
common idea that humans have their origin in the earth, they
use different metaphors to illustrate that origin. The traditions
also differ with regard to how humans emerged from the earth.
One tradition uses sexual metaphors to describe the birth of
humans from the earth. The other tradition prefers agricultural
metaphors.

In later Mesopotamian myths of human creation both of
these traditions can be found. In the myth of *Atrahasis*, for
instance, humans are born out of the earth. The myth begins
like *Enki and Ninmah* by describing how the major gods
impose the work of the earth on the minor gods. These minor
gods are charged with the tasks of digging out the river beds of
the Tigris and Euphrates and of clearing the silt from the
irrigation canals. Unlike the gods in *Enki and Ninmah*, how-

ever, the gods in this myth revolt against the great gods. Incited by an unnamed god, the gods burn their tools, lay aside their spades, and besiege the dwelling of Enlil, who was given dominion over the earth. Enlil is disturbed in his sleep by the noise of their rebellion, and he summons the great gods, Anu and Enki, to decide the dispute. The rebel gods present their case: The gods declare war because their burden is too difficult. Anu agrees with their complaint: "Their work was indeed too hard, their trouble was too much." Nevertheless, the gods' revolt cannot simply be dismissed; a penalty must be paid. Thus on the recommendation of Enlil, Anu decides that one god, the leader of the rebellion, should be killed as an example.

Enki now addresses the other great gods. He agrees with Anu that the minor gods' complaint is justified, but rather than simply kill the leader as an example, he suggests an alternative plan: Let the birth goddess create humans to carry the burden of the gods. The great gods embrace Enki's plan and summon the birth goddess, here called Nintu-Mami, to instruct her for her task, but Nintu claims that she cannot create a human by herself:

> It is not proper for me to make him.
> The work is Enki's;
> He makes everything pure!
> If he gives me clay, then I will do it. (Dalley 1991:15)

In turn, Enki responds:

> On the first, seventh, and fifteenth of the month
> I shall make a purification by washing.
> Then one god should be slaughtered.
> And the gods can be purified by immersion.
> Nintu shall mix clay
> With his flesh and his blood.
> Then a god and a man
> Will be mixed together in clay.
> Let us hear the drumbeat forever after,
> Let a ghost come into existence from the god's flesh,
> Let her proclaim it as his living sign,
> And let the ghost exist so as not to forget the slain god.
>   (Dalley 1991:15)

All the great gods endorse the plan. They kill the rebel leader. Nintu-Mami then mixes his blood with clay supplied by Enki. This is the mixture she uses to create humans, on whom the work of the gods will be imposed.

The interpretation of the creation of humans in this text is problematic. The references to the drumbeat and the ghost are not further clarified. One possible interpretation that finds support elsewhere in the myth is that this text describes human nature. Accordingly, the drumbeat is the human heart, and it serves as a sign that humans are created from the rebel god, who is present in humans in the form of a ghost. The beat of the heart serves to remind humans of their purpose in life, to serve and do the work of the gods, and also provides a warning of the possible consequences of rebellion against the gods (Moran 1970).

When Nintu-Mami creates the humans, she takes the clay and mixes it with blood. But the text goes on to state that the great gods spat on the clay. These are undoubtedly metaphors for the conception of a fetus in the womb. The clay is the fetal material supplied by the womb. We would identify the clay with the human egg, but the ancients thought in terms of an inert matter, like the earth's soil that needs seed in order to produce. The gods' spit, then, should be identified with semen. (In the Egyptian myths we will see how Atum's semen was later thought to have come from his mouth.) Only with the spit of the gods are humans able to be created from the clay. Although the mixing of clay and spit represents the conception of humans, the rest of the birth process is not described in this account. Once the gods spit on the clay, Mami states that she has succeeded in creating humans and so relieved the gods from their toil.

The myth of *Atrahasis* then continues with what appears to be a different account of the creation of humans, but on closer examination this second account is revealed to be parallel to the first account. The first account presents the creation of humans in an abstract and general way, whereas the second account is more specific and concrete (Kikawada 1983). In particular, the second account details the process by which humans are created out of clay: It begins as follows:

> Far-sighted Enki and wise Mami
> Went into the room of fate.
> The womb-goddesses were assembled.
> He trod the clay in her presence;
> She kept reciting an incantation,
> For Enki, staying in her presence, made her recite it.
> When she had finished her incantation,

> She pinched off fourteen pieces of clay,
> And set seven pieces on the right,
> Seven on the left.
> Between them she put down a mud brick.
> She made use of a reed, opened it to cut the umbilical cord,
> Called up the wise and knowledgeable
> Womb-goddesses, seven and seven.
> Seven created males,
> Seven created females,
> For the womb-goddess is creator of fate. (Dalley 1991:16–17)

This passage uses several complex metaphors. It begins by describing the process of making bricks. Like a brick-maker, Enki prepares the clay by stomping it with his feet, but in this context his actions serve as a metaphor for the shaping of the fetus in the womb. Mami recites incantations so that the fetus will be born properly. This was a common task of Near Eastern midwives (Beckman 1983). After her incantation, she pinches off fourteen pieces of clay, which is analogous to the movement of the fetus into the birth canal. Finally, Mami puts down a mud brick as a birth stool (Lambert and Millard 1969:153) and then delivers seven males and seven females. Although the mother of these newly created humans is never specified, the reference to clay suggests that it is the earth itself. But rather than draw attention to Mami's role as mother earth, the text emphasizes only her role as the divine midwife.

Our interpretation of this second account of human creation is confirmed by the following lines of the myth, which give concrete instructions for performing the rituals appropriate for a woman giving birth to a baby. When a woman gives birth, a mud brick should be put in the birthing house for seven days in honor of Mami, and the mother shall sever herself from the baby by cutting the umbilical cord. The next lines of the myth repeat Mami's role in the creation of humans, but with more specific detail:

> The womb-goddesses were assembled
> And Nintu was present. They counted the months,
> Called up the tenth month as the term of fates.
> When the tenth month came,
> She slipped in a staff and opened the womb.
> Her face was glad and joyful.
> She covered her head,

> Performed the midwifery,
> Put on her belt, said a blessing. (Dalley 1991:17)

In this text Nintu-Mami unambiguously acts as a divine midwife and delivers the birth of the humans. More ritual instruction follows and concludes the myth's focus on the creation of humans.

A brief account of human creation is included in the *Enuma Elish*. After Marduk's victory over Tiamat and his creation of the microcosm, the gods praise him for his majesty and great works. In response to this praise, Marduk considers an even greater achievement. Consulting with Ea, another name for Enki, Marduk decides to free the gods from their labor by creating humans:

> Let me put blood together, and make bones too.
> Let me set up primeval man: Man shall be his name.
> Let me create a primeval man.
> The work of the gods shall be imposed on him, and so they
>   shall be at leisure.
> Let me change the ways of the gods miraculously,
> So that they are gathered as one yet divided in two.
>   (Dalley 1991:260–61)

The last line of this text means that all the gods will be able to rest as one, yet they will still be divided into two classes: the gods above the earth and the gods below. Ea agrees with Marduk's plan but adds the further provision that the one responsible for arousing Tiamat to battle should be killed so that humans can be created. The assembly of gods indict Kingu as the one who started the war by inciting Tiamat.

> They bound him and held him in front of Ea,
> Imposed the penalty on him and cut off his blood.
> He created mankind from his blood,
> Imposed the toil of the gods on man and released the gods
>   from it. (Dalley 1991:261)

Then out of gratitude for being freed from their work, the gods themselves build Babylon and its temple Esagila and throw a banquet to celebrate Marduk's kingship.

In the *Enuma Elish* the process of human creation is not described. Although only divine blood is mentioned for the composition of humans, this text undoubtedly stands within the same Mesopotamian tradition described above in which humans have their origin in the earth. Whether humans were born from clay or sprouted like plants, we cannot determine. The sole mention of divine blood and the task of humans—to bear the gods' toil—was sufficient for the myth's purpose.

One final Mesopotamian myth of human creation that needs to be considered is a bilingual text discovered at Assur and dating back to approximately 800 BCE. This myth begins by describing how the great gods, after they create the earth, deliberate on what they should create next. Together, they recognize the need for humans to perform the work of the gods in maintaining the earth:

> In Uzumua, the bond of heaven and earth,
> Let us slay two Lamga gods [= divine craftsmen].
> With their blood let us create mankind.
> The service of the gods will be their portion,
> For all times to maintain the boundary ditch,
> To place the hoe and the basket into their hands
> For the dwelling of the great gods,
> Which is fixed to be an exalted sanctuary,
> To mark off field from field,
> For all times to maintain the boundary ditch,
> To give the trench its right course,
> To maintain the boundary stone,
> To water the four regions of the earth,
> To raise plants in abundance. (Heidel 1951:69–70)

Although this text suggests that humans will be created from the blood of two gods, the role of blood is not mentioned in the actual description of human creation. Rather, humans sprout from the ground like plants:

> Aruru, the lady of the gods, who is fit for rulership,
> Ordained for them great destinies:
> Skilled worker to produce for skilled worker and unskilled
>   worker for unskilled worker,
> Springing up by themselves like grain from the ground,
> A thing which, like the stars of heaven, shall not be changed
>   forever. (Heidel 1951:70–71)

This myth uses a variety of metaphors to describe human creation: the agricultural metaphors embodied in Uzumua, the "(place where) flesh sprouted forth"; the sprouting of grain; the blood of slain gods; and the reference to Aruru, who is associated with the birth process. The point of this myth appears to be that Aruru has ordained human reproduction so that humans will be able to procreate and reproduce, unaided by the gods, like grain that sprouts from the ground. The blood from the divine craftsmen—note that in this myth they are not rebel gods—transfers to humans the necessary skills for maintaining the earth; humans are given divine skills so that the gods may rest.

EGYPT

In comparison to the creation myths of Mesopotamia, the Egyptian creation myths are much more difficult to understand. In part, this is because the Egyptians found no need to describe the process of creation in its entirety. Although most of the Egyptian myths are basically cosmological or cosmogonical myths—that is, concerned with the composition or creation of the world—this was only a secondary purpose. Most of the myths were primarily formulated to serve a ritual or cultic function (Lesko 1991:91). This is true for the Mesopotamian creation myths as well, but unlike them the Egyptian myths usually make only passing reference to creation. The Egyptian ideas of creation must be reconstructed from numerous disparate sources.

The Egyptian creation myths are also more difficult to understand because the myths have undergone a long history of harmonization and abstraction. In predynastic Egypt, prior to the third millennium BCE, there probably existed a variety of local, independent traditions of creation, each with its own gods and unique depiction of creation. However, with the unification of Egypt and the founding of the first dynasty under Menes, many of the local myths were brought together into an elaborate system, and the numerous gods were arranged into a hierarchy (Lesko 1991:90). Moreover, the myths were continuously reformulated in response to and in conjunction with Egypt's intellectual tradition. The result was a complex national mythology.

MYTHS OF WORLD CREATION

A thorough treatment of Egypt's creation myths is beyond the scope of this chapter and undoubtedly would try the patience of most readers. Nevertheless, a few examples of this mythology will aid in constructing a cross-cultural model for interpreting the creation metaphors of the Bible. One early example of Egypt's creation mythology is known as the Heliopolitan cosmogony because it originated in the cult of Atum at Heliopolis, the biblical On. This myth presents the classical Egyptian doctrine of the procreation of the world. According to this myth, the creation of the world began at Heliopolis as a hillock emerged out of the primeval ocean Nun. On this hillock the lone god Atum procreated by himself: "Atum is he who once came into being, who masturbated in On. He took his phallus in his grasp that he might create orgasm by means of it, and so were born the twins Shu and Tefnut" (Faulkner 1969:198). Shu (male) is identified with the air and Tefnut (female) with moisture. Because this first couple was thought to have been born from Atum's mouth, later formulations of the myth state that Atum spit them out (Morenz 1973:163). Shu and Tefnut then gave birth to the earth, Geb (male), and the sky, Nut (Female). They in turn gave birth to two sons, Osiris and Seth, and two daughters, Isis and Nephthys, thus completing the Ennead (family of nine gods). These siblings possibly represent the political powers of the terrestrial world (Morenz 1973:162), though they have also been identified with natural powers (Lesko 1991:93). Finally, Osiris and Isis gave birth to Horus, who is identified with the king of Egypt.

Another creation myth focuses on the work of Ptah, the chief god of Memphis. In the Berlin *Hymn to Ptah*, Ptah, the self-created one, is praised as the one who creates the world like a potter fashioning a vessel:

> Greetings, Ptah, father of the gods,
> Tatenen, eldest of the originals, . . .
> who begot himself by himself, without any developing
>   having developed;
> who crafted the world in the design of his heart,
> when his developments developed.
> Model who gave birth to all that is,
> begetter who created what exists . . .
> Who built his body by himself,
> without the earth having developed, without the sky having
>   developed,
> without the waters having been introduced.
> You tied together the world, you totaled your flesh,

you took account of your parts and found yourself alone,
place-maker, god who smelted the Two Lands [= upper and
    lower Egypt].
There is no father of yours who begot you in your developing,
no mother of yours who gave you birth:
your own Khnum [= the potter god],
active one who came forth active.

(Allen 1988:39–40; with modifications)

An important characteristic of Egyptian creation myths that can
be observed from this text is the mixture of both craftsman and
birth imagery. Ptah both fashions the world and gives birth to it.
Ptah is also compared to Khnum, the potter god who fashions
gods and humans on his potter's wheel. Khnum, as we will
illustrate below, is also responsible for creating the semen and
fashioning the fetus in the womb (Morenz 1973:162, 183–84).
These two types of creation are thoroughly integrated in the
Egyptian myths and thus probably stem from a single cultural
model of creation.

A third Egyptian creation myth that combines elements
from the previous two myths is the *Memphite Theology*. Although this myth is only preserved in a very late and badly
damaged inscription, it might stem from the Old Kingdom
when Memphis was the capital that united Upper and Lower
Egypt. According to this myth, Ptah is the creator of even Atum
and the rest of the Heliopolitan Ennead, but the mode of
creation has been abstracted from the concrete craftsman and
birth metaphors to an intangible intellectual creative principle.
The creation comes into being through Ptah's efficacious word.

There took shape in the heart, there took shape on the tongue
the form of Atum. For the very great one is Ptah, who gave life
to all the gods and their *kas* through this heart and through this
tongue, in which Horus [= command] had taken shape as Ptah,
in which Thoth [= perception] had taken shape as Ptah. Thus
heart and tongue rule over all limbs in accordance with the
teaching that the heart is in every body and the tongue is in
every mouth of all gods, all men, all cattle, all creeping things,
whatever lives, thinking whatever he [= Ptah] wishes and com-
manding whatever he wishes. His Ennead is before him as teeth
and lips. They are the semen and the hands of Atum. For the
Ennead of Atum came into being through his semen and his
fingers. But the Ennead is the teeth and lips in this mouth which
pronounced the name of every living thing, from which Shu

and Tefnut came forth, and which gave birth to the Ennead . . .
Thus all the gods were born and his Ennead was completed. For
every word of the god came about through what the heart
devised and the tongue commanded. (Lichtheim 1980:54)

In this myth Ptah is identified with the creative principle which
is actualized through his thoughts and speech. The Ennead of
Atum serves as the agent through which Ptah's word is translated into material reality. The model for this abstract understanding of creation appears to be the actual workings of the
human mind. Just as humans conceptualize and plan and then
act on those plans so also Ptah's conceptualizations result in the
creation of the world. Similarly, the Ennead is the agent in Ptah's
creating just as the human senses serve as agents of the mind
(Allen 1988:45): "Sight, hearing, breathing—they report to the
heart, and it makes every understanding come forth. As to the
tongue, it repeats what the heart has devised" (Lichtheim
1980:54).

MYTHS OF HUMAN CREATION

Egyptian myths have little to say about the creation of
humans; their primary content is world creation and the
emergence of the gods (Kákosy 1964:205). However, short
references to human creation can be gleaned from a variety of
Egyptian texts. In the *Instruction Addressed to King Merikare*,
for instance, humans are compared to god's cattle:

Well tended is mankind—god's cattle,
He made sky and earth for their sake,
He subdued the water monster,
He made breath for their noses to live.
They are his images, who came from his body,
He shines in the sky for their sake;
He made for them plants and cattle,
Fowl and fish to feed them. (Lichtheim 1973:106)

Although the process of human creation in this text is not
explicitly detailed, the language suggests that humans are
formed through procreation by the god. Another text, from the
Instruction of Amenemope, compares humans to a building that
god constructs:

Man is clay and straw,
The god is his builder.
He tears down, he builds up daily,
He makes a thousand poor by his will,
He makes a thousand men into chiefs,
When he is in his hour of life. (Lichtheim 1976:160)

It is interesting to note that neither of the previous texts identifies the god responsible for human creation. Elsewhere, the *Book of the Gates* identifies Horus as the creator of humans (Morenz 1973:48). In the texts discovered at el-Amarna it is the sun-disk, Aten, who is the creator. In the *Short Hymn to Aten*, Aten is praised for creating all life, including humans:

August God who fashioned himself,
Who made every land, created what is in it,
All peoples, herds, and flocks,
All trees that grow from soil;
They live when you dawn for them,
You are mother and father of all that you made . . .
You are One yet a million lives are in you,
To make them live you give the breath of life to their noses;
By the sight of your rays all flowers exist,
What lives and sprouts from the soil grows when you shine.
                    (Lichtheim 1976:91–92)

There is an oscillation in this hymn between Aten's natural life-giving power as the sun and Aten's paternal character. Because King Akhenaten, the chief patron of the Aten cult, proclaimed Aten to be the sole god of Egypt, Aten is described as both a father and a mother. This aspect of Aten is further elaborated upon in the *Great Hymn to the Aten*, where Aten is praised for characteristics similar to both Enki and Nintur, his Mesopotamian counterparts in the creation process:

Who makes seed grow in women,
Who creates people from sperm;
Who feeds the son in his mother's womb,
Who soothes him to still his tears.
Nurse in the womb,
Giver of breath,
To nourish all that he made.
When he comes from the womb to breathe,
On the day of his birth,
You open wide his mouth,
You supply his needs. (Lichtheim 1976:97–98)

Like Enki, Aten supplies the semen that enables conception in the womb. And like Nintur, Aten shapes the fetus in the womb and acts as a divine midwife to deliver and care for the child at birth.

The preeminent creator of humans in Egypt is Khnum. He is most characteristically portrayed as a potter who fashions both gods and humans on his potter's wheel: "He has fashioned humankind on the wheel; he has engendered gods in order to people the land and the sphere of the Great Ocean" (Sauneron and Yoyotte 1959:73). In a hymn from his temple in Esna, Khnum is praised for creating every living thing on his wheel:

> You are the master of the wheel,
> Who is pleased to model on the wheel,
> The beneficent god who organizes the land,
> Who puts the seeds in contact with the land . . .
> You are the all-powerful one,
> And you have made humans on the wheel.
> You have created the gods;
> You have modeled the small and large cattle;
> You have formed everything on your wheel each day
> In your name of Khnum the potter.
>   (Sauneron and Yoyotte 1959:73)

In addition to fashioning humans on the potter's wheel, Khnum also supplies them with the breath necessary for life. He is the "god who forms bodies, the god who equips nostrils" (Lichtheim 1980:115). "The sweet breath of wind goes out from him for the nostrils of gods and humans" (Sauneron and Yoyotte 1959:74).

As a potter, Khnum has been called a craftsman god. But Khnum also plays a role in the birth process. In fact, these two aspects of Khnum's character are inseparable. Khnum's fashioning of humans on the potter's wheel was thought to be analogous to his work within the womb:

> He fashioned gods and men,
> He has formed flocks and herds;
> He made birds as well as fishes,
> He created bulls, engendered cows.
> He knotted the flow of blood to the bones,
> Formed in his workshop as his handiwork,
> So the breath of life is within everything,
> Blood bound with semen in the bones,
> To knit the bones from start.

> He makes women give birth when the womb is ready,
> So as to open ... as he wishes;
> He soothes suffering by his will,
> Relieves throats, lets everyone breathe,
> To give life to the young in the womb. (Lichtheim 1980:112)

Ancient Egyptians believed that Khnum had a necessary and critical task within the birth process. Like a potter shapes a vessel on his wheel so Khnum forms the fetus in the womb. Moreover, without Khnum's contribution, conception cannot take place. For example, the *Admonitions of Ipuwer* state: "Lo, women are barren, none conceive, Khnum does not fashion because of the state of the land" (Lichtheim 1973:151).

Khnum's role in the birth process has been beautifully illustrated on a number of wall carvings in the temple of Deir el Bahari that depict the birth of Hatshepsut, Egypt's only female king (Naville 1896: pls. XLVI–LV). In the first relevant scene, the chief god Amun is tastefully depicted having intercourse with the Queen Iahmes, Hatshepsut's mother. The Egyptians believed their kings had two fathers, a divine father who gives the king divine attributes and a human father from whom the new king will inherit the throne (Gordon 1977). In this scene Amun assumes the form of the queen's husband in order to impregnate her with divine semen. After the intercourse, the next scene portrays Khnum fashioning Hatshepsut on his potter's wheel. Then in the following scenes, Khnum leads the pregnant queen, with his spouse Heket, a birth goddess, to the birth place where she delivers Hatshepsut. According to these carvings, Khnum is clearly the one who forms and shapes the fetus in the womb. His work and skill as a potter serve as a metaphor for his activity in the birth process (Morenz 1973:183–84; Gordon 1982:206).

A CANAANITE MYTH OF CREATION

The Canaanite culture is the culture most familiar to ancient Israelites. We will use, as an exemplary myth of creation, its *Baal* myth. However, whether the Ugaritic *Baal* myth is a creation myth is hotly debated among scholars. Because the *Baal* myth lacks a specific description of the process of creation, some scholars have argued that it cannot properly be called a creation myth (Kapelrud 1980; Margalit 1981; Levenson 1988:9–10). Moreover, the Ugaritic myths usually designate El as the creator god rather than Baal, the central character of the *Baal* myth. Although the evidence is scant, El is called the father of gods and humans and the creator of creatures (Pope 1955:47–54; De Moor 1980). In addition, other scholars have argued that a distinction needs to be made between theogonic creation—the birth and succession of the gods—and cosmogonic creation—the creation of the world through divine conflict. El's creation is thus classified as a theogony, whereas Baal's creation is called a cosmogony (Fisher 1965; Cross 1976; Grønbæk 1985). This distinction, however, does not account for all the evidence, for El also acts in divine combat (P. Miller 1973:48–58; Wyatt 1987b:189–90); nor does it explain the absence of an explicit description of Baal creating. This latter problem need not detain us. The *Baal* myth is clearly concerned with the structures and order of the world and as such can be called a cosmogony. The fact that the myth contains no reference to the actual process of creation is insignificant, for it is unreasonable to expect a myth to offer a detailed explanation of its own significance (Wyatt 1985:376–77). In other words, the creation of the world is the significance of the myth; it is what results from Baal securing the order of the world. It is sufficient for our purposes simply to focus on Baal's activity.

The unity of the *Baal* myth is also debated. Even the order of the six tablets of the myth, two of which are quite fragmentary, is uncertain. The myth itself appears to be a complex weaving of loosely related mythic traditions. Nevertheless, two prominent episodes of divine conflict stand out, one dealing with control of the macrocosm and one with control of the microcosm.

The first episode begins with all the gods dining at a banquet on El's mountain. Sea, symbolic of the unruly cosmic powers and similar in character to Tiamat, sends two messengers to challenge El's power over the macrocosm. He demands that El hand over Baal, the storm god, to be his captive. All the gods cower at the messengers' arrival, and El has no recourse but to deliver Baal into Sea's control. Baal, however, does not give in to Sea so easily. He rebukes the other gods and assaults Sea's messengers. After a break in the text, the myth resumes with Kothar-wa-Hasis, the divine craftsman, prophesying Baal's victory over Sea:

> Behold, your enemy, Baal,
> > behold, you will kill your enemy,
> > behold, you will annihilate your foes.
> You will take your eternal kingship,
> > your dominion forever and ever. (Coogan 1978:88)

Kothar-wa-Hasis then provides Baal with two clubs with which he strikes and kills Sea:

> (The club) struck Prince Sea on the skull,
> > Judge River between the eyes.
> Sea stumbled;
> > he fell to the ground;
> his joints shook;
> > his frame collapsed.
> Baal captured and drank Sea;
> > he finished off Judge River. (Coogan 1978:89)

With the defeat of Sea, Baal secures order. El remains head of the macrocosm's pantheon of gods, and Baal is proclaimed king over the microcosm, or physical world of humans.

At the beginning of the second episode, Baal declares that his authority over the microcosm is unrivaled:

> No other king or non-king
> > shall set his power over the earth.
> I will send no tribute to El's son Death,
> > no homage to El's Darling, the Hero.
> Let Death cry to himself,
> > let the Darling grumble in his heart;
> for I alone will rule over the gods;
> > I alone will fatten gods and men;
> > I alone will satisfy earth's masses. (Coogan 1978:105)

Baal's boast, however, is premature. Death, the chthonic power of sterility, disease, and drought, demands that Baal surrender his authority to him. Baal is unable to resist his power and submits to Death's ultimatum. Death is pleased by Baal's unhappy decision and thus issues the terms of his surrender:

> As for you [Baal], take your clouds,
> > your wind, your bolts, your rain;
> take with you your seven lads,
> > your eight noble boars;
> take with you Pidray, maid of light;
> > take with you Tallay, maid of rain;

then head toward Mount Kankaniya:
raise the mountain with your hands,
    the hill on top of your palms;
then go down to the sanatorium of the underworld;
    you will be counted among those who go down into the earth.
And the gods will know that you have died.
                 (Coogan 1978:108)

Baal obeys Death's command and dies in the underworld.

Baal's demise causes the microcosm to wither at the hands of Death. The once rich fields that had produced bountiful crops with the aid of Baal's rain are now turned into a desert. Life on earth cannot be sustained with Death as Lord. Hence, the gods mourn the death of Baal:

Baal is dead: what will happen to the peoples?
Dagon's son: what will happen to the masses?
Let us go down into the earth in Baal's place.
                 (Coogan 1978:109)

Anat, Baal's sister and wife, demands that Death release her brother, but he refuses. She then takes action into her own hands:

She seized El's son Death:
    with a sword she split him;
    with fire she burned him;
    with a hand mill she ground him;
    in the fields she sowed him.
"May the birds not eat his remains,
    may the fowl not consume his parts:
    let flesh cry out to flesh!" (Coogan 1978:112)

By defeating Death, Anat releases Baal from his grip. Baal's resurrection is foreseen by El in a vision of a fruitful earth:

The heavens rained down oil,
the wadis ran with honey. (Coogan 1978:113)

Baal returns to his throne to exercise his dominion over the microcosm. After seven years, Death seeks justice from Baal for the shame he suffered at the hands of Anat. Unwilling to supply Death with other victims, Baal engages Death in combat. Neither, however, is able to overcome the other. Finally, the threat of El's intervention forces Death to yield to Baal.

Both episodes of the *Baal* myth envelope the same basic structure: The authority of El/Baal over the world is challenged by Sea/Death, both being symbols of chaos; Baal/Anat defeats Sea/Death; and El/Baal is restored to his position (Petersen and Woodward 1977:239–43). The similarities between the episodes relate to one another as a macrocosm does to a microcosm, further emphasizing the structure and order of the world. The differences between the episodes concern the intention of each. The first episode focuses on the rise of Baal as king over the microcosm. Closely connected with this episode is another in which Baal builds his temple as a sign of his rule over the microcosm. The second episode, however, focuses on the precariousness of life on earth. Life is frequently vanquished by death. Nevertheless, Anat's victory over Death and Baal's resurrection affirm the microcosm's capacity for sustaining life (Clifford 1984a:193–95).

AN ANCIENT NEAR EASTERN MODEL OF CREATION

From these ancient Near Eastern creation myths, and in anticipation of our discussion of the creation myths and metaphors in the Bible (chapter 3), a culturally shared model of creation in which these metaphors were rooted can be reconstructed. The basis of this model is a cultural understanding of the human body and its replication onto the earth. In other words, the human body is related analogically to the earth, as a microcosm is related to a macrocosm. The earth is viewed as a large model of the human body, or conversely, the human body is viewed as a small model of the earth. This model is illustrated in figure 6.

	Human Body Microcosm	Earth Macrocosm	
		Metaphorical	Personification
External Perspective	Order Boundaries Differentiation	Order Boundaries Differentiation	Threat to Order Threat to Boundaries Threat to Differentiation
Internal Perspective	Semen Conception Gestation Birth	Seed as Semen Plowing as Conception Sprouting as Birth	Semen as Moisture Gestation as Shaping of Clay Birth as Pinched Off Clay

Figure 6. An Ancient Near Eastern Creation Model

The human body, according to this model, is viewed from two related perspectives, each accentuating a distinctive feature of the body. From an external perspective, the body is a highly ordered and symmetrical entity with fixed boundaries that differentiate it from other entities. The body also has a number of orifices in its boundaries that can be penetrated and that discharge internal bodily fluids.[4] These orifices make the body vulnerable to external attack (i.e., from unclean food or rape) and so must be protected. From an internal perspective, the body, animated by the thoughts of the heart, is able to reproduce through the intentional act of procreation. The male body is able to inseminate the female body, which serves as a womb for a new human to be conceived and to develop. Birth then becomes the means of introducing further differentiation, by establishing boundaries between the female body and the separate human body that is born from it.

These characteristics of the human body are analogically related to similar features of the earth. From the external perspective, the same kinds of order, boundaries, and differentiation are discovered on the earth. The diverse geography of the land differentiates one region from another and establishes boundaries. The seasonal cycle and the regular courses of the sun, moon, and stars further delimit the basic order and structure of the world. Rivers and springs issue from the orifices of the earth. From the internal perspective, the earth functions like a womb in that seeds, which are planted in the ground, germinate into vegetation.[5] This analogical relationship between the human body and the earth led to the personification of the earth. The earth and the elements within it are presented as active agents in the creation. Elements of the earth, usually the waters, are personified as unruly or life-threatening monsters that must be conquered before order and differentiation

---

[4] This aspect of the creation model is reflected in term of rules of purity (Eilberg-Schwartz 1990:177–94) and need not concern us here.

[5] Unlike scientific conceptions of procreation, the people of the ancient Near East, as well many modern societies, embrace a theory of procreation that has been labeled "monogenetic." A woman is like the earth in providing the soil for life, but the man must plant the seed (semen) which contains the essential substance of the new born child (Delaney 1987:38–39).

can be established on the earth. Similarly, the land is personified as a female who is inseminated and gives birth to humans.

As a heuristic model of the ancient Near Eastern cultural
understanding of creation, this model is able to account for
both the interrelationship and the meaning of the individual
creation metaphors. The external perspective of the model is
reflected in the metaphors of separation and differentiation. In
the Sumerian epic tale of *Gilgamesh, Enkidu, and the Nether
World*, for example, creation is described with these metaphors: The earth was separated from heaven when An carried
off heaven and Enlil carried off earth. Similarly, in the *Creation
of the Pickax* Enlil, the god of the air, separates an originally
united heaven and earth. In both of these myths, the creation
metaphors present creation as the process of differentiation
through the establishment of boundaries.

The foremost example of this type of creation is found in
the *Enuma Elish* where the creation of the world consists of
splitting and arranging the corpse of Tiamat and controlling
the flow of her waters by restricting them within boundaries.
But unlike the Sumerian examples, creation in the *Enuma
Elish* is set within the context of the conflict myth, and so it
links metaphors of conflict with the creation metaphors of
separation and differentiation. According to this myth, Marduk must first fight and slay Tiamat, who poses a threat to the
great gods, before he can create the world from her corpse. A
similar linkage of conflict and creation metaphors is present in
the biblical texts. In Psalm 74:12–17 God's creation is described according to the metaphors that stem from the external
perspective of the ancient Near Eastern creation model: God
divides the sea, cuts open the earth for springs and torrents,
establishes the courses of the heavenly luminaries, and fixes
the boundaries of the earth. Yet integrated into this description
are metaphors of conflict; God breaks the heads of the dragons
in the waters and crushes the heads of Leviathan. Other biblical creation texts hint at the conflict metaphors. Psalm 104:7
refers simply to the waters fleeing at God's rebuke; Job 38:8–11
credits God with locking up an unruly sea. In Genesis 1, of
course, no trace of conflict is present, despite the references to
the "deep" (Hebrew *tehom* which is cognate to Babylonian
tiamat, "sea" and the name of Marduk's nemesis) and the "sea
monsters." Like the gods in the Sumerian examples, the biblical

God creates by peacefully dividing and fixing the boundaries of an otherwise undifferentiated primordial unity.

Previous biblical scholars have assumed that the creation metaphors of separation and differentiation were rooted in the conflict myth, that the establishment of order was the natural outcome of the divine warrior's victory over chaos. As a result, they have interpreted the diminishing presence of conflict metaphors in the biblical texts to be the result of the process of demythologization. In Genesis 1, the culmination of this process, the sea monsters are no longer symbols of primordial chaos but simply creatures created by God on the fifth day, and the waters that are also symbolic of chaos have no personality and offer no opposition to God (this passage will be discussed in detail in chapter 5).

The model of creation, however, suggests an alternative interpretation. The metaphors of separation and differentiation are primary. The conflict metaphors result from the personification of the primordial unity that is to be differentiated. From the perspective of the *Enuma Elish*, life was only possible when the primordial waters were controlled and restricted within boundaries. Tiamat and, to a lesser degree, Apsu are the personification of these waters. The conflict myth is a secondary development, a personification, of these primary creation metaphors of separation and differentiation.[6]

The creation metaphors that reflect the internal dimension of the creation model are by far the more numerous. These are the metaphors of procreation. Therefore, Apsu and Tiamat give birth to four generations of gods, representing the major elements of the world, from the intermingling of their waters. Similarly, in the Heliopolitan cosmogony the gods representing the creation are born from Atum. Because Atum is a lone god, he procreates by himself through masturbation; Shu (air) and Tefnut (moisture) are born from his semen. But these gods

---

[6] Our conclusion does not support Westermann's conclusion that the motif of divine conflict—the struggle with a dragon or chaos—was originally unconnected to the creation theme (1984:28–33). Westermann is unable to marshal convincing evidence of a conflict myth that is unrelated to creation. For example, the Egyptian myth of Re's daily struggle with Apophis is presented in the context of the creation of the world. Re's defeat of Apophis repeatedly secures the created order and the boundaries between day and night.

give birth to Geb and Nut through conventional means. These gods, the personified earth and sky respectively, then give birth to the remaining elements of creation. In the *Theology of Dunnu* the Plow and a personified Earth begin to create all the elements of the world through procreation, but in this case the process of conception is described in agricultural terms; the Plow "plows" the Earth.

The internal perspective of the creation model is also reflected in the ancient Near Eastern metaphors that present the creation of humans. Through the personification of the earth, humans are formed from clay and born from the earth like a fetus from a womb. The clay in these metaphors is analogous to the human embryo, which must develop before it is born. The *Atrahasis* myth describes the birth process in detail. The clay is fertilized by the gods' spittle, Enki shapes it during the period of gestation, and finally Nintu-Mami pinches off pieces and delivers humans from the womb of the earth. In the *Creation of the Pickax* and the bilingual Assyrian text from Assur, however, humans sprout from the earth like grain. Human semen is like seed that is planted and germinates from the ground. Both of these metaphors, reflecting different aspects of the creation model, are also present in the Bible. There are numerous biblical metaphors describing God planting humans in the ground, and Psalm 139:13–15 compares the human womb, in which God knits together the fetus, to the womb of the earth.

Most biblical references to God creating humans from clay, however, have not been interpreted in relation to either the birth or the agricultural metaphor. God's role in creating humans is, rather, compared to the dominant Egyptian tradition in which potter god Khnum fashions both gods and humans on his potter's wheel. This comparison is appropriate, but Khnum's role in the creation of humans is often misunderstood. As several hymns to Khnum demonstrate, Khnum's role as potter was thought to be analogous to his role in the birth process. Like a potter shapes a vessel on his wheel, so Khnum forms the fetus in the womb. Moreover, Khnum's role in the birth process has been clearly illustrated on the wall carvings in the temple of Deir el Bahari. According to these carvings, Khnum is the one who forms and shapes the fetus in the womb. His work and skill as a potter serve as a metaphor for his activity in the birth process. Similarly, the biblical references to God forming humans from clay should be interpreted according to this same model. The fashioning of clay represents the abstraction of one aspect of the birth process.

A further abstraction of the birth process is detectable in metaphors of creation by command. In the *Hymn to Ptah*, Ptah is praised as the self-created god who gave birth to all that exists. Yet Ptah's procreation of the world is explicitly linked to the thoughts of his heart. He is the one "who crafted the world in the design of his heart" and the "model who gave birth to all that is, begetter who created what exists." In the later *Memphite Theology*, this principle of creative thought is abstracted from the procreative process of creation. Ptah creates not through sexual intercourse or masturbation, but by the rule of his heart and tongue, that is, by his efficacious command. Nevertheless, traces of the procreation metaphors are still present, for the thoughts of the heart and the commands of the tongue are actualized by the teeth and lips that "are the semen and the hands of Atum." This abstraction of procreation can also be detected in a Ugaritic myth where, by command alone, El impregnates two handmaidens who then give birth to monsters (De Moor 1980:177–79).[7] Sexual intercourse in the procreative process has been abstracted to the desire of the heart that initiates it.

The creation metaphors of divine fiat in Genesis 1 can be interpreted in relation to this process of abstraction. Although these metaphors have been abstracted and applied to non-procreative contexts, vestiges of the procreation metaphor in which they are rooted can still be detected. On the third day God commands, "Let the earth put forth vegetation" (v. 11), and the earth produces vegetation. This scenario is analogous to El's impregnation of the handmaidens; this is an abstraction of God's procreative activity of impregnating the earth with seed. Similarly, on the fifth day God commands, "Let the waters bring forth swarms of living creatures" (v. 20) and on the sixth day, "Let the earth bring forth living creatures" (v. 24). Yet in fulfillment of these commands the text states that God "created" the sea monsters and fish (v. 21) and God "made" all the earth creatures (v. 25). These metaphors represent a further abstraction of procreation so that the waters and the earth no longer give birth to their creatures.

---

[7] KTU 1.12.

The correspondence of the diverse ancient Near Eastern creation metaphors to our heuristic model across cultural lines suggests that these metaphors are derived from a single, yet complex, cultural understanding of creation. Moreover, the creation myths and metaphors that we have examined reflect *either* the internal *or* the external perspective of the model, suggesting the development of two distinct, yet related, creation traditions in the ancient Near East. One tradition placed emphasis on procreation, whereas the other tradition placed emphasis on order and differentiation. The *Enuma Elish* could be considered the exception in that both perspectives of the model are present—the creation of the macrocosm through the procreation of the gods and the creation of the microcosm through the ordering and differentiation of Tiamat's carcass—but these two types of creation remain distinct in the myth.

This heuristic model does not suggest, however, that the ancient Near Eastern peoples could not conceive of creation differently, only that this model is sufficient to account for the interrelationship and meaning of these extant metaphors. The biblical writers' particular use of these metaphors, then, should be interpreted within the context of this shared cultural understanding. Only when the culturally shared meaning of the metaphor is accounted for can the biblical writers' own unique use of the metaphor be adequately understood.

In the next chapter, we will use this ancient Near Eastern creation model to interpret the biblical views of creation. This creation model will enable us to understand the diverse biblical creation metaphors and myths by placing them within the cultural context of the ancient Near East. In other words, this model provides the culturally appropriate scenarios for interpreting creation in the Bible. It schematizes the common ancient Near Eastern understanding of reality that formed the cultural basis of the distinct creation myths outlined above. Furthermore, the high correspondence between this heuristic model and the biblical metaphors—demonstrated in the next chapter—suggests that these metaphors are based on a similar culturally shared perception of reality. By presenting the basic understanding of reality that was shared by the biblical writers, this model can serve as a key for understanding the basic structure of the Israelites' worldview.

3
CREATION
IN THE BIBLE

THE PROBLEM WITH CREATION IN THE BIBLE

Creation in the Bible is described with metaphors and myths similar in kind to those used in the Mesopotamian, Egyptian, and Canaanite cultures. God fights the sea-dragon, battles the chaotic waters, separates the heavens from the earth, divides the primeval waters, acts through the spoken word, fashions people out of clay, gives birth to people, delivers humans out of the womb, plants a garden, and causes the earth to produce animal and plant life. Each of these metaphors has its basis in a culturally shared perception of reality that can be elucidated by the creation model reconstructed in the previous chapter. This thesis will be discussed and illustrated in the following sections. At this juncture, however, attention needs to be turned to the character of these metaphors and the significance of these similarities.

Biblical scholars have long noted that the biblical descriptions of creation have numerous similarities with other ancient Near Eastern creation myths. In fact, many scholars would acknowledge the resemblances listed above, but few attribute any significance to these parallels. Rather, scholars have chosen to emphasize the uniqueness of the Bible's views of creation, focusing on how it differs from other ancient Near Eastern literature. Until recently, the predominant view of biblical scholars has been that the Israelites appropriated the alien creation myths and metaphors of their Near Eastern neighbors, but in so doing, they transformed this material in a profound way.

The close similarities between the biblical and other ancient Near Eastern creation myths were first analyzed by Hermann Gunkel. He argued that the numerous biblical passages that allude to God's defeat of the sea-dragon or separation of the waters, especially Genesis 1, have their origin in the *Chaoskampf*—best exemplified by Marduk's battle and victory over Tiamat in the *Enuma Elish*. This myth was borrowed by the Israelites and transferred to Yahweh, the God of Israel, but in the process this conflict was stripped of most of its mythological and polytheistic character. According to Gunkel, early adaptations of the conflict myth have survived in a number of poetic fragments in the Bible (Pss 74:13–14; 89:9–10; Isa 51:9–10). Although these fragments, attesting to an early poetic recension, still exhibit some mythological flavor, Gunkel maintained that by the time of the myth's final reworking in Genesis 1 it had been completely "Judaicized."

Because Gunkel intended to demonstrate Israel's dependency on Babylonian mythology for its understanding of creation, he emphasized the similarities between the biblical creation myths and the *Enuma Elish*. Although Gunkel could not ignore the Bible's differences with the *Enuma Elish*, and so characterized Genesis 1 as a more profound presentation of creation, he valued the Bible's Babylonian heritage. As he himself pointed out, "one does no honor to his parents by thinking poorly of his ancestors" ([1895]1984:47). The scholars that have followed Gunkel, however, have not shared his respect for the ancient Near Eastern creation myths. Building on Gunkel's own observations, they have typically argued that the biblical creation myths and metaphors were foreign imports that had to be sanitized so that they could be acceptably employed in the presentation of the biblical faith. In contrast to Gunkel, these scholars have tended to emphasize the differences between the biblical and other ancient Near Eastern creation myths in order to demonstrate the superiority of the biblical faith.

For example, Walther Eichrodt devoted a chapter in his influential *Theology of the Old Testament* to "Cosmology and Creation" in which he argued extensively for the distinctive character of the Israelite belief in creation (1967:93–117). According to Eichrodt, the central distinction between the Israelite view of creation and the Babylonian view of creation, as preserved in the *Enuma Elish*, concerns the relationship of the deity to nature:

Whereas Israel's covenant God makes himself known in personal and moral action, and can therefore be experienced as spiritual personality independent of Nature, the Babylonian conception of God remains bogged down in naturalism. The Babylonian epic of the origin of the universe is an explicit Nature myth, in which natural forces are personified and made to play an active part. Hence the gods are not eternal, but emerge like everything else from the chaotic primordial matter. By the same token there is also no possibility of overcoming polytheism and its religious fragmentation; the diversity of Nature has obscured the uniqueness of the Creator. Hence the creating deity must remain a Demiurge, with quasi-human features, fashioning whatever material is available. (1967:116)

In contrast to the Babylonian cosmology, Eichrodt emphasized that the Bible states that God is completely autonomous from the natural world. Rather, the creation is dependent upon God and so is subject to the will of the creator. Because the God of the Bible acts independently on the creation, Eichrodt maintained that the creation is "from the very first integrated into a spiritual process in which each individual event acquires its value from the overall meaning of the whole; that is to say, into history" (1967:100–101). In other words, the *Enuma Elish* simply describes in dramatic fashion the order and cycles of the natural world, whereas the biblical creation accounts (Eichrodt denied that they were myths) present God's first actions in the historical drama of salvation.

The famous Israeli scholar Yehezkel Kaufmann similarly argued for a distinction between the biblical and non-biblical creation myths, by focusing on the character of the gods of each. According to him, the ancient Near Eastern gods were the personal embodiments of the seminal forces of nature— gods of the sky, of the sun, of the earth, of the river, of the sea, of the storm, of the vegetation. The gods had their origin in the primordial matter of the cosmos and emerged from this matter through procreation. Thus, the gods were born from the same substance that formed the natural world, eliminating all boundaries between them and their creation (1960:21–40). The God proclaimed by the Bible, however, is vastly different.

The basic idea of Israelite religion is that God is supreme over all. There is no realm above or beside him to limit his absolute sovereignty. He is utterly distinct from, and other than, the world; he is subject to no laws, no compulsions, or powers that transcend him. He is, in short, non-mythological. (1960:60)

The implication of Kaufmann's assessment, of course, is that the biblical creation accounts are different in their essential character from the ancient Near Eastern creation myths.

The most prominent and prolific interpreter of creation in the Bible from the previous generation was Bernhard Anderson. Like the scholars who preceded him, Anderson was concerned to describe the uniqueness of the Israelite view of creation. In his influential book entitled *Creation Versus Chaos*, popular with both scholarly and general audiences, he argued that the uniqueness of creation in the Bible can be attributed to Israel's exclusive emphasis on God's activity in human history. Unlike the creation myths of the ancient Near East and the *Enuma Elish* in particular, which served to express the human condition within the recurrent cycles of nature, creation in the biblical tradition was historicized.

Anderson argued that the ancient Near Eastern cultures interpreted the rhythms of nature according to a cosmic drama that was structured on a pattern: creation, lapse, restoration. In the beginning the creator god defeated the powers of chaos and established order. But the powers of chaos were not eliminated; they were merely confined within certain boundaries. Consequently, these chaotic powers were able eventually to break through the boundaries and to reassert their dominance over the creation. Order reverted to confusion. The creator god continually had to do battle with chaos, renewing creation with each victory. In nature this drama was manifest in the changing of the seasons, from the fertility of the agricultural season to the sterility of the hot, dry summer. In the religious practices of the people, this drama was reenacted each year at the New Year festival by reciting the creation myth. Each year Marduk defeated Tiamat again in order to reestablish the created order. This New Year festival, according to Anderson, was the means by which the ancients remained in harmony with the rhythms of nature. "Each year man, along with the cosmos, falls away from reality and must be purified and reborn. But at the turn of the New Year the victory over chaos is won again and the world is renewed" ([1967]1987:29). With the securing of nature at the Near Year, human life and peace were also secured.

The Israelites, in contrast, recited a historical drama. According to Anderson, Israel experienced the reality of God not in the natural cycles but in historical events. "Israel came to know the reality of God in the realm of the profane, the secular, the historical. And the consequence of this 'knowledge of God' ... was that the realm of nature, which ancient people regarded as sacred, was desacralized, or emptied of divinity" (1987:31). Rather than celebrate the establishment of the natural order, the Israelites chose to remember and celebrate events that happened at a definite place and time. Although they too were dependent upon the rhythms of nature for survival, they "broke with paganism, and its mythical view of reality, at the crucial point: nature is not the realm of the divine. The God Israel worships is the Lord of nature, but he is not the soul of nature" (1987:32). Thus Anderson claimed that Israel's idea of creation was transformed from a mythical event to a historical event and the creation stories themselves attest to this. They are inseparably bound to the historical narratives that follow them. Set in the form of historical accounts, their primary purpose is to describe the beginning of a historical process that God is directing toward its fulfillment.

From this brief, representative survey it should be clear that previous scholarship attributed little significance to the Bible's creation myths and metaphors. Although these metaphors and myths appear to resemble their Mesopotamian, Egyptian, and Canaanite counterparts, numerous scholars have argued that these similarities are superficial because the Israelites demythologized them, stripping them of much of their cosmogonic meaning, and employed them in historical contexts. One scholar even argued that these metaphors do not refer to creation in any meaningful sense. They were merely convenient figures of speech, borrowed from neighboring cultures, that Israel used to illustrate Yahweh's saving activity, but Israel never felt any religious reality behind them (McCarthy 1967). More recent scholarship, however, has rejected these conclusions by challenging their basic assumptions.

The common devaluation of the Bible's creation metaphors and myths has been based on two assumptions: First, in contrast to the nature gods of the other ancient Near Eastern cultures, the God of Israel acts in history; and second, the biblical literature has a historical rather than a mythological character. But these assumptions cannot be sustained upon a close examination of the evidence. In other words, one cannot account for the differences between the Israelite and neighboring cultures according to the distinction between history and nature.

Although many of the gods of the ancient Near Eastern cultures were associated with some phenomenon of the natural world, it is doubtful that all were identified completely with the natural phenomenon.[1] In reference to the Mesopotamian cultures, Thorkild Jacobsen insisted that the gods were not simply the personification of nature:

> It is not correct to say that each phenomenon was a person; we must say that there was a will and a personality in each phenomenon—in it and yet somehow behind it, for the single concrete phenomenon did not completely circumscribe and exhaust the will and personality associated with it. (1946:131)[2]

---

[1] Two gods from the Canaanite religion of Ugarit, the chief god El and the divine craftsman Kothar-wa-Hasis, cannot be equated with any element of the natural world. Although El is frequently called "Bull," there is no evidence to suggest that he was ever equated with the bull. Rather, this title was used metaphorically to describe the nobility and virility of El. He is the creator and father of gods and humans; he is wise, just, and compassionate. The attributes and functions of both El and Kothar-wa-Hasis are derived from human society, not from the phenomena of nature (Hillers 1985:262–63). They could be characterized more accurately as gods of history rather than as gods of nature. Moreover, in the Ugaritic myths El acts in history, in human affairs, in much the same way as Yahweh acts in the patriarchal narratives of Genesis. Like Yahweh, El promises the childless protagonist an offspring, appears in dreams, guides him in his acquisition of a wife, and heals him of sickness (Parker 1989; Cross 1973:177–83).

[2] This distinction between the deity and its natural representation is further clarified by Jacobsen's discussion of the relationship between the god and its cult statue (1987a). To the ancients the god and its cult statue, or natural representation, were two different and distinct things. While the deity was one, its representations were many. This distinction is even represented in the text of *Gilgamesh,* which uses one expression to refer to the sun-god Shamash and another to refer to the god's natural representation, the sun. Although elsewhere in the literature a god and his representation appear to be equated, this should be explained in terms of transubstantiation. Through ritual "the statue mystically becomes what it represents, the god, without, however, in any way limiting the god, who remains transcendent" (1987a:22). The cult statue, or its natural representation, was considered to be a theophany of the deity.

The object or phenomenon of nature was perceived to be a manifestation of the divine presence, a theophany, but the deity itself remained transcendent and independent of its representation (Jacobsen 1970:320–21).

Some of the ancient Near Eastern gods were embodiments of the elements of nature, but many like the God of Israel transcended the natural world. It is simply incorrect to assume that the biblical creation myths and metaphors must be different from their ancient Near Eastern counterparts because the Bible's creator god remains distinct from the creation. From this perspective, Yahweh is no different from El, Baal, Marduk, Enki, Nintur, Atum, Ptah, or Khnum. Moreover, recent studies have demonstrated that Israel's Near Eastern neighbors also believed that their gods acted in human history (Albrektson 1967; Gnuse 1989). It cannot be argued that in the ancient world the God of Israel alone acted in human history or that Israel's view of creation was unique because Yahweh acted in history. The assumption that the Bible presents a god of history in contrast to the nature gods of Israel's neighbors is unsubstantiated.

The character of the biblical literature, whether it is mythological or historical, is largely an issue of definition and perspective. Some scholars have defined myth in such a way that its presence in the Bible is precluded. This type of definition, however, is unhelpful for it obscures the similarities that the Bible shares with other literature. Similarly, the distinction between myth and history, as these terms have been employed by biblical scholars, tends to distort the character of each. Myth and history are often interrelated in that myth can be set in historical guise and history can have a mythic dimension (Roberts 1976). Myth and history do not prove to be valid criteria for distinguishing between the biblical and non-biblical literature of the ancient Near East.

INTERPRETING CREATION IN THE BIBLE

In light of the discussion in the previous section, how should we interpret creation in the Bible? First, we cannot ignore or minimize the similarities between the biblical creation myths and metaphors and their Near Eastern counterparts. The cross-cultural model of creation that we reconstructed in the previous chapter suggests a significant degree of cultural continuity among ancient Israel's Near Eastern neighbors. Each culture's views of creation were based on the same fundamental conception of reality. Moreover, the correspondence of the Bible's creation metaphors to this creation model suggests that there was a cultural continuity between Israel and its neighbors.

On the one hand, the traditional scholarly explanation for the similarities between Israel's and its neighbors' creation metaphors has been that Israel borrowed from or was influenced by the alien ideas of its neighbors. However, this explanation in itself is inadequate, for it does not elucidate the mechanism by which the Israelites borrowed or were influenced. Recent studies on the origin of the Israelites, on the other hand, emphasize the cultural affinities they shared with the inhabitants of the eastern Mediterranean, indicating that they were probably indigenous to the region themselves, making such borrowing or influence unnecessary (see the survey by Gnuse 1991 and the synthesis by Coote 1990). An alternative explanation for these similarities is offered by the creation model. This common creation model suggests that the Israelites shared a similar conception of reality, rooted in basic experiences of the human body and the earth, as their ancient Near Eastern neighbors. Indeed, the Israelites were part of the larger ancient Near Eastern cultural milieu in that they shared similar understandings of the world with their neighbors. The differences between the Bible and other Near Eastern literature can only be understood from within the context of their similarities. These differences reflect the cultural particularities of each people, not extensively different and unrelated cultures.

Second, we must take seriously the metaphorical character of the biblical references to creation. They should not simply be dismissed as convenient figures of speech or hollow tropes, as if they were historicized "useful fictions." They are not mere illustrations. As metaphors, they were used to convey significant analogies, and we must interpret them as such in order to understand their meanings.

As outlined in the Introduction, von Rad observed that only in a few late wisdom texts that exhibit Egyptian influence was Israel's belief in creation expressed as an independent doctrine in the Bible ([1955]1984). His observation that Israel's belief in creation rarely occurs as an independent doctrine

remains valid, though many of his conclusions derived from
this observation—namely, that Israel's belief in creation was a
late development, subordinate to the doctrine of salvation—
can no longer be accepted.[3] But this observation is not surprising; there were few creation myths in the ancient Near East in
which the creation of the world was considered for its own
sake. Most creation myths served political, cultic, or etiologi-
cal purposes; they were used to justify the exaltation of a
certain deity or temple or to explain the present state of affairs.
The *Enuma Elish*, for example, was primarily concerned with
the elevation of Babylon and its cult of Marduk over the older
Mesopotamian cities and cults. Similarly, most of the Egyptian
creation myths were employed for some cultic or ritual function. The Israelites also repeatedly used creation metaphors in
extraneous (i.e., noncreation) contexts, but in so doing, they
did not devalue creation or strip the metaphors of their metaphorical character. Rather, they used creation metaphors to ascribe cosmological significance to the new contexts—to place
the extraneous material within the context of God's activity in
creation. The lack of an *independent* doctrine of creation in the
Bible has no bearing on the *significance* that the Israelites
placed on creation.

Rather than presenting creation for its own sake,[4] the
biblical authors regularly employed creation metaphors in
order to put their subject matter within the context of God's
activity in creation. The use of these metaphors indicates that
there is some analogy between creation and the subject matter

---

[3] Delbert Hillers refuted von Rad's contention that the biblical
doctrine of creation has Egyptian antecedents (1978). W. F. Albright
and his students have demonstrated that the name of Israel's God,
Yahweh, itself refers to the creation. Grammatically, the name is a
causative verb that literally means "he who brings into existence," or
"he who creates" (1978:168–72; Cross 1973:60–75). It is no longer
possible to claim with von Rad that the doctrine of creation was a late
development in the religion of Israel (Anderson [1967]1987:51–52).
Von Rad's thesis that Israel's belief in creation was subordinate to its
belief in salvation has also been challenged (Harner 1967; Ludwig
1973), and will be further dealt with in this chapter.

[4] Those passages that might be seen as presenting creation for its
own sake—Psalms 8; 19:1–6; 33:6–9; 104; 136:4–9—actually refer to
the creation in order to praise God. God's acts of creation demonstrate
God's majesty and supremacy over the earth.

to which the metaphors relate. The subject of most of the passages containing creation metaphors is either the human condition—the status of humankind in relation to God—or God's activity in the redemption of Israel. By using creation metaphors to express these subjects, the biblical authors have presented the human condition and redemption *in terms of* God's activity in creation. In other words, humankind's status in relation to God and God's activity in redemption are analogous to God's relationship to and activity in creation. Creation in the Bible therefore serves as a paradigm or model of the human condition and of redemption.

CREATION AS THE PARADIGM OF THE HUMAN CONDITION

Like their Near Eastern counterparts, the Bible's creation metaphors also tend to separate out into two distinct traditions. One tradition follows the internal perspective of the creation model and uses metaphors connected to birth and plant growth, while the other tradition follows the external perspective and uses metaphors related to order and differentiation. Whereas God's redemption of Israel is expressed with metaphors reflective of both the internal and the external perspective of the model, the human condition is expressed only by metaphors reflective of the internal perspective. The Bible uses metaphors connected with human birth and plant growth to describe the status of humans in relation to God; humans are utterly dependent upon the creator who brings both infants from the womb and plants from the earth.

METAPHORS OF THE BIRTH PROCESS

Human dependency upon God is illustrated in several narrative tales that describe God's power over the womb. God closes the womb of Rachel (Gen 30:2) but opens the womb of Leah (Gen 29:31–35). In due time, God opens Rachel's womb as well (Gen 30:22). Similarly, God had closed the womb of Hannah but opens her womb after hearing her petition (1 Sam 1). God closes the wombs of the women in the house of Abimelech because Abimelech had taken Sarah as a wife (Gen 20:18). God causes both Sarah and Rebekah to conceive after having been barren (Gen 21:2; 25:21). Although none of these passages describe creation itself, they all employ the creation metaphor of God working in the womb—by opening or closing the womb—in order to emphasize the human condition. All of these tales illustrate that God, the creator, is in control of human reproduction, and thus humans must depend upon God for their very being. Humans are only creatures whom the creator has brought into existence.

In addition to controlling the opening of the womb, according to numerous biblical passages, God works actively in the womb to form the fetus. The call of Jeremiah attests to this:

> Before I formed you in the womb I knew you,
> and before you were born I consecrated you;
> I appointed you a prophet to the nations. (Jeremiah 1:5)

Not only Jeremiah's existence but also his profession is attributed to God's activity in the womb. By juxtaposing Jeremiah's call to prophesy with God's activity in the womb, the text emphasizes Jeremiah's dependency on God. Just as Jeremiah had no role in his birth so also he had no choice in being a prophet. Jeremiah's life and destiny are in God's control. As a result, when Jeremiah is tormented by the burden of his profession, he curses the day of his birth; it would have been better to have been killed in the womb so that his mother would have been his grave than to come forth from the womb to spend his days in shame (Jer 20:14–18). Similarly, the anonymous prophet of the exile known as Second Isaiah[5] likens the servant to one who was destined while still a fetus in the womb:

> [1]The LORD called me before I was born,
> while I was in my mother's womb he named me. . . .
> [5]And now the LORD says,
> who formed me in the womb to be his servant,
> to bring Jacob back to him,
> and that Israel might be gathered to him . . .
> (Isaiah 49:1, 5)

---

[5] Second Isaiah, or Deutero-Isaiah, is the name given to the anonymous prophet that scholars believe is responsible for writing Isaiah 40–55. Unlike Isaiah of Jerusalem, whose oracles are set in Jerusalem and reflect the political circumstances of the eighth century, Second Isaiah's oracles are set in Babylon and reflect the political circumstances of the sixth century.

Like Jeremiah, the servant is directed by God from birth, and God's claim on the servant is that God created the servant by forming him in the womb.

One of the Bible's most profound statements on the human condition occurs in the dialogues of the book of Job. In this context, Job questions why God has caused his sufferings, but at the same time, Job recognizes his absolute dependency on God:

> [8]Your hand fashioned and made me;
> and now you turn and destroy me.
> [9]Remember that you fashioned me like clay;
> and will you turn me to dust again?
> [10]Did you not pour me out like milk
> and curdle me like cheese?
> [11]You clothed me with skin and flesh,
> and knit me together with bones and sinews.
> (Job 10:8–11)

Job confesses that he is the handiwork of God. Note that God's activity in the womb is compared to the work of a potter. This metaphor is based on the analogous relationship between the human body and the earth that is illustrated in the creation model. The earth, when it is personified, serves as a womb in which the fetus gestates. The task of a potter in shaping and fashioning clay is thus analogous to the growth and development of the fetus within the womb. This passage from Job, however, describes not God's creation of humankind but rather God's activity in the birth of the single human Job. Job was born from a human womb, not from the earth, unlike the humans in *Atrahasis* or *Enki and Ninmah*. Nevertheless, this creation metaphor is employed in order to give cosmological significance to Job's human condition. By highlighting how God shaped Job in the womb from the material of the earth, this creation metaphor further emphasizes the fragile nature of human existence and human dependency on God.

Humans are like a clay vessel fashioned by a potter. If the potter chooses, the vessel can be smashed into the dust from which it came. Job concludes, then, that he has no recourse against God. How can the vessel challenge its maker? Such human impotence finally leads Job to question the value of life:

[18]Why did you bring me forth from the womb?
    Would that I had died before any eye had seen me,
[19]and were as though I had not been,
    carried from the womb to the grave. (Job 10:18–19)

If God can act indiscriminately, then surely human life is worthless, for humans as the creation of God are subject to the creator's every whim.

At the end of the book of Job (chs. 38–42), Yahweh addresses Job from a whirlwind. But Yahweh does not defend his actions with regard to Job, nor does God answer Job's challenge concerning why he suffers. Rather, God questions Job on the matters of creation. Job had presumed to understand the nature of the created order. He had presumed that God's actions were unjustified, that God placed no purpose in Job's sufferings. But Job, as part of the creation, is incapable of understanding the purposes of the creator. With every question about the creation Job finds himself unable to respond until at last he confesses:

[2]I know that you can do all things,
    and that no purpose of yours can be thwarted . . .
[3]Therefore I have uttered what I did not understand,
    things too wonderful for me which I did not know.
                    (Job 42:2–3)

Not only are the human creatures unable to challenge the creator, the speeches of Yahweh further claim that humans are incapable of comprehending God's purposes for creation.

In contrast to human ignorance of God's ways, God is intimately familiar with humans. The psalmist proclaims:

[2]You know when I sit down and when I rise up;
    you discern my thoughts from far away.
[3]You search out my path and my lying down,
    and are acquainted with all my ways. (Psalm 139:2–3)

God knows the depths of human thought and the intent of human actions. Moreover, the psalmist claims that humans remain continually under God's watchful presence; they are unable to escape from God. What accounts for God's encompassing knowledge and presence? God is the creator! Because God created humans, nothing they think or do is beyond God's grasp.

[13]For it was you who formed my inward parts;
    you knit me together in my mother's womb.

> ^{14}I praise you, for I am fearfully and wonderfully made.
>> Wonderful are your works;
> that I know very well.
> ^{15} My frame was not hidden from you,
>> when I was being made in secret,
>>> intricately woven in the depths of the earth.
>>>> (Psalm 139:13–15)

God is intimately familiar with humans because God formed them in their mothers' wombs. The creation metaphor of God's working in the womb roots this feature of the human condition in the creation itself. The cosmological significance of the human condition is further emphasized by the connection between the mother's womb and the depths of the earth. Through this analogy—reflecting the microcosm/macrocosm relationship between the human body and the earth—the psalmist implies that God's activity in the human womb replicates God's activity in creating humans from the womb of the earth.

Humans, being what they are, try to escape their human condition by throwing off their dependency on God. The prophets of Israel continually condemn the people for following their own ways rather than the ways of God. One particular oracle of judgment that is important for our purposes again connects the human condition with God's activity in creation:

> ^{15}Ha! You who hide a plan too deep for the LORD,
>> whose deeds are in the dark,
>> and who say, "Who sees us? Who knows us?"
> ^{16}You turn things upside down!
>> Shall the potter be regarded as the clay?
> Shall the thing made say of its maker,
>> "He did not make me";
> or the thing formed say of the one who formed it,
>> "He has no understanding"? (Isaiah 29:15–16)

The prophet Isaiah mocks human attempts to act autonomously, to live in opposition to God's desires. Such behavior is compared to the absurdity of confusing the creator with the creation. Because God has created humans, they are dependent upon God.

The metaphor of a potter fashioning clay is also taken up by the prophet Jeremiah in order to condemn the people's rebellion against their creator, but in this passage the metaphor has been fully abstracted from its original creation context.

³I went down to the potter's house, and there he was working at his wheel. ⁴The vessel he was making of clay was spoiled in the potter's hand, and he reworked it into another vessel, as seemed good to him. ⁵Then the word of the LORD came to me: ⁶Can I not do with you, O house of Israel, just as the potter has done? says the LORD. Just like the clay in the potter's hand, so are you in my hand, O house of Israel. . . . ^{11b}Look, I am a potter shaping evil against you. Turn now, all of you from your evil way, and amend your ways and your doings. (Jeremiah 18:3–6, 11b)

Like a potter who shapes a vessel in any way that seems desirable, Yahweh can act however he chooses on the world scene. Implicit in this metaphor is the relationship between the creator and its creation. The people of Israel, and humans in general, are merely the creation of God and thus are dependent upon the creator.

Another oracle, addressed to the people of Judah who were exiled in Babylon, elucidates the analogous relationship between the work of a potter, the birth process, and God's activity in creation:

⁹Woe to you who strive with your Maker,
  earthen vessels with the potter!
Does the clay say to the one who fashions it, "What are you
    making"?
  or "Your work has no handles"?
¹⁰Woe to anyone who says to a father, "What are you
    begetting?"
  or to a woman, "With what are you in labor?"
¹¹Thus says the LORD,
  the Holy One of Israel, and its Maker:
Will you question me about my children,
  or command me concerning the work of my hands?
¹²I made the earth,
  and created humankind upon it;
  it was my hands that stretched out the heavens,
  and I commanded all their host. (Isaiah 45:9–12)

Second Isaiah had proclaimed that God was about to save the people in exile by the hand of Cyrus, king of the Persian empire (Isa 45:1–7). But the people evidently did not accept this message. Perhaps they doubted God's power to effect change in history; perhaps they doubted God's choice of Cyrus to inaugurate the change. In any case, the people deny God the ability to act in the creation. Therefore, the prophet rebukes the people.

Using explicit parental metaphors, Second Isaiah proclaims that Yahweh is the creator, humans are merely the creation. How dare they call God's power into question! As the creator, God can shape human affairs and history according to God's own purposes. In fact, God's control over creation will be demonstrated through Cyrus's liberation of the exiles, which is done for no other purpose than to fulfill God's desire (Isa 45:13).

All of the previous examples use creation metaphors to describe God working in the womb. Other biblical metaphors following the internal perspective of the creation model present God as both midwife and mother. In Psalm 22, for example, the psalmist refers to God as a midwife. This Psalm is an individual lament in which the psalmist bemoans his plight. He is surrounded and tormented by enemies and feels abandoned by God: "My God, my God, why have you forsaken me?" (Ps 22:1). But rather than reject God, the psalmist recognizes his dependency upon God and thus employs the metaphor of a midwife in order to recall God's prior protection and so plead for God's present help:

>[9]Yet it was you who took me from the womb;
>>you kept me safe on my mother's breast.
>
>[10]On you I was cast from my birth,
>>and since my mother bore me, you have been my God.
>
>[11]Do not be far from me,
>>for trouble is near
>>and there is no one to help. (Psalm 22:9–11)

God's activity in creation is comparable to Nintu-Mami's role in the *Atrahasis* myth. God, as midwife, delivers humans from the womb of the earth. In this psalm, however, this creation metaphor is put in the context of the psalmist's own birth in order to root his vulnerable plight in the human condition. Just as a newborn depends upon a midwife to bring it from the womb so that it might live so also the psalmist depends upon God for deliverance.

Psalm 22 also employs a maternal metaphor for God. Verse 9 describes how the psalmist was taken from the womb by God and placed on his mother's breasts. But in verse 10 it is on God that the psalmist is placed. The poetry implies that God is the mother from whose womb the psalmist was born (Trible 1978:60–61). This passage implies that the psalmist is dependent upon God as a child depends upon its mother.

Elsewhere, God is explicitly described as the mother who gave birth to the people of Israel. In Deuteronomy 32 the history of Israel, both God's actions on behalf of Israel and Israel's repeated rejection of God, is reviewed. This review culminates in an indictment in which Israel's apostasy is compared to a child who forgets its mother:

> You were unmindful of the Rock that bore you;
>   you forgot the God who gave you birth.
>   (Deuteronomy 32:18)

In a strikingly different context, Moses rebukes God for neglecting to care for the people of Israel as a mother should care for her child:

> [11]Moses said to the LORD, "Why have you treated your servant so badly? Why have I not found favor in your sight, that you lay the burden of all this people on me? [12]Did I conceive all this people? Did I give birth to them, that you should say to me, 'Carry them in your bosom, as a nurse carries a sucking child,' to the land that you promised on oath to their ancestors?" (Numbers 11:11–12)

In both of these passages, the relationship between God and the people of Israel is compared to that of a mother and her child. This dependent relationship requires certain responsibilities from both sides. Israel, the creation of God, should be faithful to God just as a child is naturally drawn to its mother. Conversely, God as the creator and mother of Israel has the responsibility of providing for Israel's basic needs. The creator has an obligation toward the creation.

God's care for the creation is the flip side of the human condition. Because humans are the creation of God, they are ultimately dependent upon God for their existence, and so God must nourish, comfort, and protect them. In this tradition, Second Isaiah compares God's love and care for the people to a mother's care for the child of her womb. The people of Judah had been exiled to Babylon, and as a result, they questioned God's care for them. Had God abandoned them? To these people the anonymous prophet offers a message of hope:

> Can a woman forget her nursing child,
>   or show no compassion for the child of her womb?
> Even these may forget,
>   yet I will not forget you. (Isaiah 49:15)

Because God had given birth to Israel, God could not abandon them. Despite the present circumstances, God will show compassion on the people. Note that Second Isaiah acknowledges the imperfection of this creation metaphor. Human mothers might in fact abandon their children, but God's compassion for these offspring far surpasses the compassion of human mothers. God will never abandon the people.

Similarly, God is described not only as the one who bore the people of Israel from the womb but also the one who carries them throughout their life:

> [3]Listen to me, O house of Jacob,
>   all the remnant of the house of Israel,
> who have been borne by me from your birth,
>   carried from the womb;
> [4]even to your old age I am he,
>   even when you turn gray I will carry you.
> I have made, and I will bear;
>   I will carry and will save. (Isaiah 46:3–4)

As the creator, God is responsible for the creation and so carries the people like a mother carries her child. But unlike a mother, God continues to carry God's people even into old age.

AGRICULTURAL METAPHORS

The birth of an infant from its mother's womb is analogous to the sprouting of vegetation from the earth. According to the creation model, these two processes of creation have a microcosm/macrocosm relationship. The several ancient Near Eastern references to humans sprouting like plants or being fashioned from clay portray humans originating from the earth. This relationship also occurs in the Bible. Psalm 139, for example, compares the mother's womb with the depths of the earth. The frequent references to God's fashioning humans from clay all stem from the same basic analogy between the earth and the womb. This metaphorical relationship between humans and plants is also used to emphasize the final product of growth rather than the initial germination or the process of growth. Humans are thus compared with grass, various sorts of trees, and vines (Frymer-Kensky 1987b).

In the Bible, grass serves as a dominant metaphor for expressing the fragility and impermanence of the human condition.

Just as grass quickly withers and is easily destroyed so humans are powerless in the presence of God.

> [5]You sweep them away; they are like a dream,
>   like grass that is renewed in the morning;
> [6]in the morning it flourishes and is renewed;
>   in the evening it fades and withers. (Psalm 90:5–6)

Humans are impermanent like grass; they are here today but gone tomorrow.

> [15]As for mortals, their days are like grass;
>   they flourish like a flower of the field;
> [16]for the wind passes over it, and it is gone,
>   and its place knows it no more. (Psalm 103:15–16)

Moreover, grass serves as an appropriate metaphor to contrast the impermanence of humankind with the permanence of God:

> [6]All people are grass
>   their constancy is like the flower of the field.
> [7]The grass withers, the flower fades,
>   when the breath of the LORD blows upon it;
>   surely the people are grass.
> [8]The grass withers, the flower fades;
>   but the word of our God will stand forever.
>   (Isaiah 40:6–8)

In contrast to grass, trees may function metaphorically to describe whether or not people are faithful to their creator. Those who avoid sin and delight in the law of God are compared to a healthy, fruitful tree:

> They are like trees
>   planted by streams of water,
> which yield their fruit in its season,
>   and their leaves do not wither. (Psalm 1:3)

Similarly, those who trust in God are blessed:

> They shall be like a tree planted by water,
>   sending out its roots by the stream.
> It shall not fear when heat comes,
>   and its leaves shall stay green;

> in the year of drought it is not anxious,
>> and it does not cease to bear fruit. (Jeremiah 17:8)

However, those who do not trust in God, those who have rejected the ways of God and have followed their own desire, are cursed.

> They shall be like a shrub in the desert,
>> and shall not see when relief comes.
> They shall live in the parched places of the wilderness,
>> in an uninhabited salt land. (Jeremiah 17:6)

Each of these metaphors serves as a paradigm of the human condition, illustrating human dependency upon God. Humans are like trees that must rely upon God, who provides water and nutrients for growth. If humans follow the ways of God, they will be luxuriant and fruitful, resilient even to drought. But if humans reject God, they also reject their creator. Thus God will withhold from them the basic necessities of life. They will be like a shrub in the desert, without water, bearing little foliage.

As the creator, God plants humans in the ground and nurtures their growth. But if the human plant does not produce or is displeasing to God, the creator has the prerogative to uproot the plant. This relationship between the plant and the one who plants it thus became a fitting metaphor describing God's relationship to Israel.

> [16]The LORD once called you, "A green olive tree, fair with goodly fruit"; but with the roar of a great tempest he will set fire to it, and its branches will be consumed. [17]The LORD of hosts, who planted you, has pronounced evil against you, because of the evil that the house of Israel and the house of Judah have done, provoking me to anger by making offerings to Baal. (Jeremiah 11:16–17)

God planted Israel, and it grew into a lush olive tree. But Israel turned away from God to follow Baal; Israel rejected the creator that planted and nurtured it. As a result, God will destroy Israel by burning the tree to the ground.

A similar use of the plant metaphor appears in the "Song of the Vineyard." In this song Israel is like a vine that God planted with the hope that it would produce sweet grapes for wine:

> [1]My beloved had a vineyard
>   on a very fertile hill.
> [2]He dug it and cleared it of stones,
>   and planted it with choice vines;
>   he built a watchtower in the midst of it,
>   and hewed out a wine vat in it;
>   he expected it to yield grapes,
>   but it yielded wild grapes. (Isaiah 5:1–2)

God, as the creator who had planted Israel, had done all that could be expected from a good farmer. God started with fertile soil and planted the best vines. God worked the field so that the vines' roots would be unencumbered. Nevertheless, the vines did not produce good fruit; Israel did not remain faithful to its creator. Consequently, God will destroy this vineyard. If it cannot produce the good fruit for which it was planted, it is good for nothing.

> [5]And now I will tell you
>   what I will do to my vineyard.
>   I will remove its hedge,
>   and it shall be devoured;
>   I will break down its wall,
>   and it shall be trampled down.
> [6]I will make it a waste;
>   it shall not be pruned or hoed,
>   and it shall be overgrown with briers and thorns;
>   I will also command the clouds
>   that they rain no rain upon it. (Isaiah 5:5–6)

Regardless of the extraneous context in which it is employed, each of the creation metaphors discussed above exemplifies the human condition. The status of humankind in relation to God is presented in terms of God's relationship to the creation. Because God is the creator and humans are the creation, humans are utterly dependent upon God. Each of the metaphors emphasizes this dependency as the basic characteristic of the human condition: Humans are like vessels in relation to God the potter; humans are dependent upon God, who fashioned them in the womb or gave birth to them; and humans are like plants that rely upon the creator, who planted them. Moreover, each of these metaphors is based on a culturally shared perception of reality that can be explained in terms of our reconstructed ancient Near Eastern creation model.

CREATION AS THE PARADIGM OF REDEMPTION

The biblical creation myths and metaphors are also employed as paradigms of God's activity in the redemption of Israel.[6] In the same way that God created the world and humankind, God will redeem the people of Israel. Redemption is likened to a new creation with metaphors reflecting both the internal and the external perspective of the creation model. According to the internal perspective, God is a mother or midwife who is about to give birth to a redeemed Israel. God's redeeming activity is also described in terms of God's planting the people in the land. From the external perspective, God is presented as a warrior who battles against the chaos that threatens the created order. In both cases, creation myths and metaphors give cosmological significance to God's redemption of Israel.

AGRICULTURAL METAPHORS

Second Isaiah compares Israel's redemption to plants that sprout from the earth:

> Shower, O heavens, from above,
>   and let the skies rain down righteousness;
> let the earth open, that salvation may spring up,
>   and let it cause righteousness to sprout up also;
>   I the LORD have created it. (Isaiah 45:8)

God has created a fertile earth that produces vegetation when the heavens shower upon it. In the same way God's creative activity produces salvation for God's people.

Other prophets also use agricultural metaphors to liken God's redemption of Israel to a new creation. Amos compares Israel to a new plant:

> I will plant them upon their land,
>   and they shall never again be plucked up
>   out of the land that I have given them,
> says the LORD your God. (Amos 9:15)

---

[6] Redemption in ancient Israel was concrete and corporate rather than spiritual and individualistic. It entailed primarily God's deliverance of Israel from the oppression of its enemies and, as we will see in a later chapter, the restoration of Israel's despoiled land.

Similarly, Jeremiah compares Israel to a plant: "I will rejoice in doing good to them, and I will plant them in this land in faithfulness, with all my heart and all my soul" (Jer 32:41). In a different course, Jeremiah likens the people of Israel and Judah to a land that God is going to replant:

> 27The days are surely coming, says the LORD, when I will sow the house of Israel and the house of Judah with the seed of humans and the seed of animals. 28And just as I have watched over them to pluck up and break down, to overthrow, destroy, and bring evil, so I will watch over them to build and to plant, says the LORD. (Jeremiah 31:27–28)

The Babylonians, at God's direction, had devastated the land of Israel. The people and their livestock had been slaughtered. But in the coming days God will redeem Israel, bringing new life to it as to a field, sowing it with seed and producing humans and animals.

Because Israel had sinned against God, the prophets had announced the coming of God's judgment. As discussed in the previous section, Israel was compared to a plant or tree that God would burn to the ground (Jer 11:16–17) or devastate (Isa 5:5–6). However, when God redeems the people, they are compared to a well-rooted tree that produces abundant fruit:

> In days to come Jacob shall take root,
>> Israel shall blossom and put forth shoots,
>> and fill the whole world with fruit. (Isaiah 27:6)

In the context of this oracle God's role in the redemption of Israel is described only in terms of a keeper and guard of a vineyard (Isa 27:2–3). In a similar oracle, God's redeeming activity is compared to elements of the creation itself. God will be the dew and the shade of a tree so that the normally short-lived flowers of the lily (Zohary 1982:176), likened to Israel, can blossom and flourish:

> 5I will be like the dew to Israel;
>> he shall blossom like the lily,
>> he shall strike root like the forests of Lebanon.
> 6His shoots shall spread out;
>> his beauty shall be like the olive tree,
>> and his fragrance like that of Lebanon.

⁷They shall again live beneath my shadow,
>   they shall flourish as a garden;
> they shall blossom like the vine,
>   their fragrance shall be like the wine of Lebanon.
>   (Hosea 14:5–7)

In a salvation oracle by Second Isaiah Israel's redemption is again compared to the sprouting of a plant, but this redemption is placed in the context of God's creation of Israel in the womb:

> ²Thus says the LORD who made you,
>   who formed you in the womb and will help you:
> Do not fear, O Jacob my servant,
>   Jeshurun whom I have chosen.
> ³For I will pour water on the thirsty land,
>   and streams on the dry ground;
> I will pour my spirit upon your descendants,
>   and my blessing on your offspring.
> ⁴They shall spring up like a green tamarisk,
>   like willows by flowing streams. (Isaiah 44:2–4)

This text further demonstrates the microcosm/macrocosm relationship between the human body and the earth. Moreover, it explicitly demonstrates that creation serves as a paradigm of redemption. God created Israel by forming it in the womb (microcosm). In the same way, God will redeem Israel by causing it to sprout up from the womb of the earth (macrocosm), after supplying the water necessary for germination.

METAPHORS FROM THE BIRTH PROCESS

God is described as a midwife who redeems Israel by delivering it from the womb of its mother. In Isaiah 66, Zion is presented as the mother who will swiftly bear a redeemed Israel with Yahweh's aid:

> ⁷Before she was in labor
>   she gave birth;
> before her pain came upon her
>   she delivered a son.
> ⁸Who has heard such a thing?
>   Who has seen such things?
> Shall a land be born in one day?
>   Shall a nation be delivered in one moment?

Yet as soon as Zion was in labor
   she delivered her children.
⁹Shall I open the womb and not deliver?
   says the LORD;
shall I, the one who delivers, shut the womb?
   says your God. (Isaiah 66:7–9)

The poet in this passage uses maternal metaphors to emphasize the certainty and the suddenness of God's redemption of Israel. Just as no one expects a woman to deliver a baby before she goes into labor, so Israel's redemption will be sudden and unexpected when Zion gives birth to Israel without labor. Israel's redemption is certain just as it is certain that a pregnant woman will deliver her child—once the birth process begins, it cannot be stopped. In this text the personified Zion is the mother of Israel. But Zion is also the dwelling place of God and a symbol of God's presence. Thus in a following verse, Yahweh takes on the role of Israel's mother:

As a mother comforts her child,
   so I will comfort you;
   you shall be comforted in Jerusalem. (Isaiah 66:13)

As in Psalm 22, quoted above, God's role in redemption shifts from that of the midwife who delivers Israel out of the womb to that of the comforting mother who raises and nurtures him.

Second Isaiah compares God to a woman in labor in order to emphasize the imminence of God's redemption of Israel:

For a long time I have held my peace,
   I have kept still and restrained myself;
now I will cry out like a woman in labor,
   I will gasp and pant. (Isaiah 42:14)

During the people's suffering in exile, God had been silent. But now God's role in Israel's situation is about to change. God's silence is compared to the nine months of woman's pregnancy, when she waits for the fetus within her to develop. God is about to save the people, just as a woman who is in labor will soon and inevitably deliver the child. The redemption of Israel is likened to a new creation, in which God gives birth to a redeemed people.

METAPHORS OF CONFLICT

The verses surrounding the metaphor of God's giving birth in Isaiah 42:14 also employ creation metaphors. These metaphors reflect the external perspective of the creation model and accentuate further the cosmological significance of God's redemption of Israel:

[13]The LORD goes forth like a soldier,
     like a warrior he stirs up his fury;
he cries out, he shouts aloud,
     he shows himself mighty against his foes. . . .
[15]I will [dry up] mountains and hills,
     and dry up all their herbage;
I will turn the rivers into [coastlands],
     and dry up the pools.[7]
[16]I will lead the blind
     by a road they do not know,
by paths they have not known
     I will guide them.
I will turn the darkness before them into light,
     the rough places into level ground. (Isaiah 42:13, 15–16)

This juxtaposition between metaphors from the internal and the external perspectives of the creation model demonstrates that both of these types of metaphors have their unity in the single perception of reality that is elucidated by the creation model. Nevertheless, these metaphors tend to remain distinct, as in this passage.

Most of the biblical metaphors that reflect the external perspective of the creation model make up what has frequently been termed the conflict myth—the struggle between order and chaos. Although this myth varies in detail in each of its extant expressions, certain themes unambiguously signal its presence. Of primary importance is the battle between the deity and some antagonist. The basis of the external perspective of creation is the establishment of order, differentiation, and boundaries in the world. However, the antagonist—usually a personified element of the world such as the sea, drought, plague, pestilence, darkness, or death itself—poses a threat to

---

[7] The translation of the NRSV has been altered slightly in this verse to follow the interpretation of Clifford (1984b:95).

the order of the world. This personified monster seeks to dismantle the boundaries of light and darkness, life and death; it disregards the differentiation between the seasons, between land and water, between nature and culture. The deity must defeat this monster in order to create the world. Through the deity's victory, the chaotic element is confined within specified boundaries. The monster's power against humankind and the earth is limited. The world is securely ordered.

In the biblical literature the most complete form of the conflict myth contains a challenge to Yahweh's kingship over creation, Yahweh's march into battle as the divine warrior, the convulsions of the natural world in conjunction with Yahweh's theophany, God's defeat of the enemy, Yahweh's victorious procession to his mountain sanctuary, God's enthronement, a banquet celebration, and finally, Yahweh's creation and bestowal of peace on the earth (Cross 1973:91–111, 156–63; Hanson 1979:300–315). But often only a few of these motifs are employed. In the previously quoted passage from Isaiah 42, for example, God goes forth to battle against the enemies, the representatives of chaos (v. 13). The following verse (v. 15) then describes God's securing of the created order by confining chaos within fixed limits. The sea that had overcome the land is forced back into its proper location with the result that the hill country and its vegetation become dry and suitable for habitation again. Similarly, pools of water in the land will be dried up so that the land can be used for agriculture or pasturage. The reference to God's turning rivers into coastlands fits into this same motif; God will confine the waters to the edge of the coastland.

In verse 16 the theme of the passage shifts from God's activity in creation to God's activity in redemption, but these themes are integrated in such a way that creation again serves as a paradigm of redemption. Specifically, God's redemption of Israel is incorporated into the conflict myth as an aspect of God's cosmogonic activity. Yahweh, who defeated his foes and so secured the land from the threatening sea, will lead his people in a victory procession from exile to the newly created land. God's people are blind because they have failed to see and comprehend God's activity in the world. Nevertheless, God will secure their redemption by removing all obstacles. The darkness that characterizes their blindness will be turned to light. The rough terrain that would hinder their journey will be turned into level ground.

In the Bible's use of the conflict myth, God's redemption of Israel is set explicitly within the context of God's activity of creation. In each case, God's redeeming work is described as a new creation, a new battle against chaos. Before we can proceed to illustrate God's cosmogonic activity, an important caveat must be offered. In God's battle against chaos, whatever form it might take, God defeats but does not annihilate chaos. God merely confines or restricts chaos to fixed bounds. Chaos remains a latent element within the creation, ready to break its fetters and wreak havoc on the creation (Day 1985:88; Levenson 1988:3–50). Consequently, the Israelites, or their ancient Near Eastern neighbors for that matter, did not perceive the world as a static creation—created once at the beginning of time. The creation is repeatedly being threatened by chaotic forces, and so God, as its creator, must repeatedly fight in new cosmogonic battles. In the history of Israel, the people's enemies were identified with chaos. All of Israel's enemies were considered God's enemies and thus a threat to God's kingship over creation. It is for this reason that the conflict myth served as an appropriate metaphor for describing God's redemption of Israel. By redeeming Israel from its enemies, God was defeating the powers of chaos and restoring order to the world (Hiebert 1992b:877). Each act of redemption was considered a new creation.

The classic biblical example of creation presented with the metaphors of the conflict myth, which serves as a paradigm of redemption, is the "Song of the Sea" in Exodus 15:1–18. This is an archaic poem celebrating Yahweh's victory over Pharaoh and his army at the sea. Uncharacteristic of the Near Eastern conflict myth (as in the *Enuma Elish* or the *Baal* myth) but typical of the Bible's presentation of this myth, chaos is symbolized by a historical foe, the king of Egypt (cf. Fretheim's interpretation of the role played by Pharaoh in the Exodus narratives [1991a]). The sea, which is ordinarily the symbol of chaos par excellence, in this poem functions primarily as the setting of the conflict. From this observation numerous scholars conclude that the Near Eastern conflict myth was historicized by Israel, stripped of its cosmological significance. These scholars claim that the myth was transformed from a myth of cosmic creation to an account of God's creation of a historical people (Anderson 1984b:4–5; [1967]1987:37–38).

This interpretation of the "Song of the Sea" is problematic. As discussed earlier in this chapter, such an interpretation fails to reckon with the metaphorical character of the language. Cosmic metaphors are applied to a historical account in order to attribute cosmic meaning to the historic events. It does not diminish their cosmic character (Fretheim 1991b:357). Specifically, the cosmic metaphors in Exodus 15:1–18 place God's deliverance of Israel from Egypt at the sea within the context of God's activity in creation. Israel's redemption is compared to a new creation. God engages in a cosmogonic battle against the enemy, Pharaoh, that threatens the created order. The result of God's victory is a redeemed people in an ordered world, secured from the threat of chaos (Fretheim 1991b: 358–59).

Most of the elements of the conflict myth are present in the "Song of the Sea." The song begins with the adoration of God, who has triumphed over Pharaoh and his army—the symbols of chaos. Like chaos, which threatens the order of the world, Pharaoh and his policies have threatened the existence of God's people. Therefore, God acts to secure the integrity of the creation, to redeem the people from the clutches of chaos. God marches out against Pharaoh like a warrior:

> [3]The LORD is a warrior;
>   the LORD is his name.
> [4]Pharaoh's chariots and his army he cast into the sea;
>   his picked officers were sunk in the Red Sea.
> [5]The floods covered them;
>   they went down into the depths like a stone.
>   (Exodus 15:3–5)

In this passage God is depicted as casting the enemy into the sea. In the following verses God's actions are more specifically associated with those of a storm god like Marduk or Baal:

> [8]At the blast of your nostrils the waters piled up,
>   the floods stood up in a heap;
>   the deeps [foamed] in the heart of the sea.[8]

---

[8] The translation of the NRSV has been altered to reflect the interpretation of Cross (1973:128–29). There is no substantial evidence to support the traditional reading of "congeal."

[9]The enemy said, "I will pursue, I will overtake,
    I will divide the spoil, my desire shall have its fill of them.
    I will draw my sword, my hand shall destroy them."
[10]You blew with your wind, the sea covered them;
    they sank like lead in the mighty waters. . . .
[12]You stretched out your right hand,
    the earth swallowed them. (Exodus 15:8–10, 12)

These verses tell of a storm god who stirs up the sea so that it capsizes the boat on which the Egyptians are crossing. This is the characteristic language of the conflict myth in which the divine warrior uses the thunderstorm to defeat chaos. The result is that the Egyptians sink to the bottom of the sea and drown; they disappear into the sea as if they were swallowed by the earth.

That the conflict myth has not simply been historicized should be clear from the manner by which God defeats the Egyptian army. God does not destroy the Egyptians by historical means, nor does God act exclusively in *human* history. Rather, God acts in creation and marshals the creation in the cosmogonic battle. The creation itself, through the form of a violent storm at sea, is used to defeat the threat to the created order. In this manner God demonstrates a kingship and supremacy over creation and thus redeems the people of God.

Other elements of the conflict myth in the "Song of the Sea" include the procession of Yahweh's people to his mountain sanctuary and the manifestation of God's kingship:

[13]In your steadfast love you led the people whom you
        redeemed;
    you guided them by your strength to your holy abode. . . .
[17]You brought them in and planted them on the mountain of
        your own possession,
    the place, O LORD, that you made your abode,
    the sanctuary, O LORD, that your hands have established.
[18]The LORD will reign forever and ever. (Exodus 15:13, 17–18)

Scholars dispute whether the sanctuary in this song is an early tribal sanctuary, such as Gilgal, or Solomon's temple itself on Mount Zion. In any case, these references give further evidence for interpreting this song in light of the creation myth. God's acts of redemption for the people—their deliverance from the control of the Egyptians, the guidance to the promised land, and establishment there—typically viewed as "historical" acts, are presented according to the paradigm of creation. These events are thus given cosmological significance. Israel's redemption is part of God's new act of creation.

It has long been an axiom of biblical theology that the exodus experience, God's redemption of Israel at the sea, forms the core of the biblical faith. Although some scholars have begun to challenge this belief, its influence on later biblical thought is unquestionable. In particular, God's cosmogonic victory over the Egyptians at the sea became the archetype for all of God's battles against Israel's enemies. Whenever the Israelites were oppressed by the more powerful nations around them, they looked for God to fight in a new cosmogonic battle on their behalf just as God had fought against the Egyptians. God's activity in creation, as portrayed by the conflict myth, served as the paradigm of God's repeated acts of redemption for Israel; and God's victory at the sea was the preeminent example of this cosmogonic activity. Even in the "Song of the Sea" God's defeat of Israel's future enemies is foreshadowed:

> [14]The peoples heard, they trembled;
>> pangs seized the inhabitants of Philistia.
> [15]Then the chiefs of Edom were dismayed;
>> trembling seized the leaders of Moab;
>> all the inhabitants of Canaan melted away.
> [16]Terror and dread fell upon them;
>> by the might of your arm, they became still as a stone
> until your people, O LORD, passed by,
>> until the people whom you acquired passed by.
>> (Exodus 15:14–16)

The message of the song is clear: just as God defeated Pharaoh and his army at the sea, God conquered all Israel's enemies in the battles of conquest; and so also God will defeat all of Israel's future enemies. These battles are modeled on God's victory over chaos in the primordial battle of creation.

In the "Song of the Sea" God's victory in the cosmogonic battle is celebrated by the Israelites as a present reality. God had defeated chaos so that the created order remained secure. But this was rarely the experience of the people of Israel. Frequently the world was not stable; God's victory over chaos was not evident. God was summoned to act as the creator rather than to be praised. In Psalm 74, for example, reference to God's prior activity in creation serves as a subtle reproach for God's failure to redeem the people from their present sufferings (Levenson 1988:23–25). This psalm is a national lament, probably written in response to the destruction of Jerusalem at the hand of the Babylonians in 587 BCE, though some scholars suggest a postexilic date. In any case, the psalmist repeatedly questions the lack of God's redeeming action on behalf of the afflicted people of God:

> [1]O God, why do you cast us off forever?
>> Why does your anger smoke against the sheep of your
>>> pasture?
> [2]Remember your congregation, which you acquired long ago,
>> which you redeemed to be the tribe of your heritage.
> Remember Mount Zion, where you came to dwell.
>> (Psalm 74:1–2)

Yahweh had redeemed his people in the past. Although not explicitly, the psalmist does refer to Yahweh's redemption of the people at the sea where Yahweh defeated chaos and so redeemed Israel to be his people. But now Yahweh is silent, failing to act on behalf of his people and even on behalf of his own name:

> [10]How long, O God, is the foe to scoff?
>> Is the enemy to revile your name forever?
> [11]Why do you hold back your hand;
>> why do you keep your hand in your bosom?
>>> (Psalm 74:10–11)

Into the midst of this psalm, the psalmist inserts a short hymn that describes God's activity in creation:

> [12]Yet God my King is from of old,
>> working salvation in the earth.
> [13]You divided the sea by your might;
>> you broke the heads of the dragons in the waters.
> [14]You crushed the heads of Leviathan;
>> you gave him as food for the creatures of the wilderness.
> [15]You cut openings for springs and torrents;
>> you dried up ever-flowing streams.
> [16]Yours is the day, yours also the night;
>> you established the luminaries and the sun.
> [17]You have fixed all the bounds of the earth;
>> you made summer and winter. (Psalm 74:12–17)

United in this hymn are the themes of divine kingship, defeat of the sea dragon, and world ordering—all elements of the conflict myth. God is proclaimed to be the creator, the one who defeated chaos and established the bounds of the earth. But Israel's affliction at the hand of the nations indicates that chaos is loose in the world; the dragon has broken its fetters and escaped. As the creator, God must again fight in a cosmogonic battle. Chaos must again be defeated and bound. Consequently, the psalmist calls on God to act as the creator by redeeming Israel:

> [22]Rise up, O God, plead your cause;
>> remember how the impious scoff at you all day long.
> [23]Do not forget the clamor of your foes,
>> the uproar of your adversaries that goes up continually.
>> (Psalm 74:22–23)

According to this psalm, God's activity in creation is not only the paradigm of God's redemption of Israel, it is also the basis by which God can redeem and the reason for which God should redeem.

In the oracles of Second Isaiah, the prophet of the exile similarly summons Yahweh to redeem his people from their oppressors just as he subdued the dragon in the battle of creation long ago:

> [9]Awake, awake, put on strength,
>> O arm of the LORD!
> Awake, as in days of old,
>> the generations of long ago!
> Was it not you who cut Rahab in pieces,
>> who pierced the dragon?
> [10]Was it not you who dried up the sea,
>> the waters of the great deep;
> who made the depths of the sea a way
>> for the redeemed to cross over?
> [11]So the ransomed of the LORD shall return,
>> and come to Zion with singing;
> everlasting joy shall be upon their heads;
>> they shall obtain joy and gladness,
>> and sorrow and sighing shall flee away. (Isaiah 51:9–11)

Sleep is characteristic of creator gods (Batto 1987b). After they defeat the chaos monsters and secure the order of creation, they enjoy the divine prerogative of rest. However, for the people of Judah suffering in exile, world order did not appear to be secure. Chaos had been unleashed and was assaulting them from every corner. God had no right to slumber while chaos raged over the earth. God must be aroused from sleep in order to defeat the dragon as in the days of old.

The oracle in Isaiah 51 attests to several integrally connected dimensions of God's creation and redemption. At one
level God defeated the chaos dragon, here named Rahab, in the
primordial battle of creation. According to the second level of
the oracle, God delivered the Israelites from the Egyptians at
the sea. God's drying up the sea and making a way in its depths
replicated God's primordial victory over Rahab. Finally, the
oracle announces that God's people will participate in a new
exodus, a new creation, as they return to their land. God's
activity in creation, the exodus, and the people's future redemption is viewed according to a single paradigm: God's defeat
of chaos. Some scholars, following von Rad, have used this
passage to demonstrate the historical character of creation
(Harrelson 1970:248–52; Stuhlmueller 1959), but this interpretation neglects the significance of the creation metaphors.
God's redemption, rather, is given a cosmological character as
a new creation. God's activity in creation served as the paradigm
by which Israel was redeemed from bondage at the exodus, and
in the same way God will redeem this people from exile.

Our interpretation of this passage is supported by the
following oracle in Second Isaiah. In this passage God addresses the people with a message of hope. Because Yahweh is
the creator, the people do not need to fear human oppressors.

> [12]I, I am he who comforts you;
>> why then are you afraid of a mere mortal who must die,
>> a human being who fades like grass?
> [13]You have forgotten the LORD, your Maker,
>> who stretched out the heavens
>> and laid the foundations of the earth. (Isaiah 51:12–13)

Yahweh the creator has not slumbered from his tasks. The
people have simply forgotten that Yahweh is the creator and that
Yahweh is in control of human affairs and able to redeem them
from their oppression.

One final text that illustrates how God's activity in creation
serves as the paradigm of redemption is found in Psalm 77.
This psalm is a personal lament in which the psalmist questions God's character and intention to redeem:

> [7]"Will the Lord spurn forever,
>> and never again be favorable?
> [8]Has his steadfast love ceased forever?
>> Are his promises at an end for all time?

[9]Has God forgotten to be gracious?
  Has he in anger shut up his compassion?" (Psalm 77:7–9)

In the midst of despair, however, the psalmist finds hope in God's previous deeds on behalf of his people:

[14]You are the God who works wonders;
  you have displayed your might among the peoples.
[15]With your strong arm you redeemed your people,
  the descendants of Jacob and Joseph. (Psalm 77:14–15)

Because God had marvelously redeemed the people in the past, the psalmist hopes that he too will be redeemed from his affliction.

But what had God done to inspire such hope in the psalmist? How had God redeemed the people of God? In historical terms, God's redemption of Israel had come to be known as the exodus, but the psalmist presents this prior act of redemption in the language of creation:

[16]When the waters saw you, O God,
  when the waters saw you, they were afraid;
  the very deep trembled.
[17]The clouds poured out water;
  the skies thundered;
  your arrows flashed on every side.
[18]The crash of your thunder was in the whirlwind;
  your lightnings lit up the world;
  the earth trembled and shook.
[19]Your way was through the sea,
  your path, through the mighty waters;
  yet your footprints were unseen.
[20]You led your people like a flock
  by the hand of Moses and Aaron. (Psalm 77:16–20)

In the "Song of the Sea" the sea becomes the setting for God's battle against Pharaoh and his army. Yahweh employs the sea as a weapon, but does not fight against it. But according to this hymn, Yahweh's battle is against the sea itself. In the tradition of Baal and Marduk, Yahweh fights against the waters, the symbol of chaos (May 1955), as a divine warrior in the cosmogonic battle, employing all the typical weapons of the storm god—rain, lightning, thunder, and wind. Unlike Baal and Marduk's victory, however, God's victory over the sea results, not in the construction or the ordering of the cosmos, but in Israel's redemption. The waters are made to recede so that Yahweh can lead his people to his holy abode unimpeded. The historical referent of this creation language does not devalue or historicize creation; rather, it places God's historical act of redemption at the exodus within a cosmological context. Creation is the paradigm of redemption. God was able to redeem Israel in the past because God was and continues to be the creator. Consequently, there is hope for the psalmist that God will also redeem him.

CREATION AND ANCIENT ISRAEL'S WORLDVIEW

Metaphors are rooted in culture; they are based on a culturally shared perception of reality. This is also true for the creation metaphors of the Bible. Moreover, the frequently illustrated correspondence between these metaphors and our reconstructed creation model suggests that the biblical writers shared with their ancient Near Eastern neighbors a single, yet complex, perception of reality that was rooted in fundamental experiences of the human body and the earth. Whether the Israelites could or did conceive of creation differently is not at issue. We have used the creation model only to elucidate the explicit creation metaphors in the biblical text. A model is simply a conceptual map, a heuristic tool, for organizing diverse data into a meaningful pattern (Carney 1975:1–11). In particular, the creation model enables us to understand the interrelationship of the various biblical creation metaphors and in turn the culturally shared perception of reality on which they are based. But it does not preclude the possibility that the Israelites also thought of creation in vastly different terms. For our purposes, it is sufficient to note that the creation model can explain the wide variety of biblical creation metaphors according to a single frame of reference.

In the previous chapter I argued that creation myths and metaphors provide the key for elucidating the worldview and values of the biblical writers. Because these myths and metaphors focus on the basic domains of reality—God, humans, and the natural world (the assumptions of the Classification universal)—and their interrelationship (the assumptions of the Relationship universal), they make explicit what is otherwise assumed by the biblical writers. In particular, they disclose the fundamental assumptions of the ancient Israelites' worldview. Therefore, the creation model itself, by detailing the interrelationship of these basic domains of reality, also elucidates ancient Israel's worldview.

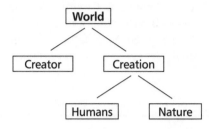

Figure 7. Domains of Israel's Worldview

The Classification scheme of ancient Israel's worldview is diagrammed in figure 7. The primary differentiation in the world is between the creator God and the creation. God creates the inhabitable world yet remains distinct from it. The creation itself is secondarily divided between humans and nature. But this differentiation should not obscure the essential unity of the creation. Humans and nature are of the same substance.

According to the creation model, one focal assumption of the Relationship universal is the correlation between humans and the natural world. Humans are both part of nature, created along with the rest of the natural world, and are also distinct from nature, singled out as different in kind. We refer to this distinction as culture, the ability of humans to create their own artificial environment that is superimposed on the natural world (Niebuhr 1951:29–39). The biblical writers, as we will discuss in chapter 5, attributed this distinction to the human character; humans were created to be distinct from the rest of the natural world. Nevertheless, the Israelite worldview is not defined in terms of a radical dichotomy between nature and culture. The creation model entails a neutral type of relationship between humans and nature. Because the human body has a microcosm/macrocosm relationship to the earth, the relationship between humans and the natural world is characterized by harmony. Despite their cultural attempts to transcend it, humans are integrally connected to the natural world.

The other focal assumption of the Relationship universal that can be discerned from the creation model concerns the hierarchical interrelationship between God and the creation.

As the creator, God acts on and transforms the creation. The creation is dependent upon God, who in turn is responsible for the creation. This Relationship assumption finds expression in the Bible's particular use of creation metaphors. By employing these metaphors in extraneous contexts, the biblical writers emphasize humankind's and, by extension, nature's dependency upon God. Both humans and nature are God's creation and are thus dependent upon God's care. Similarly, when the creation is corrupted by human or natural agents, humankind and the natural world are dependent upon God for redemption through a new act of creation (this latter point will be taken up in detail in chapter 6). From the human perspective, this assumption can be characterized as a negative type relationship, but from God's perspective, it is a positive type of relationship. Humans and nature are subordinate to God, and God is dominant over creation.

The two main Relationship assumptions of ancient Israel's worldview, which are outlined above, can be diagrammed as in figure 8. The assumptions divide the world primarily between God the creator and the creation. These primary domains are arranged vertically to illustrate the hierarchical (positive-negative) relationship between God and the creation. The creation itself is divided secondarily between humans and the rest of the natural world, which are arranged horizontally to illustrate the harmonious (neutral) relationship between them.

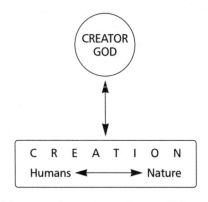

Figure 8. The Basic Israelite Worldview

The double-arrow lines in the diagram illustrate the assumptions of Causality. The only causal assumption embedded in the creation model itself is that God is a causal agent in the creation. Nevertheless, we can make a few preliminary remarks concerning the other paths of causality in anticipation of our discussion in the following chapters. Just as God is a causal agent in relation to the creation, that is, God's actions have a consequent effect for creation, humans are causal agents in relation to the rest of the natural world. Nature as such is not a causal agent. But because of the harmonious relationship between humans and nature, human agency produces ramifications in nature that affect humans. Human causal agency in nature is thus reciprocal. Finally, all of creation serves as a causal agent in relation to God. Although creation is subordinate to God, creation, through the agency of humans, can produce change in God.

The worldview that we have deduced from the creation model represents the "plain vanilla" worldview of the ancient Israelites. It incorporates only their most basic assumptions of reality expressed in their creation metaphors. Because it is derived from the cross-cultural model of creation, it represents by implication a worldview that the Israelites shared with their Near Eastern neighbors. This worldview does not reflect, however, the many complexities of the real world in which they lived. For example, it does not take into account the fundamental distinction between ingroups and outgroups that pervades the Classification assumptions of collectivist societies such as ancient Israel. Nor does it take into account the diverse segments of Israelite society. These aspects of their worldview remain to be investigated. Nevertheless, this basic worldview can serve as the foundation on which to build.

4
GOD, HUMANS, AND THE NATURAL WORLD

HISTORY AND NATURE

Until recently, few biblical scholars gave any attention to the Bible's views of the natural world or to the role of the natural world in the religion and culture of ancient Israel. Attention instead was directed toward Israel's view of history and its interpretation of God's activity in history. This scholarly focus has been shaped in part by the Bible's own emphasis on historical events. At the heart of the Bible's presentation of Israelite religion stands Israel's story in which God is repeatedly acting in historical events to create, discipline, and redeem Israel to be the people of God. For example, God calls Abraham to leave his ancestral home in Mesopotamia for the purpose of creating a new people in the land of Canaan. When Abraham's descendants are later enslaved in Egypt, God intervenes in human history by delivering them from the oppressive power of Pharaoh. At Sinai God establishes a covenant with Israel; Yahweh chooses Israel to be his people, and Israel pledges to faithfully worship Yahweh alone. God again acts in history by settling the Israelites in the land of Canaan, fighting on their side to drive out the Canaanites. God also designates David to be king over Israel, to be God's regent and a shepherd for God's flock. God empowers him to build a large empire and establishes a dynasty in his name. Throughout Israel's existence God's actions are discerned in the events of history. Times of famine, drought, and oppression from enemies are not random or without purpose. The prophets recognize in these events God's actions of judgment against the people. Similarly, times of agricultural bounty, prosperity, and peace are interpreted as God's blessings. According to the biblical tradition, the events of history are filled with meaning and purpose, for "everything Israel experienced in history is an act of Yahweh" (Ringgren 1966:113).

History clearly plays a prominent role in the Bible's presentation of Israelite religion. But the emphasis that scholars have placed on the importance of history for understanding the religion of Israel has excluded the role of the natural world from consideration. Although the reasons for this narrow emphasis on history are manifold, the overriding impetus has been an apologetic concern to distinguish Israelite religion from the religion of its ancient Near Eastern neighbors. If the religion of Israel could be shown to be significantly different from the polytheistic religions of its neighbors, then the truth of the biblical faith was thought to be more persuasive. Biblical scholars thus drew upon a conceptual dichotomy between history and nature, derived from the philosophy of Hegel, as a model for differentiating between Israelite and other ancient Near Eastern religions (Simkins 1991:3–30).

A logical reflex of this dichotomy between history and nature is the distinction between linear and cyclical time. Linear time is the time of history. It has a definite beginning and end. Although like a graph it might have many ups and downs, it nevertheless marches unrelentingly forward. Because it is unidirectional, each moment is new and unique. It is the time of change and progress and so brings freedom. Cyclical time, on the other hand, is the time of nature ("nature" understood in a pre-Darwinian sense). With no beginning and no end, an ordained order of events continually repeat themselves. Each moment is merely the latest reiteration of a primordial moment. Nothing is new or unique. Like the changing seasons, time is an endless repetition with no progress. Therefore, cyclical time enslaves for it is devoid of change.[1]

According to this conceptual model, the Israelite religion was a religion of history. The Israelites worshipped a God

---

[1] Cyclical time, when projected onto ancient societies, is anachronistic. It is an image derived from our mechanical view of the world. This type of time is better understood as oscillating time—"rhythmically swinging back and forth between recurrent markers" (Kearney 1984:99).

who acted and was revealed in the events of human history in order to guide that history towards its appointed goal. Each event was new and filled with human potential. The natural world was viewed simply as the stage for the historical drama. It possessed no divine meaning. It was neither a manifestation of God nor an active agent in the fulfillment of the purposes of God. In contrast, the ancient Near Eastern polytheistic religions, the religions of Israel's neighbors, were embedded in nature. The gods were personified natural powers, and the peoples were servants to the never ending cycles of nature.

The biblical scholars who employed the history-versus-nature model to interpret Israelite religion recognized that Israel was born from these ancient Near Eastern nature religions—for example, Abraham came from Mesopotamia and his descendants were enslaved in Egypt—but they claimed that a new religion was born at the exodus. As slaves in Egypt, the Israelites were immersed in the static cyclical world of nature. According to the Egyptian cosmologies, societal roles were determined in the primordial era. A slave was destined to remain a slave; change within the established order was not possible. However, when Yahweh delivered the Israelites from bondage and made them his people, the myth of nature and cyclical time was shattered. The natural world was not divine; the given was not the inevitable. History offered the possibility of change, and Yahweh was the agent of change. By disenchanting the natural world, the Israelites opened themselves to the potential of history, and by recognizing God's activity in history, the Israelites were able to interpret all the events of history to be the unfolding of God's purposes. Therefore, according to this model, the religion of Israel emerged in contradistinction to the other ancient Near Eastern religions.

Although I have discussed and rejected this model in the preceding chapters, I introduce it again here to illustrate why previous biblical scholarship has neglected the role of the natural world in the religion of Israel. In an attempt to distinguish between Israelite and other ancient Near Eastern religions, biblical scholars have claimed that the Israelites, in contrast to their neighbors, had little interest in the natural world. G. Ernest Wright, the most vocal proponent of this model, made the following comparison:

The contemporary polytheisms, having analyzed the problem of life over against nature, had little sense of or concern with the significance of history. Nature with its changing seasons was cyclical, and human life, constantly integrating itself with nature by means of cultic activity and sympathetic magic, moved with nature in a cyclical manner. But Israel was little interested in nature, except as God used it together with his historical acts to reveal himself and to accomplish his purpose. Yahweh was the God of history, the living God unaffected by the cycles of nature, who had set himself to accomplish a definite purpose in time. (1957:71)

Not only did the Israelites have a different, i.e., superior, understanding of the natural world—that it was merely raw material to be used by humans and God—but they also viewed their God differently. Whereas the polytheistic gods were immanent in nature, Israel's God transcended the natural world. This distinction is also made by Wright:

In polytheism the central and original metaphors and symbols for depicting the gods were drawn for the most part from the natural world. With the growth of social complexity the gods increasingly took on social functions, and such terms as king, lord, father, mother, judge, craftsman, warrior, and the like, were used. Yet Baal of Canaan and Enlil of Mesopotamia never shook off their primary relation to the storm which typifies nature's force. Anu, the head of the pantheon in Babylon, originated as the numinous feeling for the majesty of the sky. He was thus given form as heaven, though subsidiary forms were the king and the bull of heaven. The mother of the gods was Ninhursaga, who arose from the feeling for the fertility of the earth and was thus given form as the earth, with subsidiary forms ascribed as mother, queen and craftsman. Ea was the sweet waters, who could be given form in the ram and the bison, but more especially as the knowing-one, the craftsman, the pundit and the wizard. . . . In the Bible, on the contrary, God is known and addressed primarily in the terms which relate him to society and to history. The language of nature is distinctly secondary. God is Lord, king, judge, shepherd, father, husband, and the like, but these appellatives are not superimposed upon a central image in nature. Nature as God's creation contains no forms on which one can focus a religious attention. (1952: 48–49)

Biblical scholars, therefore, gave no attention to the role of the natural world in the religion of Israel. Their use of the dichotomy between history and nature as a model for interpretation precluded any such role. The natural world was an appropriate category of discussion only for polytheistic religions.

As argued in the preceding chapters, the history-versus-nature model is inadequate for interpreting both Israelite and other ancient Near Eastern religions. The Israelite religion was not simply a religion of history, nor were the ancient Near Eastern polytheistic religions merely religions of nature. The dichotomy between history and nature does not correspond to the differences between the religion of Israel and the religions of its neighbors.

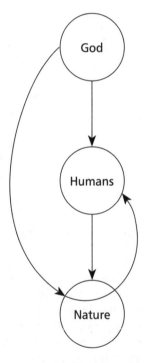

Figure 9. A History-Oriented Worldview

A long-lasting effect of biblical scholarship's use of the history-versus-nature model for interpreting Israelite religion has been the presumption of particular worldviews for Israel and its neighbors along these dichotomous lines. The world-

view of ancient Israel, diagrammed in figure 9, which scholars
had presumed in their use of this model, ascribed no active
role to the natural world. Nature was perceived simply as raw
material. Like humans it was the product of God's creation, but
it remained distinct from humans. Moreover, humans could
act as independent causal agents in nature. Although nature,
as God's instrument, could affect humans, it had no intrinsic
capacity to affect change. Acting as God's representatives in
this world, humans could autonomously utilize nature's resources for their own purposes. The material world was subject to both divine and human control.

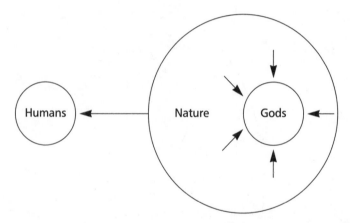

Figure 10. A Nature-Oriented Worldview

Scholars who embraced the history-versus-nature model
presumed a worldview of Israel's neighbors that stands in
contrast to their presumed worldview of Israel. As illustrated
in figure 10, this commonly presumed polytheistic worldview
credited the natural world with an active role in the interaction
with both gods and humans. (Of course, the apologetic agenda
of these scholars suggests that this worldview gives a *too active*
role to nature.) According to this worldview, the gods were
merely the personified forces of nature. Even when they took
on social roles such as king, judge, or craftsman, they were
unable to transcend their connection to nature. The gods thus
affected humans through the manifold forms of the natural
world. Humans, from the perspective of this worldview, were

completely subject to nature. They were not able to escape the unending cycles of nature or to effect lasting change in the world. Human society was characterized by its static quality; it lacked progress.

The presumed Israelite worldview was, for apologetic reasons, interpreted in a positive light by biblical scholars; it has not received such a favorable treatment at large. As discussed in the Introduction, this worldview was accused of fostering the current environmental crisis. Indeed, this presumed worldview does promote an ethic of exploitation, and has justifiably been rejected by people concerned about the condition of the natural environment. But this worldview is not the worldview of the ancient Israelites! It is derived from a dichotomous model that cannot account for the diversity within the religion of Israel. Israelite religion is concerned with both history *and nature.* An understanding of the religion of Israel cannot be developed through exclusively historical categories but must take into consideration the role of the natural world.

In chapter 3, I constructed a model for understanding the basic worldview of the ancient Israelites. This model, diagrammed in figure 8, illustrates the basic assumptions of the Classification and Relationship universals. In contrast to the history-oriented and nature-oriented worldviews illustrated in figures 9 and 10, the basic Israelite worldview posits a fundamental distinction between the creator and the creation. The essential unity of the creation is only secondarily differentiated into humans and nature. As a result, God's activity cannot be accounted for in strictly historical or natural terms. God's activity is in relation to the whole creation.

God the creator is the primary and most comprehensive biblical metaphor that describes God's activity in and on behalf of the creation; God the creator brings the creation into existence (through the many ways discussed in the preceding chapters) and acts in the creation to sustain it and to shape it according to God's purposes (Westermann 1971:23–24). As this opening statement implies, creation in the biblical tradition, and in the ancient Near East in general, is not just a single event that happened at the beginning of time. The deist's image of God as a cosmic clockmaker is foreign to the biblical text. According to the Bible, God's activity in creation includes both sequential events in the linear course of time, such as the

numerous occasions in which God redeemed Israel, and ongoing processes that are more characteristic of cyclical time—more
appropriately called "oscillating" time—such as the seasonal
cycle of agriculture and the life cycle of animals and humans.
For this reason, some scholars have described the Israelites'
view of time as spiral—an oscillating repetition that is infused
with change and development (Cross 1988:95–96; Fretheim
1991b:358). It is necessary to examine both of these disparate
aspects of God's activity in creation in order to elucidate fully
God's role as creator.

In the following sections of this chapter I have chosen to
present God's interaction with the creation according to two
categories or models: theophany and covenant. Each category
describes a particular feature of God's role as creator. Moreover, each category cuts across the distinction between linear
and oscillating time, blending characteristics of each dimension into a holistic presentation of God's activity in creation.
By exploring the metaphor of God the creator from the perspective of these categories, I will further detail God's relationship
to the creation and, by extension, humankind's relationship to
the natural world.

THE SIGNIFICANCE OF THEOPHANY

Theophany literally refers to God's appearance. Both
Christian and Jewish theology claim that God is always and
everywhere present in the world. Theophany is simply an
intensification of God's presence at a particular place during a
particular time. God's presence in the world is made known in
such a way that humans recognize it as distinctive (though not
always immediately). It is a means by which God engages in
human affairs. But this intensification of God's presence also
affects the natural world. God's presence is often revealed
through a spectacular display of meteorological phenomena,
and reverberations of God's presence echo throughout the
natural world.

Two issues have dominated scholarly discussion of theophany: the origin and the categorization of the diverse biblical
accounts of theophany. Some scholars argue that the biblical
descriptions of God's appearance originated in the ritual cele-

brations of Yahweh's kingship in the New Year festival and that the theophanies themselves were modeled on God's revelation on Mount Sinai (Weiser 1950; Mowinckel [1962]1992: I.142–43), whereas other scholars trace their origin to either celebrations of Yahweh's victory in the pre-monarchical holy wars (Jeremias 1965:118–50) or Canaanite descriptions of the theophany of Baal as storm god (Cross 1973:147–77). Although some scholars would lump together all biblical examples of theophany (Kuntz 1967), most recognize at least two different types of theophanies. Westermann distinguishes the biblical theophanies according to the purpose of God's appearing. The term "theophany" is reserved for those accounts in which God appears to the people through a mediator for the purpose of self-revelation and communication. God's appearance to Moses and the people on Mount Sinai (Exod 19, 34) is the fullest example of this type of theophany. The biblical accounts in which God appears in order to aid the people, such as God's fighting against Sisera and the Canaanites (Judg 5), Westermann prefers to call "epiphanies" (1965:99; Fretheim 1984:80–81). Jeremias similarly distinguishes between two types of theophanies according to the function of their basic form. One type of theophany is intended for individuals and represents for them a special demonstration of God's favor. A second type of theophany is God's appearance as a warrior through the powers of nature which causes alarm among Israel's enemies (1976:896).

Although this scholarly discussion of the origin and categorization of theophany is not without merit, it has tended to direct attention away from other aspects of theophany. Specifically, little discussion has been given to the significance of God's appearance in the creation, especially with regard to the implied relationship between God and the creation. Two exceptions are noteworthy.

In a recent dictionary article on theophany, Theodore Hiebert focused on the form and location of theophanies rather than on their origin and function (1992a). In his differentiation of the diverse biblical theophanies, he recognized both natural forms (phenomena associated with the thunderstorm) and societal forms (king, warrior, judge) of God's appearance. Although this differentiation is not absolute—the natural and social forms coalesce in most descriptions of theophany—this categorization draws attention to the crucial role that the natural world plays in the manifestation of God's presence. The importance of the natural world in relation to God's appearance is further highlighted by Hiebert's discussion of the location of theophanies. According to Hiebert, "one of the fundamental characteristics of theophany in Israel is its occurrence at locations in the natural environment which were considered particularly sacred, particularly conducive to contact and communication between the divine and human spheres of reality" (1992a:505). God appears at springs, rivers, trees, and especially mountains, and by so doing endows the natural world with sacredness. The natural world serves as a symbol of God's presence.

The other exception is the work of Terence Fretheim. Although he has followed scholarly convention by highlighting the function of theophanies, he has also explored the particular significance of the natural forms of God's appearance. By emphasizing the metaphorical character of the biblical descriptions of theophany—noting that natural metaphors are frequently used to describe God—Fretheim has argued that there is a definite correspondence between God and the natural world. The biblical theophanies function primarily to reveal God, and nature often serves as the means by which God is revealed. But the natural world does not function simply as a tool in theophanies. According to Fretheim, if the "natural metaphors for God are in some ways descriptive of God, then they reflect in their very existence, in their being what they are, the reality which is God" (1987:22). The natural world is internally related to God and is thus capable of revealing God (1984:37–44). "The fact that theophanies function as revelatory events means that the function of nature in theophany is only an intensification of what is true of nature otherwise" (1987:25).

Both Hiebert and Fretheim have persuasively argued that the natural world is more than raw material that God might use to achieve historical purposes. The natural forms of theophany give intrinsic value to the natural world. Nature is capable of symbolically representing the creator because God has bound Godself to the creation (Fretheim 1984:38). Of course, it has long been recognized that humans are capable of revealing God. This is in part the meaning behind the statement that humans are created in the "image of God" (Gen 1:26–27), and it is given fullest expression in the incarnation. Hiebert and

Fretheim have simply demonstrated that this insight extends to the rest of the natural world. All of creation—the natural world and humans together—stands in relationship to God and is a suitable vehicle of God's presence.

The focus that Hiebert and Fretheim have given to the natural aspects of God's appearance is a good starting point for our discussion of theophany and its value for understanding Israel's worldview. They have drawn attention to three significant facets of theophany that will form the basic parameters of our investigation: The natural setting of theophanies, the natural form of theophanies, and the implicit relationship between the creator and the creation that is revealed by theophanies. Exploring theophany according to these parameters will enable us to confirm and to illustrate our basic model of the Israelite worldview and at the same time to give further nuance and precision to the model.

THEOPHANY AND SACRED SPACE

An appropriate place to begin our investigation of theophany is with the location of theophanies. Hiebert has already pointed out that theophanies frequently occur at a variety of settings in the natural environment and especially at mountains. These locations are considered to be holy, i.e., set apart as distinctive from the rest of the natural environment, by both those who directly experienced the theophanies and those who pass on their tradition. The classic biblical example of a theophany is God's appearance to Moses in the burning bush:

> [1]Moses was keeping the flock of his father-in-law Jethro, the priest of Midian; he led his flock beyond the wilderness, and came to Horeb, the mountain of God. [2]There the angel of the LORD appeared to him in a flame of fire out of a bush; he looked, and the bush was blazing, yet it was not consumed. [3]Then Moses said, "I must turn aside and look at this great sight, and see why the bush is not burned up." [4]When the LORD saw that he had turned aside to see, God called to him out of the bush, "Moses, Moses!" And he said, "Here I am." [5]Then he said, "Come no closer! Remove the sandals from your feet, for the place on which you are standing is holy ground." (Exodus 3:1–5)

The theophany ascribes meaning and value to the place at which the theophany occurred. The location of the theophany is no longer simply one place among many in the natural environment. It is distinctive and extraordinary; it is holy ground.

In the scholarly jargon these holy sites have been called sacred spaces, and they are not unique to the religion of Israel. Mircea Eliade, a pioneer in this field of study, has demonstrated that most cultures of the world, both past and present, have had some notion of sacred space (1959:20–65). Human awareness of sacred space is simply the recognition that space is not homogeneous. Some space is qualitatively different from other spaces. Profane space is arbitrary, undifferentiated, ordinary space. Sacred space is the place where the sacred ("God" in the biblical tradition) has broken into profane space by bringing order and differentiation. By breaking into the randomness of profane space, the sacred provides an absolute fixed point of reference around which human life can orient itself. Sacred space enables a "world" to be found; it enables humans to order and structure the arbitrariness of ordinary space.

Sacred space represents a symbolic perception of reality. It is the reification of a people's myths and rituals.[2] Humans have a fundamental need for orientation in the world; order and structure are necessary for a meaningful life. Without a point of orientation randomness would dominate. Value and meaning would become relative. The experience of the sacred provides the necessary point of orientation and thereby enables humans to create an orderly, meaningful, and thus *real* world. Through their myths and rituals, people give structure and order to the world around them.

The experience of the sacred and the awareness of sacred space are common experiences of humankind. Sacred space fulfills a basic human need. The creation of an orderly world around the sacred space, however, is an expression of its significance for a particular people. Although similarities can be detected across diverse cultures, reflecting the common

---

[2] According to Eliade, the awareness of sacred space is a primordial human experience, preceding all theoretical reflection on the world (1959:20–21). In other words, humans first experience the distinctiveness of sacred space and then begin to theorize and formulate the significance of that experience through myths and rituals.

human experience of sacred space, each culture orders its world in relation to sacred space according to its own particular concerns.

As in the understanding of creation, the cultures of the ancient Near East, including Israel, shared a similar understanding of sacred space. This is not coincidental. Sacred space and the world ordered in relation to it are the geographical expressions of creation. Through the process of creation certain places are endowed with sacredness. According to the *Enuma Elish*, for example, Marduk chose Babylon to be the special place of his temple and organized the rest of the creation around it. In the *Creation of the Pickax* humans sprout from the ground at Uzumua, and Duranki is the place at which heaven and earth were originally attached. In the Egyptian creation myths, the land of Egypt is the hillock that first emerged out of the primeval ocean Nun. Babylon, Uzumua and Duranki (both sites in Nippur), and the land of Egypt (Klimkeit 1975:268–70) are each considered to be sacred space. Each place is a symbolic geographical expression of the structure of creation. This relationship between creation and sacred space, however, should not be interpreted to mean that a people's understanding of creation was prior to their perception of sacred space. The ideas of creation and the experiences of sacred space are mutually dependent. People's perceptions of sacred space affirm their particular views of creation, and creation myths explain and ascribe significance to their awareness of sacred space.

A HORIZONTAL MODEL OF SACRED SPACE

There are two related and complementary models at work in the ancient Near Eastern perception of sacred space. The more primitive perception of sacred space is represented by a horizontal model, illustrated in figure 11, in which the life-sustaining creation is located at the center of a plateau (the "real" world) and diminishes in its significance and effect as one moves to the periphery (Wyatt 1987a:378; cf. also Leach 1976: 81–93; Davies 1977; Jenson 1992). The sacredness of creation is experienced as divine, and at the center of the world it provides the absolute nexus around which the world is oriented. The creator makes the land at the center holy in a cosmological sense. The land is characterized by divine order;

it is the point from which the creation originated. The divine sacredness of the center contrasts with the sacredness of the periphery, which is experienced as demonic and diabolical (Smith 1993:97–98, 109). The periphery is chaotic, hostile to life. It is symbolized by both the desert and the sea, which form the boundary between the land of the living and the netherworld (Haldar 1950). The boundary at the periphery is a sterile region inhabited by demons, wild animals, and sea monsters (Pedersen 1926:454–59; Talmon 1966:43). Humans are unable to dwell there apart from divine assistance.

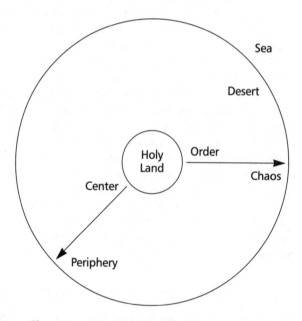

Figure 11. A Horizontal Model of Sacred Space

It is important to note that both the center and the periphery are experienced as sacred, although each in different ways. The sacred has an ambivalent character. In his classic and influential study, *The Idea of the Holy*, Rudolf Otto described this ambivalent encounter with the sacred as *mysterium tremendum et fascinans*. This formulation, which does not readily yield a satisfactory English translation, attests to the fundamental human experiences that are inspired by the sacred. The encounter with the sacred can produce both terror and joy, dread and wonder. Although seemingly contradictory, these paradoxical experiences actually complement one another. The God who lovingly bestows peace and bounty on faithful servants is also the one before whose wrath enemies tremble. This is analogous to the experience of the sacred at the center and the periphery. Although the sacred is a unity, humans are often unable to reconcile its diverse, opposing aspects, choosing instead to hold them in tension. The divine aspects of the sacred are ascribed to the center, the demonic to the periphery. Each is an extension of the other; each is defined in contrast to the other. As recognized by the insightful few (cf. Job 9:22–24; Isa 45:5–7), however, the unity of the sacred transcends both the center and the periphery.

The symbolic perception of space represented by the horizontal model undoubtedly originated in the human perception of the body and by extension personal space (Wyatt 1987a:378), but it also derives from the actual human experience of the ancient Near Eastern environment. In this environment both the desert and the sea were inhospitable to human life. The sterile desert was the domain of noxious plants and beasts. The sea was even more threatening. Although teeming with life, it was both violent and unpredictable, unable to be tamed. The fertile and habitable land was experienced as an oasis surrounded by the hostile periphery. Although this model is anchored in the ancient Near Eastern environment, it describes a symbolic rather than an actual geography. It attests to the sacredness that the people of the ancient Near East perceived in the natural environment.

The clearest and most elaborate example of this symbolic geography is attested in the biblical literature in Israel's foundational story of exodus from Egypt, wandering in the wilderness, and conquest of the land of Palestine. This story begins with the Israelites' escape from Egypt and Yahweh's destruction of the Egyptian forces at the *yam suph*, "Red Sea" (Exod 15:4). Although the *yam suph* has traditionally been associated with the Red Sea, scholars have preferred to interpret it as referring to an unknown sea of reeds along the course of the modern day Suez Canal. But there is no evidence to support this interpretation (Batto 1983:27–31). Nor does it appear that the specific reference to the *yam suph* in Exodus 15 originally referred to the Red Sea, for none of the narrative traditions preserved in Exodus 14 make this connection. Instead, the *yam suph* probably denotes the sea at the edge of the world. The noun *suph* is attested with the meaning of "edge, end, border" and carries the connotations of "non-existence, extinction, destruction" (Batto 1983:32–34; Snaith 1965:395–98). The *yam suph* reflects symbolic geography; God defeated Pharaoh at the chaotic sea that encompassed the world. This sea was later identified in the biblical tradition with the Red Sea and the southern oceans.

For the Israelites, Egypt is the land of death; it is symbolically identified with the netherworld (Exod 14:11; Wyatt 1987a:375–76). By defeating the Egyptians at the sea, God delivers the Israelites from the land of the dead and begins to lead them to the land of the living, the land of God's abode (Exod 15:13, 17). But the Israelites first have to pass through the desert that, bordering on the sea, stands between the world of chaos and the real world of the holy land. Although the actual geography of the Sinai peninsula, the region between Egypt and the land of Israel, is characterized by desert, the references to the desert in the wilderness wandering narratives do not simply describe the setting of the Israelites' trek to the promised land. Rather, they ascribe a symbolic significance to Israel's journey. Through the wilderness wanderings the Israelites participate in a symbolic rite of passage from death to life (Cohn 1982:7–23). The desert in these narratives is ambiguous. The desert is chaos in contrast to the order of the promised land. It is characterized by hunger and thirst, dangerous creatures, and hostile peoples. The desert is reminiscent of the death of Egypt. On the other hand, the desert is where the people of Israel experience divine favor. God provides food and water in the wilderness. God makes a covenant with the people at God's desert abode. Moreover, God's presence remains with the people, represented by both the pillar of fire and cloud and the ark of the covenant. The people's experience of God in the desert foreshadows God's presence in the promised land (Propp 1987).

Through the trek in the desert Israel is in transition, in liminality (V. Turner 1969:94–97). Israel is neither living nor dead, but betwixt and between. The desert life is not the ideal but the means of entry into the holy land. The land is holy because it is the land of God's dwelling, the land where God is experienced. The holy land is the land flowing with milk and honey, the land of creation. It is the land of the living and the only place where *real* life is possible. For this reason, when the prophets threaten Israel with exile, they threaten to cut Israel off from life itself. Exile from the holy land is equivalent to returning to the land of Egypt. Consider the prophecy of Hosea:

> [1]When Israel was a child, I loved him,
>   and out of Egypt I called my son.
> [2]The more I called them,
>   the more they went from me;
>   they kept sacrificing to the Baals,
>   and offering incense to idols. . . .
> [5]They shall return to the land of Egypt,
>   and Assyria shall be their king,
>   because they have refused to return to me.
>   (Hosea 11:1–2, 5)

Although the Israelites will be exiled to the land of Assyria, the prophet can characterize it as Egypt because it is symbolically the land of death. Israel will return to the netherworld from which it came.

Two further examples will suffice to illustrate the horizontal model of sacred space. In an oracle from Second Isaiah, the prophet of the exile proclaims that Yahweh is going to gather his people from the edges of the earth:

> [5]Do not fear, for I am with you;
>   I will bring your offspring from the east,
>   and from the west I will gather you;
> [6]I will say to the north, "Give them up,"
>   and to the south, "Do not withhold;
>   bring my sons from far away
>   and my daughters from the end of the earth—
> [7]everyone who is called by my name,
>   whom I created for my glory,
>   whom I formed and made." (Isaiah 43:5–7)

This oracle attests to a symbolic geography in which the holy land, the land of Israel, is placed at the center (cf. Ezek 5:5). The exiles are at the chaotic periphery, far from the land of the living. But their situation is temporary. The prophet proclaims that Yahweh is going to bring them to the center just as he did in the original exodus-conquest story (chapter 6 will present a fuller discussion of the new exodus-conquest theme).

In the book of Joel the prophet laments the destruction of agriculture by a severe locust plague. Moreover, Joel identifies this locust plague with the day of Yahweh (Simkins 1991:101–69). Joel attributes cosmological significance to their destructive activity; their ravaging of all vegetation signals the collapse of the created order. The desolation left in their wake is evidence of this:

> Fire devours in front of them,
>> and behind them a flame burns.
> Before them the land is like the garden of Eden,
>> but after them a desolate wilderness,
>> and nothing escapes them. (Joel 2:3)

This passage presents more than a simple description of the all-consuming destruction caused by the locusts. Rather, the locusts are presented as agents of chaos. They are marching from the periphery to the center, assaulting the life-giving powers of the center. The center is being transformed into the sterile desert of the periphery. For the prophet this event must surely be the day of Yahweh (chapter 6 will present a thorough discussion of the day of Yahweh).

A VERTICAL MODEL OF SACRED SPACE

Although the horizontal model reflects the more primitive human understanding of sacred space, the vertical model elucidates the more dominant understanding within the biblical tradition. According to this model, the world is oriented around a cosmic mountain. The mountain is cosmic in the sense that it is a microcosm of the whole world and participates in the government and stability of the world. Figure 12 illustrates the vertical dimension of this understanding of sacred space. The base of the mountain is the ordinary world of humans beings. It is profane space. As one ascends to the summit of the mountain, one approaches heaven, the dwelling of the gods. Thus, temples and shrines are frequently erected on mountain peaks. Beneath the mountain lies the underworld, the realm of the dead. Often a spring issues from the base of the mountain, originating from a source of water in the underworld. Uniting heaven, earth, and the underworld is the *axis mundi*, the center pole around which the world is oriented, making communication among the three realms of the world possible.

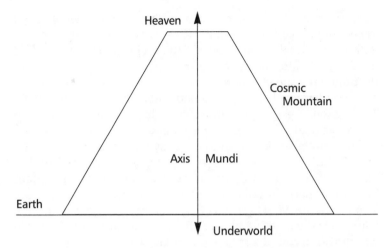

Figure 12. A Vertical Model of Sacred Space

The correlation of heaven, earth, and the underworld along a central axis is most clearly illustrated in an Isaianic oracle directed against the king of Babylon:

[12]How you are fallen from heaven,
    O Day Star, son of Dawn!
How you are cut down to the ground,
    you who laid the nations low!
[13]You said in your heart,
    "I will ascend to heaven;
I will raise my throne
    above the stars of God;
I will sit on the mount of assembly
    on the heights of [assembly in the far north];[3]
[14]I will ascend to the tops of the clouds,
    I will make myself like the Most High."
[15]But you are brought down to Sheol,
    to the depths of the Pit. (Isaiah 14:12–15)

---

[3] The text of the NRSV has been altered slightly to read "assembly in the far north" rather than "Zaphon." The background of this oracle, which has its origin in a myth of the rebellion of an astral deity, centers upon El's unnamed mountain dwelling, the meeting place of the divine assembly, which is located in the far north, rather than Baal's mountain abode, Zaphon, which is also located in the north. See Cross (1973:38).

According to this oracle, the king of Babylon considers himself to be more powerful than God. He intends to ascend the cosmic mountain and take God's place in the divine assembly. But God does not tolerate this hubris. Instead of ascending to the top of the mountain, the king is sent below the mountain to the depths of the underworld and is reckoned among the dead (Isa 14:19). The symbolic geography underlying this oracle is clearly oriented vertically. The top of the mountain symbolizes heaven, and the depths beneath the mountain symbolize the underworld.

Building on the work of Eliade, Richard Clifford has outlined five distinct characteristics of the cosmic mountain in the comparable religions of Israel and Ugarit (Canaanite): The mountain is (1) the meeting place of the gods or divine beings; (2) the meeting place of heaven and earth; (3) the place where the divine decrees are issued; (4) the battleground of conflicting natural forces; and (5) the source of fertilizing waters (1972:3). Each of these characteristics will be illustrated below. Although there were several cosmic mountains throughout the history of Israel—Sinai, Horeb, Carmel, Gerizim, Ebal, Paran, Seir—the most important and influential mountain for the religion of Israel was Mount Zion. Zion is a medium sized hill in Jerusalem on which Solomon built his temple. Today it is the site of the Dome of the Rock, the spot from which Mohammed, according to Islamic tradition, ascended into heaven. But during the period of Israelite occupation of the land of Palestine, Zion was the sacred place where Yahweh dwelled.

Numerous psalms acclaim Yahweh's selection of Mount Zion from all the hills in Israel to be his special dwelling:

> [1]In Judah God is known,
>   his name is great in Israel.
> [2]His abode has been established in Salem,
>   his dwelling place in Zion. (Psalm 76:1–2)

> [1]On the holy mount stands the city he founded;
> [2]the Lord loves the gates of Zion
>   more than all the dwellings of Jacob.
> [3]Glorious things are spoken of you,
>   O city of God. (Psalm 87:1–3)

Zion, and especially the temple built on Zion, was the foremost place in Israel where God's presence was experienced. Zion was sacred space; it provided the focal point of orientation for the people of Israel.

The abode of God, Zion served as the meeting place for all the divine beings and the place where heaven and earth intersect. These first and second characteristics of the cosmic mountain are most clearly illustrated in Isaiah 6, the passage describing Isaiah's call to prophesy:

> [1]In the year that King Uzziah died, I saw the Lord sitting on a throne, high and lofty; and the hem of his robe filled the temple. [2]Seraphs were in attendance above him; each had six wings: with two they covered their faces, and with two they covered their feet, and with two they flew. [3]And one called to another and said:
>
> "Holy, holy, holy is the LORD of hosts;
>   the whole earth is full of his glory."
> [4]The pivots on the thresholds shook at the voices of those who called, and the house filled with smoke. [5]And I said: "Woe is me! I am lost, for I am a man of unclean lips, and I live among a people of unclean lips; yet my eyes have seen the King, the LORD of hosts!" (Isaiah 6:1–5)

This text suggests that Isaiah served as a priest in the temple on Mount Zion. On the occasion described by this text, Isaiah is in the temple, possibly engaged in his usual priestly duties, when he unexpectedly finds himself standing in the midst of the divine assembly. The correlation between the earthly temple on Zion and God's heavenly temple becomes transparent; the gap between heaven and earth is removed.

With Yahweh and his retinue filling the temple, Isaiah is privy to the deliberation of the divine assembly. According to the ancient Near Eastern conception of deity, God does not govern the world alone. Rather, God is supported by an assembly of divine beings who deliberate with God and enact God's commands (cf. Gen 1:26; 3:22; 1 Kgs 22:19–23; Job 1:6–12; 2:1–6; Ps 82). In Isaiah's vision, Yahweh, the king and leader of the divine assembly, poses a question to the members of the assembly: "Whom shall I send, and who will go for us?" (Isa 6:8). Isaiah is not about to let this exceptional opportunity pass, and so he volunteers to be the assembly's messenger. In this manner Isaiah was called to prophesy God's judgment against the people of Israel (cf. Koch 1982:108–13).

When Yahweh commissions Isaiah in the temple on Zion
to be his herald, it is also an example of the third characteristic
of the cosmic mountain—the place where divine decrees are
issued. The famous mountain of divine decrees, however, is
Mount Sinai. From Sinai Yahweh gave his law, *torah*, to the
people of Israel and established his covenant with them. In the
biblical tradition, Sinai functions as an archetype for the giving
of the law. Regardless of when the laws were formulated
during the history of the people of Israel, they are all attributed
to God's revelation on Sinai (Levenson 1985:17–19). Even
though during the monarchy Zion inherited the earlier traditions of Sinai, Sinai continued to remain the locus of the law.
The decrees issued from Zion, in contrast, focus on God's
judgment of the people because of their rebellion against the law.
Psalm 50 attests to this type of decree; God judges the people
from Zion.

Although the cosmic mountain is the battleground of
opposing forces, in the biblical tradition this fourth characteristic of the cosmic mountain is expressed in terms of the
inviolability of Zion. Because God dwells in Zion, it is uncon-
querable. Yahweh will defend his mountain city against all
assaults. Israel's enemies, who are also God's enemies, will be
unable to assail it; the very appearance of Zion will spark panic
among them. A number of psalms attest to this theme of
Völkerkampf, "war of the nations" (Pss 2; 46; 48; 76).

Underlying the *Völkerkampf* is the conflict myth. The
nations are agents of chaos bent on assailing Yahweh's kingship and rule over the creation. In response, Yahweh fights
against the nations in a new cosmogonic battle, securing the
order of creation. Because Yahweh defends his holy mountain
against the ravages of chaos, Zion serves as a refuge for the
people. Zion is a haven of order in a chaotic world. In the first
stanza of Psalm 46 the psalmist extols God as a secure refuge
even when the creation itself begins to crumble:

> [1]God is our refuge and strength,
>   a very present help in trouble.
> [2]Therefore we will not fear, though the earth should change,
>   though the mountains shake in the heart of the sea;
> [3]though its waters roar and foam,
>   though the mountains tremble with its tumult.
>   (Psalm 46:1–3)

Because Yahweh is the creator, he can protect his people against the collapse of the creation. In the second stanza the creation's reversion to chaos is connected to the nations' assault on Zion:

⁴There is a river whose streams make glad the city of God,
the holy habitation of the Most High.
⁵God is in the midst of the city; it shall not be moved;
God will help it when the morning dawns.
⁶The nations are in an uproar, the kingdoms totter;
he utters his voice, the earth melts.
⁷The LORD of hosts is with us;
the God of Jacob is our refuge. (Psalm 46:4–7)

At the end of the psalm God is again exalted as the one who is both a victor over all the nations of the earth and a refuge for the people.

The fifth and final characteristic of the cosmic mountain is that the mountain is often the source of a spring or river endowed with special fertilizing powers. In Psalm 46:4, quoted above, a river is associated with Zion. In an Isaianic oracle the inviolability of Zion is also connected to a river:

²⁰Look on Zion, the city of our appointed festivals!
Your eyes will see Jerusalem,
a quiet habitation, an immovable tent,
whose stakes will never be pulled up,
and none of whose ropes will be broken.
²¹But there the LORD in majesty will be for us
a place of broad rivers and streams,
where no galley with oars can go,
nor stately ship can pass.
²²For the LORD is our judge, the LORD is our ruler,
the LORD is our king; he will save us. (Isaiah 33:20–22)

In both of these passages the river flowing from Zion is used metaphorically of the peace and security offered by Zion.

A perennial spring actually does erupt from the base of Mount Zion. The spring is known as Gihon, and it flows into the pool of Siloam. It served as a water source for the city of Jerusalem and so symbolized the city's ability to withstand a lengthy siege. The spring of Gihon also became a symbol of God's power to fertilize the earth. This is especially true in late prophetic texts. In the book of Joel, Yahweh's defeat of the nations in a cosmogonic battle will result in a fertile land: "In that day the mountains shall drip sweet wine, the hills shall flow with milk, and all the stream beds of Judah shall flow with water; a fountain shall come forth from the house of the LORD and water the Wadi Shittim" (Joel 3:18). A similar vision is heralded in an anonymous oracle appended to the prophecies of Zechariah: "On that day living waters shall flow out from Jerusalem, half of them to the eastern sea and half of them to the western sea; it shall continue in summer as in winter" (Zech 14:8; cf. Ezek 47). In these prophetic oracles the vertical model of sacred space is integrated with the horizontal model. Out of the center of the mountain of God will flow a river that will bring fertility and life to the barren periphery.

By employing the horizontal and vertical models of sacred space, we have described ancient Israel's symbolic understanding of the structure of God's presence in the creation. The significance of this cannot be overstated. According to the biblical tradition, God is not transcendent, if by "transcendent" one means "unattached to the world." God is transcendent only in the sense that God is in the creation, related to the creation, yet remains distinct in substance from the creation (Fretheim 1984:70–71). It is God's presence in the creation that ascribes the creation with value. The creation itself becomes a symbol of God's presence,[4] where God can be encountered. God's presence in creation is further displayed in the natural form of theophanies.

GOD'S FORM IN THEOPHANY

The form of God's appearance in theophany is problematic. In many biblical accounts of theophany God's form is clearly anthropomorphic. This type of theophany is described most frequently in the patriarchal narratives (Gen 18; 28:10–17; 32:22–32 are the most explicit examples). Many more theophanies, however, describe God's appearance in natural terms. Specifically, God's appearance is preponderantly depicted as a thunderstorm. Does this imply that God's form is the thunderstorm? Most biblical scholars answer, "No" (Barr 1960:33). Fretheim, in making the best argument for this conclu-

[4] A similar insight is encompassed in the metaphor of Lady Wisdom (Murphy 1985:8–10; Yee 1992:90).

sion, argues that God appears in human form but is veiled by natural phenomena. For example, Exodus 3:2 claims that God appeared "in" a flame of fire out of a bush. Similarly, Exodus 19:18 states that Yahweh descended "in" smoke and fire, and Exodus 24:9–11 claims that even though God is veiled, Moses and others see the feet of God (Fretheim 1984:93–97).

Fretheim's observations are decisive in recognizing that God is not identified with the natural phenomena that are characteristic of God's theophany. In this sense, God is transcendent. But Fretheim's arguments are not convincing with regard to the form of God. That God's appearance is described with both anthropomorphic and natural images does not imply that God appears in human form, though clothed by natural phenomena. Rather, it attests to the necessity of anthropomorphism with respect to nature. In order for nature to interact with humans it must be given human characteristics, it must be personified. Humbaba, the guardian of the cedar forests of Lebanon in the *Epic of Gilgamesh*, for example, is envisioned as a mighty cedar tree. Nevertheless, the Humbaba tree is personified with human traits: Humbaba can speak and fight; Humbaba has a neck and a heart. Humbaba is not a divine figure that is simply clothed in the guise of a tree. Similarly, the biblical descriptions of theophany suggest that Yahweh appears in natural form.

Perhaps the question, Does God appear in natural form? is misleading. The ancient Israelites do not appear to be addressing this question. As James Barr notes, "form" and "appearance" are correlative in Hebrew thought (1960:32). The Israelites would have made no distinction between God's form and appearance. The above discussion on God's form, on the contrary, assumes this distinction. A more appropriate question might be: Did the ancient Israelites recognize an intensification of God's presence in natural phenomena? The answer to this question is undoubtedly, "Yes."

The most prominent natural phenomenon associated with Yahweh's theophany is the thunderstorm. Even many of the other biblical examples of God's appearance in natural form, such as the pillar of fire and cloud, the so-called volcanic eruptions on Sinai, and the repeated references to the wind of God, can be traced to the thunderstorm (Mann 1971; Cross 1973: 163–69; Luyster 1981). Psalm 18 (= 2 Samuel 22) presents the fullest example of this type of theophany:

⁷Then the earth reeled and rocked;
    the foundations also of the mountains trembled
    and quaked, because he was angry.
⁸Smoke went up from his nostrils,
    and devouring fire from his mouth;
    glowing coals flamed forth from him.
⁹He bowed the heavens, and came down;
    thick darkness was under his feet.
¹⁰He rode on a cherub, and flew;
    he came swiftly upon the wings of the wind.
¹¹He made darkness his covering around him,
    his canopy thick clouds dark with water.
¹²Out of the brightness before him
    there broke through his clouds
    hailstones and coals of fire.
¹³The LORD also thundered in the heavens,
    and the Most High uttered his voice.
¹⁴And he sent out his arrows, and scattered them;
    he flashed forth lightnings, and routed them.
¹⁵Then the channels of the sea were seen,
    and the foundations of the world were laid bare
  at your rebuke, O LORD,
    at the blast of the breath of your nostrils. (Psalm 18:7–15)

Numerous other biblical examples of God's appearance in the thunderstorm could be marshaled, but this example sufficiently illustrates our point. The violent phenomena of the thunderstorm—raging winds, lightning that causes smoke when it strikes the earth, hail, darkness, torrential rains, and earth-shaking thunder—signal the presence of God.

The ancient Israelites' recognition of the presence of God in the thunderstorm attests to both the particular environment of Palestine and the Israelite's own perception of the relationship between God and the creation. For eastern Mediterranean people the thunderstorm was the single most powerful natural phenomenon experienced. (Earthquakes, which were not uncommon, would appear to be an exception to this statement, but the linguistic evidence suggests that the Israelites connected the earthquake with the reverberations caused by the thunderstorm.) The thunderstorm was the source of great destructive power. Its torrential rain, fierce winds, hail, and lightning could destroy crops and demolish homes and other structures. The thunderstorm was also beneficial. It brought the seasonal rains that were essential for the region to support life. Without a regular cycle of rains, the eastern Mediterranean coastal lands quickly become arid and inhospitable (Hiebert 1992a:509).

The thunderstorm, with its destructive and life-giving powers, was a fitting symbol for God's presence in the creation. But this was only possible because the Israelites recognized God's presence in nature. God was transcendent but did not remain outside of the natural world. Instead, the creation was the means by which the creator was made known. An important axiom of biblical scholarship has been that God was made known through human affairs and actions. But this axiom does not tell the whole story. The rest of creation, the natural world, also reveals God. God's presence is manifest as equally in the formation and destruction of a nation as in the rolling thunderstorm bringing the fructifying rains of winter.

CREATION'S RESPONSE TO GOD'S THEOPHANY

In analyzing the similar theophanies of both Yahweh and Baal (both appear in the thunderstorm), Frank Cross identified a fourfold mythological pattern:

1. The Divine Warrior goes forth to battle against chaos (symbolized by the sea or waters, death, dragons like Leviathan, or historical enemies).

2. Nature convulses (writhes) and languishes when the warrior manifests his wrath.

3. The Divine Warrior returns to take up kingship among the gods, and is enthroned on his mountain.

4. The Divine Warrior utters his voice from his temple, and nature again responds. The heavens fertilize the earth, animals writhe in giving birth, and people and mountains whirl in dancing and festive glee. (1973:162–63)

According to this pattern, the natural world responds to God's theophany with both convulsions and fertility, death and life. Although not explicitly stated by Cross, this is the pattern of the conflict myth, and thus the response of nature can be explained in terms of the order of creation. In the first movement of the myth, stages 1 and 2, Yahweh marches out to battle because his kingship over creation has been challenged by chaos. The creation begins to crumble because the challenge made against God's kingship is real. This is not simply an elaborate foil for God to demonstrate supremacy. Chaos has disrupted the order of creation; the future of life is uncertain. But the collapse of creation is not due solely to the assault of chaos. Yahweh's march to battle itself appears to accelerate the collapse.[5] The order of creation can only be reconstituted through the destruction of creation (this theme will be take up further in chapter 6). Despite the challenge of chaos, God is always victorious. The second movement of the myth, stages 3 and 4, celebrates Yahweh's victory over chaos and the reestablishment of his kingship. Because Yahweh returns to his throne, the creation can flourish again. God the king and creator recreates the world. The cosmic damage done by chaos is reversed, and the creation is restored to its original condition.

Although most biblical examples of theophany attest to only one movement of this mythic pattern, the hymns that have been juxtaposed in Isaiah 34–35 present the complete pattern. The first movement of the myth is presented in Isaiah 34. In this hymn, the prophet addresses all creation—the earth and all that fills it, the world and all that sprouts from it. Yahweh is marching to battle against the nations because they have challenged his kingship by oppressing his people. They have exiled the people of Judah from the life-producing center to the sterile periphery. The nations, by assaulting the people of God, had assailed God's rule over creation. Their challenge will not succeed; Yahweh will defeat them in a new cosmogonic battle. Nevertheless, the consequence of their challenge is the disintegration of creation.

> All the host of heaven shall rot away,
>   and the skies roll up like a scroll.
> All their host shall wither
>   like a leaf withering on a vine,
>   or a fruit withering on a fig tree. (Isaiah 34:4)

---

[5] Cross connects the collapse of creation to the fear that the personified natural world experiences before the fierce anger of the Divine Warrior; see also Loewenstamm. This trembling of nature in fear is certainly present in the biblical texts, but this interpretation is not sufficient in itself to explain the biblical descriptions of theophany. Yahweh is marching to battle, nature is trembling, but the reason for both is the new cosmogonic battle the Divine Warrior must fight.

The remainder of the hymn further describes this cosmic collapse: the soil will be turned into sulfur, the rivers into pitch; the land will be drenched with blood and inhabited only by wild demonic creatures.

When Yahweh defends the created order and triumphs over the nations, however, he will return victorious to his throne, reclaim his kingship, and recreate the world.

> [1]The wilderness and the dry land shall be glad,
> the desert shall rejoice and blossom;
> like the crocus [2]it shall blossom abundantly,
> and rejoice with joy and singing.
> The glory of Lebanon shall be given to it,
> the majesty of Carmel and Sharon.
> They shall see the glory of the LORD,
> the majesty of our God. . . .
> [5]Then the eyes of the blind shall be opened,
> and the ears of tne deaf unstopped;
> [6]then the lame shall leap like a deer,
> and the tongue of the speechless sing for joy.
> For the waters shall break forth in the wilderness,
> and streams in the desert;
> [7]the burning sand shall become a pool,
> and the thirsty ground springs of water;
> the haunt of jackals shall become a swamp,
> the grass shall become reeds and rushes.
> (Isaiah 35:1–2, 5–7)

In oppressing Yahweh's people and challenging Yahweh's kingship the nations had placed themselves at the center. They had usurped the center's powers of life and death. But there they will not remain. When Yahweh goes out to defeat them, the fertile land of the nations will become a sterile desert and worse. Their land will be like the chaotic land of the periphery. In contrast, the people of God who had been exiled to the periphery will experience the fertility and life of the center. The desert of the periphery will blossom with life. God will bring order and life to the periphery so that even those aspects of chaos that afflict the human body, human ailments, will be healed.

As a result of God's recreation of the world in which the chaotic periphery is transformed into the life-giving land of the center, the exiled people of God will be able to return to Zion. The barren desert will no longer be an impassable barrier to the center. In response, the people rejoice in God's salvation:

> The ransomed of the LORD shall return,
>   and come to Zion with singing;
> everlasting joy shall be upon their heads;
>   they shall obtain joy and gladness,
>   and sorrow and sighing shall flee away. (Isaiah 35:10)

The praise of God, however, is not the prerogative of humans alone. At the beginning of this salvation oracle the personified desert itself rejoices in God. The impression from this text is that all of creation praises God in the form that God created it. The creation, both humans and the natural world, praises God in its very being as the living product of God's creative desires. The creation as it is designed by the creator is a vehicle of praise. Implicit in this oracle, creation's adoration of God is explicit in Psalm 148. Both humans and the natural world are called to praise God because they are the creation and God is the creator:

> [5]Let them (elements of nature) praise the name of the LORD,
>   for he commanded and they were created.
> [6]He established them forever and ever;
>   he fixed their bounds, which cannot be passed. . . .
> [13]Let them (humans) praise the name of the LORD,
>   for his name alone is exalted;
>   his glory is above earth and heaven. (Psalm 148:5–6, 13)

The creation itself attests to the glory of God and so praises God (Fretheim 1987:23).

THEOPHANY AND THE ISRAELITE WORLDVIEW

Our examination of theophany allowed us to refine further our model of the basic Israelite worldview, especially with regard to the relationship between God and the creation. But to ensure that we employ an appropriate model for elucidating this relationship, it is helpful to examine this relationship from the perspective of two inappropriate models. At one extreme, the relationship between God and the creation can be viewed through the model of pantheism. According to this model God is identified with the creation. Pantheism does not distinguish between the world and God; every part of the world constitutes some element of divine being. This is a model of total immanence. At the other extreme, a dualistic model suggests that God is totally independent from the creation. God and the creation are two uninvolved, unrelated parts of reality. Dualism can also imply a basic opposition or antagonism between the two parts of reality, but in this context I am using a dualistic model simply to describe what has been called God's transcendence—God remains apart from the creation. Neither pantheism nor dualism, however, can adequately explain the biblical descriptions of theophany. According to these descriptions, God is intimately involved in the creation, yet remains distinct. The creation can reveal God's presence, but the creation is not equated with God.

An organismic model for describing the relationship of God and creation is in accord with the experience of theophany (Fretheim 1984:34–35). This model emphasizes the intimate relationship between God and the creation. Clearly, the creation is dependent upon God. The habitable world was created by and is continually affected by God's actions. But God also relies upon the creation to fulfill God's purposes. God does not stand outside of the creation acting independently of it (see the similar conclusion by Murphy 1990:114). The frequently attested Hebrew expression "heaven and earth" bears witness to God's presence in the creation. This expression reveals the division between the terrestrial and the extraterrestrial realms. God reigns uncontested in the heavens, whereas God shares the domain of the earth with humans. However, this expression also attests to the totality and unity of creation (Knierim 1981:76–80; Fretheim 1984:38–39). There is no reality apart from God and the creation. There is no realm for God to dwell in other than the creation. Therefore, God's presence is necessarily in the creation, and God's actions are limited by and expressed in terms of the creation. According to our model of the basic Israelite worldview (figure 8), the relationship between God and the creation must be represented by a bi-directional line of causality.

Although theophany illustrates primarily the relationship between God and the creation, it also confirms the unity of humans and the natural world that is outlined in our model of the Israelite worldview. God's appearance occurs in both natural and societal forms. No distinction is made between God's appearance in human affairs and in the natural world. On numerous occasions, for example, the biblical text celebrates God's victory over a human army, but in the same text describes God's appearance in battle as a thunderstorm

(Hiebert 1992b). Equally significant, both humans and the natural world respond in praise to God's theophany. The praise of God is the ultimate fulfillment of creation, and as a vehicle of praise, the natural world is an intrinsically valuable aspect. Humans are not sufficient by themselves to fulfill the purposes of creation. All of creation must participate.

GOD'S COVENANT WITH CREATION

The Bible describes the relationship between God and the creation as a covenant, a formal union between two parties. Covenant has long been recognized as a central, if not *the* central, institution of the religion of Israel. The structure and meaning of the biblical covenants have been thoroughly explored by previous scholars (McCarthy 1963; Hillers 1969; Baltzer 1971; Levenson 1985) and need not be elaborated upon here. The reader is directed to these works for further discussion. For our purposes, we will focus only on those ways in which covenant defines the relationship between God and the creation and, by extension, the relationship between humans and the natural world.

The covenants described in the Bible are not all of one type. For example, God establishes covenants with individuals (Abraham and David) and a people (Israel). The covenant that concerns us first, however, is God's covenant with all creation. This covenant provides the foundation for all other covenants. It is given by God in response to God's prior destruction of the created order with a flood and occurs in two different yet complementary forms, Genesis 8:20–22 and 9:8–17.

THE YAHWIST'S COVENANT

The first passage has been attributed to the J (the Yahwist) source and is the earlier of the two texts.[6] Although the Yah-

---

[6] Through the use of source criticism, biblical scholars have been able to isolate four literary strands in the Pentateuch—J (the Yahwist), E (the Elohist), D (the Deuteronomist), and P (the Priestly writer)— each written during a different period of Israelite history and each characterized by a distinctive purpose. For a clear demonstration and assessment of this "documentary hypothesis," see Friedman. Recently, this interpretation of the literary character of the Pentateuch

wist does not use the word "covenant," his reference to God's promise is semantically equivalent (Dequeker 1974:116). The passage itself is set at the end of the flood, after Noah and his family safely leave the ark:

> [20]Then Noah built an altar to the LORD, and took of every clean animal and of every clean bird, and offered burnt offerings on the altar. [21]And when the LORD smelled the pleasing odor, the LORD said in his heart, "I will never again curse the ground because of humankind, for the inclination of the human heart is evil from youth; nor will I ever again destroy every living creature as I have done.
> [22]As long as the earth endures,
> seedtime and harvest, cold and heat,
> summer and winter, day and night,
> shall not cease. (Genesis 8:20–22)

We will have more to say about this passage in the context of the flood and the creation myths in the next chapter. At this point it is sufficient simply to note how God's relationship to creation is envisioned. According to this passage, God's covenant with creation entails two components: First, God will never again destroy the creation; and second, God will ensure a regular seasonal cycle so that the ground is no longer cursed because of humankind.

Because of the first human's rebellion against God, humankind is forced out of the garden of God to live in a dry and barren landscape. The ground is cursed; it will produce only thorns and thistles. Eventually, subsequent human rebellion leads to God's regretting the creation of the world and humankind. Because humans are continually inclined toward evil, God seeks to destroy the earth and all humans with it (Gen 6:5–7). Only Noah and his family find favor in God's sight. Despite the fact that the flood destroys all humans except Noah's family, it fails to change the basic predilection of the

---

has come under attack. Nevertheless, virtually all scholars continue to recognize the presence of two distinct strands in Genesis 1–11, J and P. The date of the Yahwist is widely debated. Traditionally, J has been assigned to the period of Solomon, though some scholars date him as early as David and others as late as the exile. Scholars are generally agreed that the Priestly writer dates from the period of the exile or the early postexilic period, though he also incorporated earlier material.

human heart (Petersen 1976:441–44). Because humans are still inclined toward evil (Gen 8:21), it is inevitable that humans will again rebel against God and God will again regret their creation. God's covenant with creation, however, rectifies this precarious situation. God acknowledges that humans are evil at heart and then promises not to destroy creation again because of human rebellion. The creation will continue because God is committed to its preservation.

What is the sign of God's preservation of the creation? The land of Palestine is a region characterized by two seasons: A cool, moist winter during which crops are planted and harvested; and a hot, dry summer during which vegetation withers but fruit ripens on the trees and vines (Baly 1974:43–53). These seasons and even the alternation between day and night are not random. According to this J passage, the regular cycles of nature, characteristic of the eastern Mediterranean seasons, and Israel's own experience of the natural world attest to God's continual ordering or preservation of the creation.

THE PRIESTLY WRITER'S COVENANT

The covenant that is implicit in the J passage is made explicit in the second passage, which is attributed to the P (the Priestly writer) source. This passage explicitly states that God established a covenant with all creation:

> [8]Then God said to Noah and to his sons with him, [9]"As for me, I am establishing my covenant with you and your descendants after you, [10]and with every living creature that is with you, the birds, the domestic animals, and every animal of the earth with you, as many as came out of the ark. [11]I establish my covenant with you, that never again shall all flesh be cut off by the waters of a flood, and never again shall there be a flood to destroy the earth." [12]God said, "This is the sign of the covenant that I make between me and you and every living creature that is with you, for all future generations: [13]I have set my bow in the clouds, and it shall be a sign of the covenant between me and the earth. [14]When I bring clouds over the earth and the bow is seen in the clouds, [15]I will remember my covenant that is between me and you and every living creature of all flesh; and the waters shall never again become a flood to destroy all flesh. [16]When the bow is in the clouds, I will see it and remember the everlasting covenant between God and every living creature of all flesh that is on the earth." (Genesis 9:8–16)

The Priestly writer's formulation of God's covenant with the creation has the same basic meaning as the Yahwist's formulation; God will never again destroy the earth with flood. The Priestly writer, however, specifically claims that God's covenant is with all of creation. It encompasses every living creature and the earth itself. Like the Yahwist, the Priestly writer asserts that the natural order, in the form of a rainbow, attests to God's covenant with creation, but whereas the natural order for the Yahwist is a sign to humans of God's preservation of creation, the bow according to the Priestly writer reminds *God* of God's own covenantal pledge. In other words, the rainbow reminds God to maintain the order of creation so that the naturally occurring storm will not escalate into a cosmic flood that threatens the life of creation (L. Turner 1993).

The corollary to God's covenant with creation is God's activity in blessing. God acts within the cycles of the natural world to sustain the created order (Wehemeier 1970; Westermann 1978; Mitchell 1987:29–78). For the Priestly writer, God's blessing is symbolized by human procreation. In the context of establishing a covenant with creation, the Priestly writer states: "God blessed Noah and his sons, and said to them, 'Be fruitful and multiply, and fill the earth' " (Gen 9:1). This is the reiteration of God's blessing at creation when God blessed both humans (Gen 1:28) and other living creatures (Gen 1:22; oddly, God explicitly blesses the fish and the birds, but not the land animals, which were possibly included with the blessing of humans in an earlier form of the text). Moreover, the Priestly writer demonstrates God's activity in sustaining the creation through two extensive genealogical lists, one placed after God's initial creation (Gen 5) and one after God's recreation of the world in connection with the flood (Gen 10–11). These genealogies are not simply chronological notes, nor do they exclusively serve antiquarian interests. Rather, they attest to God's continuing commitment to the creation. God is bound in covenant with the creation and displays the covenantal obligation to creation through blessings.

Other writers of the Bible also emphasize this correlation between God's covenant with creation and God's activity in blessing. The Yahwist, for example, highlights God's sustaining activity in creation by linking God's blessing in procreation to God's covenant with Abraham, which is itself based on God's covenant with creation (Dequeker 1974). In Psalm 65

God's blessing is presented as an extension of God's activity in creation. In verses 5–8 the psalmist praises God for defeating the enemies in a cosmogonic battle and establishing the created order. Praise of God's blessing in creation then ensues:

> [9]You visit the earth and water it,
>   you greatly enrich it;
>   the river of God is full of water;
>   you provide the people with grain,
>   for so you have prepared it.
> [10]You water its furrows abundantly,
>   settling its ridges,
>   softening it with showers,
>   and blessing its growth.
> [11]You crown the year with your bounty;
>   your wagon tracks overflow with richness.
> [12]The pastures of the wilderness overflow,
>   the hills gird themselves with joy,
> [13]the meadows clothe themselves with flocks,
>   the valleys deck themselves with grain,
>   they shout and sing together for joy. (Psalm 65:9–13)

The experience of God's blessing is not limited to procreation. As the creator, God provides the earth with fertility and water so that it will sustain life. The flourishing of life itself—human, animal, and vegetable—is the result of God's covenant with creation.

GOD'S COVENANT WITH ISRAEL

The most familiar and well-studied of the biblical covenants is the covenant God made with the people of Israel at Mount Sinai. According to the biblical tradition, God brought Israel to this desert mountain after delivering them from bondage in Egypt. At the mountain of God the people swore by oath to follow all the laws that God had given them through Moses. If they did this, God would make them the people of God and bless them. Otherwise, God would bring curses upon them. When God's covenant was offered to the people, the people could not refuse the covenant without consequences; they could accept the covenant and live, or reject the covenant and die, but they could not remain neutral.

Despite a few dissident voices, most scholars compare the structure and significance of this covenant with the suzerain-vassal treaties made by the Hittites, the Assyrians, and other ancient Near Eastern peoples. This type of treaty established a political alliance between a mighty emperor and a subordinate king who was dependent upon the emperor for his throne. The suzerain-vassal treaty is characteristically comprised of six parts: (1) a preamble by which the suzerain identifies himself; (2) a historical prologue that outlines the suzerain's previous dealings with the vassal, especially the ways the suzerain has acted benevolently on behalf of the vassal; (3) a series of stipulations that are imposed on the vassal; (4) provisions for the deposit and public reading of the treaty; (5) a list of witnesses; and (6) the curses and blessings that will befall the vassal depending on his faithfulness in following the stipulations of the treaty.

Although the Sinai covenant is not itself a treaty, biblical scholars have been correct to draw attention to the numerous similarities between the form of the Sinai covenant and the suzerain-vassal treaties. In particular, this type of political treaty serves as a model for understanding the significance of the numerous laws that form the condition of God's covenant. According to the suzerain-vassal treaty, the vassal has an obligation to keep the stipulations of the suzerain *because* the suzerain has acted graciously on his behalf. In the Hittite treaty of Mursilis, for example, Duppi-Tessub of Amurru is obligated to Mursilis because Mursilis established him on the throne over the land of Amurru:

> When your father died, in accordance with your father's word I [Mursilis] did not drop you. Since your father had mentioned to me your name with great praise, I sought after you. To be sure, you were sick and ailing, but although you were ailing, I, the Sun, put you in the place of your father and took your brothers and sisters and the Amurru land in oath for you. (Pritchard 1969:203–4)

The historical prologue describes in detail all the deeds that the suzerain had done for the vassal for the purpose of pressing upon the vassal his obligation to the suzerain. Similarly, Yahweh's covenant with Israel does not arise out of a vacuum. Yahweh has already delivered Israel from bondage in Egypt. Israel is obligated to follow the laws of God. For this reason, the people of

Israel cannot respond with indifference to God's covenant. God is the emperor, and God has already acted on the people's behalf by redeeming them. The people can either accept God's reign as suzerain and respond accordingly or rebel against God and accept the consequences. The Sinai narrative of the Pentateuch and the laws contained therein (Exod 19:1–Num 10:28) cannot be separated theologically from the story of exodus and the history of God's redemption of Israel (Exod 1–15).

God's covenant with Israel, however, cannot be understood on a strictly historical level. God's right to rule is not derived solely from God's acts in history. Rather, God's covenant with Israel is founded ultimately on God's covenant with all of creation. Israel owes God allegiance because God has secured the created order from the threats of chaos.

The Sinai covenant and the suzerain-vassal treaties are based on a similar historical pattern: the vassal is threatened by some enemy force; the suzerain intervenes on behalf of the vassal, defeats the enemy, and delivers him from the threat; and the suzerain establishes his obligatory treaty with the vassal. For Duppi-Tessub, the enemy were those who contested his succession to the throne. Mursilis intervened by securing Duppi-Tessub's position on the throne. For the people of Israel the enemy was Egypt, and God's deliverance of the people was the exodus. This historical pattern is the same pattern that lies behind the conflict myth (Levenson 1988:131–39). In the *Enuma Elish*, the most elaborate presentation of this pattern, the existence of all the gods is equally threatened by Tiamat and her army. At the request of the gods, Marduk marches out to battle and defeats Tiamat. But Marduk exacted a price for his service. In exchange for their deliverance, the assembly of the gods must grant him kingship over all the gods. Marduk's right to rule over the gods and their allegiance to him are the corollaries to his victory over the menacing Tiamat.

The demonstration of Marduk's kingship was the creation of the world. The ordered world attested to Marduk's defeat of Tiamat and his rule over all the gods. Similarly, in the biblical tradition Yahweh's right to rule over Israel and to establish his covenant with the people is demonstrated by the exodus. Through the deliverance of Israel from Egypt, Yahweh defeated the agent of chaos (Pharaoh) and restored the created order. The exodus-Sinai narrative is the historical analogue to the conflict myth.

The lists of witnesses that are present in all suzerain-vassal treaties confirm our conclusion that covenant is grounded in creation. These lists contain the names of the gods of both parties, many of which are creation deities, and elements of the creation itself. In his treaty with Duppi-Tessub, Mursilis calls upon "the mountains, the rivers, the springs, the great Sea, heaven and earth, the winds and clouds" (Pritchard 1969: 205) to bear witness. In the biblical tradition there are no other gods to witness God's covenant with Israel. Thus the creation stands as a testimony and witness of God's commitment to the people and of the people's oath to be faithful to God. In the reformulation of the Sinai covenant in the book of Deuteronomy, for example, God explicitly summoned the creation to witness the covenant: "I call heaven and earth to witness against you today that I have set before you life and death, blessings and curses" (Deut 30:19). Similarly, when Israel breaks God's covenant, the creation stands as a testimony against it:

> [1]Rise, plead your case before the mountains,
>   and let the hills hear your voice.
> [2]Hear, you mountains, the controversy of the LORD,
>   and you enduring foundations of the earth;
> for the LORD has a controversy with his people,
>   and he will contend with Israel. (Micah 6:1–2)

The creation can witness to the terms of the covenant because the covenant is grounded in the order of creation. On one level, the existence of creation attests to God's supremacy over all enemies. God has defeated all threats to the order of creation, and has thus secured the redemption of Israel. On another level, the well-being of creation is a measure of Israel's fidelity to the covenant. As long as Israel remains faithful to the covenant, the creation will flourish. If, however, Israel rebels against the covenant, the creation itself will show the effects. It will become sterile and hostile because Israel's rebellion threatens God's own supremacy over the creation.

Creation's witness to Israel's fidelity to the covenant is formalized in terms of blessings and curses. If Israel keeps the stipulations of the covenant, Israel will experience the blessings of the covenant. But, if Israel rebels against the covenant

and refuses to follow its stipulations, then Israel will experience the curses of the covenant. The blessings and curses of
the covenant indicate a direct relationship between Israel's
actions and the condition of the natural world.

> [13]If you will only heed his every commandment that I am
> commanding you today—loving the LORD your God, and serv-
> ing him with all your heart and with all your soul—[14]then he
> will give the rain for your land in its season, the early rain and
> the later rain, and you will gather your grain, your wine, and
> your oil; [15]and he will give grass in your fields for your live-
> stock, and you will eat your fill. [16]Take care, or you will be
> seduced into turning away, serving other gods and worshiping
> them, [17]for then the anger of the LORD will be kindled against
> you and he will shut up the heavens, so that there will be no
> rain and the land will yield no fruit; then you will perish
> quickly off the good land that the LORD is giving you. (Deuter-
> onomy 11:13–17)

Although this passage, and others, shows that Israel experiences covenantal blessings and curses through the medium of the natural world, changes in the natural world
should not be interpreted simply as God's reward or punishment for Israel's fidelity to the covenant. Rather, the evidence
suggests that the blessings and curses are the consequences of
Israel's actions. According to the covenant theology, God established in the structure of creation an act/consequence construct so that there is an inherent connection between an action
and its consequence. One scholar has even labeled this act/
consequence construct a cosmogony: "The act/consequence
cosmogony envisions such pervasive order in the closed cir-
cuit of creation that whatever humans do, whether for good or
for ill, will necessarily have repercussions in nature as easily
as among people" (Knight 1985:150). Consequently, when the
people of Israel rebel against God's covenant, they are corrupt-
ing the order of creation. Through transgression they do ob-
jective damage to the creation which responds accordingly.
Similarly, when the people follow the covenant, they live in
accord with the creation which flourishes as God intended.
Yahweh's role as creator, then, consists in setting in motion and
bringing to completion those effects which he established in
the created order (Koch 1983).

The covenant relationship between God and Israel provides a framework for understanding the Israelites' relation-

ship to their natural environment. By employing the value orientation preference model, we can discern ancient Israel's preference for the harmony-with-nature solution as an answer to the human-relationship-to-nature problem. In other words, the Israelites perceived the condition of the natural world to be linked to their status as a covenant people. If the Israelites were faithful to God, then the land would be fruitful and the people would prosper. Drought, plague, pestilence, infertility, and the resultant poverty and death, on the other hand, would be the inevitable results of the people's transgressions against God and the created order. The natural world would serve as a witness to, or measure of, Israel's faithfulness to God. This reciprocal relationship between Israel and the natural world is represented in the model of the basic Israelite worldview (figure 8) by the bi-directional horizontal arrow. The Israelites' actions have ramifications in the natural world, according to their faithfulness to the covenant, which will affect them in turn—causing them to prosper or to suffer, to live or to die.

JOB AND THE BREAKDOWN OF THE ISRAELITE WORLDVIEW

The book of Job challenges the Relationship assumptions of the basic Israelite worldview, namely, that the condition of the natural or material world indicates the people's fidelity to God. For Job the harmony-with-nature solution to the human-relationship-to-nature problem is inadequate in explaining his miserable plight. Job lost his family, his possessions, and his health, yet Job claims that he is innocent of any transgressions against God. His friends repeatedly try to explain his suffering in terms of the covenant theology, but Job refutes their explanations at every turn. Job's unhappy experience of the world cannot be resolved in terms of lack of faithfulness to God. Thus Job makes two charges against God: first, God has failed to rule the creation properly so that the righteous are blessed and the wicked are cursed; and second, in the case of Job's own suffering "God is guilty of criminal negligence" (Crenshaw 1992:71). Job demands a hearing before God in order to force God to justify past actions and thereby remove the implied guilt that has been placed on Job.

When God finally confronts Job, however, it is Job and not God who must account for past actions. God does not explain Job's suffering. Rather, in two speeches God assails Job's understanding of creation and his ability to create:

> [4]Where were you when I laid the foundation of the earth?
>   Tell me, if you have understanding.
> [5]Who determined its measurements—surely you know!
>   Or who stretched the line upon it?
> [6]On what were its bases sunk,
>   or who laid its cornerstone
> [7]when the morning stars sang together
>   and all the heavenly beings shouted for joy? (Job 38:4–7)

> [1]Can you draw out Leviathan with a fishhook,
>   or press down its tongue with a cord?
> [2]Can you put a rope in its nose,
>   or pierce its jaw with a hook?
> [3]Will it make many supplications to you?
>   Will it speak soft words to you?
> [4]Will it make a covenant with you
>   to be taken as your servant forever? (Job 41:1–4)

In accusing God of failing to act as the creator, Job uttered ignorant words against God. Job has no understanding of creation; how can he assert that God has failed to maintain the created order? Job has no ability or power to participate in God's creative activity; how can he accuse God of criminal negligence?

The implications of the book of Job for the Israelite worldview are twofold. First, the character of Job gives preference on the subjugation-to-nature solution of the human-relationship-to-nature problem. The created order is an uncontrollable, unpredictable mystery. There is no necessary correlation between human fidelity and the condition of creation. The righteous do experience a creation that appears to be out of order. Yet humans have no choice but to accept the creation that God provides for them. The character of Job reflects a worldview that has been challenged by the external inconsistencies of the world. Job's suffering was at odds with the basic assumption that human actions have a reciprocal effect on the natural world. Therefore, the character of Job falls back on his second order value orientation preference, subjugation-to-nature, in order to make sense of his experience of the world.

Second, the book of Job serves as a critique of some implications of the Israelite worldview. The Israelite world-view assumes a reciprocal relationship between humans and the natural world. The book of Job does not deny that human sin, for example, results in the corruption of the natural world, that nature is affected by human actions. It does deny, however, that nature is an unambiguous *witness* to the character of human actions. As reflected in the speeches of Job's friends, some formulations of the covenant theology placed humans at the center of creation and fidelity to God as the exclusive factor in determining the order of creation. The condition of creation was thought to be dependent upon human actions. The speeches of Yahweh, however, emphasize the cosmic insignificance of humankind and human actions (Crenshaw 1992:80–84). They can neither understand the workings of the creation nor repli-cate God's creation. The speeches themselves consist primarily of meteorological (snow, hail, wind, rain, lightning, dew, frost, clouds, constellations) and zoological (lion, mountain goat, wild ass, wild ox, ostrich, horse, hawk, Behemoth, Leviathan) surveys. Humans have no role in the creation of these animals and natural phenomena. Moreover, the wild animals were not created for any human benefit but for God's own delight. The world was not created with humans at the center. Therefore, the creation and its creator cannot be judged from the human perspective (Gordis 1985).

God's Covenant with the King

According to the biblical tradition, two individuals found favor with God so that God made a covenant with them: Abraham and David. These two covenants are not unrelated. Especially in the J source, God's covenant with Abraham fore-shadows God's covenant with David. For example, the Abraha-mic covenant is stated in terms of promises to be fulfilled in the future: God will make Abraham into a great nation, and he will be a source of blessing for all the families of the earth (Gen 12:1–3). It is not Abraham but his descendants who will experience the blessings of God's covenant. After Abraham left his homeland and entered the land of Palestine, God formalized a covenant with Abraham. God promised him countless descendants (Gen 15:5–6) and land:

> [18]On that day the LORD made a covenant with Abram, saying, "To your descendants I give this land, from the river of Egypt to the great river, the river Euphrates, [19]the land of the Kenites, the Kenizzites, the Kadmonites, [20]the Hittites, the Perizzites, the Rephaim, [21]the Amorites, the Canaanites, the Girgashites, and the Jebusites." (Genesis 15:18–21)

The land that God promised Abraham in fact corresponds to the borders of David's kingdom. Scholars have reasonably concluded, therefore, that the Yahwist modeled the Abrahamic covenant on the Davidic covenant so that David's kingdom would become the fulfillment of God's promises to Abraham.

The hallmark of the Davidic covenant is the unique paternal relationship that God establishes with David and his heirs. God will be a father to David and his heirs, who in turn will be sons to God. The formulation of this covenant is placed in the context of David's desire to build a temple for God. Using a play on the word "house," the Deuteronomistic historian shaped originally unrelated traditional material (Cross 1973: 241–62) in order to emphasize that although God would not allow David to build a house (i.e., temple), a task that was expected of kings (Kapelrud 1963), God will establish for David a house (i.e., dynasty):

> [11]Moreover the LORD declares to you that the LORD will make you a house. [12]When your days are fulfilled and you lie down with your ancestors, I will raise up your offspring after you, who shall come forth from your body, and I will establish his kingdom. [13]He shall build a house for my name, and I will establish the throne of his kingdom forever. [14]I will be a father to him, and he shall be a son to me. When he commits iniquity, I will punish him with a rod such as mortals use, with blows inflicted by human beings. [15]But I will not take my steadfast love from him, as I took it from Saul, whom I put away from before you. [16]Your house and your kingdom shall be made sure forever before me; your throne shall be established forever. (2 Samuel 7:11b–16)

This paternal relationship between God and the king was not unique to Israel but rather characterized the com-

mon royal ideology of the ancient Near East (Frankfort 1948). The
king was considered to be the earthly representative (i.e., son)
of God, and the deeds of the king were symbolic of the deeds
of God. This correlation between king and God is attested in
numerous psalms, but nowhere more clearly than in Psalm 2:

> [7]I will tell of the decree of the LORD:
>   He said to me, "You are my son;
>   today I have begotten you.
> [8]Ask of me, and I will make the nations your heritage,
>   and the ends of the earth your possession." (Psalm 2:7–8)

This psalm begins by describing how the nations gather together
in an assault against God's anointed king on Zion. But their
attack will not succeed because God and the king are as one.
Because the king is God's representative, an assault against the
king is an attack against God. Therefore, just as God is victorious
over all enemies so also will the king be victorious. Just as God
rules over all creation so also will the king rule over all the earth
from Zion.

Human kingship is modeled on divine kingship. But what
is the basis of kingship itself? According to the biblical tradition and the ancient Near Eastern royal ideology, kingship was
earned through military victory (Halpern 1981:51–109). In
heaven, kingship was acquired by the Divine Warrior who
defeats chaos and subsequently creates the world. The biblical
enthronement psalms (Pss 47, 93, 95, 96, 97, 98, and 99)
celebrate Yahweh's kingship because he has secured the world
from the threat of the unruly waters:

> [1]The LORD is king, he is robed in majesty;
>   the LORD is robed, he is girded with strength.
>   He has established the world; it shall never be moved;
> [2]   your throne is established from of old;
>   you are from everlasting.
> [3]The floods have lifted up, O LORD,
>   the floods have lifted up their voice;
>   the floods lift up their roaring.
> [4]More majestic than the thunders of mighty waters,
>   more majestic than the waves of the sea,
>   majestic on high is the LORD! (Psalm 93:1–4)

On earth, kingship was established and maintained through
military victory over human armies. But because of the

correlation between king and God, these armies were identified as the agents of chaos. In Psalm 89, a composite psalm reflecting numerous aspects of Israel's royal ideology, God's covenant with David is explicitly connected to God's defeat of chaos and creation of the world:

> [3]You said, "I have made a covenant with my chosen one,
>   I have sworn to my servant David:
> [4]'I will establish your descendants forever,
>   and build your throne for all generations.' " . . .
> [9]You rule the raging of the sea;
>   when its waves rise, you still them.
> [10]You crushed Rahab like a carcass;
>   you scattered your enemies with your mighty arm.
> [11]The heavens are yours, the earth also is yours;
>   the world and all that is in it—you have founded them.
>   (Psalm 89:3–4, 9–11)

God, as king in heaven, can guarantee David's kingship on earth (Levenson 1985:102–11). God will secure David's kingship by defeating all enemies:

> [22]The enemy shall not outwit him,
>   the wicked shall not humble him.
> [23]I will crush his foes before him
>   and strike down those who hate him.
> [24]My faithfulness and steadfast love shall be with him;
>   and in my name his horn shall be exalted.
> [25]I will set his hand on the sea
>   and his right hand on the rivers. (Psalm 89:22–25)

Just as God is victorious in heaven, so will David be victorious on earth. The last verse of this passage is especially significant; David is given control over the aquatic symbols of chaos. This text could simply mean that David's enemies are equated with chaos, but the verse itself focuses on David's role rather than that of his enemies. As the representative of God, David has been placed in the position of the creator in relation to the earth. David himself, enabled by God's covenant with him, secures the created order by defeating his enemies.

A different, yet complementary, argument for the integral link between the actions of the king and the order of creation has been given by Hans H. Schmid. He has argued convincingly that legal order in the ancient Near East, including covenant in the Bible, belongs to the order of creation (1968;

1984; cf. Scullion 1971). Cosmic order is characterized by righteousness, and, according to the ancient Near Eastern royal ideology, the king, whether he be the divine king or the earthly representative of the deity, was the guarantor of the created order. "Upon him and his acts depend the fertility of the land as well as the just social and political order of the state" (Schmid 1984:105). Through the promulgation of laws and his accompanying execution of justice, the king demonstrates righteousness that was not simply an attribute of moral character but the action of world ordering. For this reason, the promulgation of law is connected to the time of creation. In the prologue to his famous law code, for example, Hammurabi claims that he was appointed by the gods at the creation of the world to bring justice to the people (Pritchard 1969:164). His law is thereby equated with the order of creation.

In the biblical tradition it is foremost Yahweh who is righteous, and he demonstrates his righteousness as the ruler over creation by maintaining the covenant that ensures that the heavens will provide the needed rain for the land, that the land will be fertile and produce an abundance of crops, and that the people will know peace. But the Davidic king is Yahweh's earthly representative. His task is to demonstrate God's righteousness and thereby to secure the order of creation (cf. Ps 72).

In contrast to the covenant theology and the book of Job, the biblical texts that stem from the royal ideology reflect the mastery-over-nature solution to the human-relationship-to-nature problem. Because of the correlation between king and God, the king stands in the same relationship to the creation as does God the creator. Just as God defeated the agents of chaos, the king secures the order of creation by defeating all his enemies. The king's deeds are world ordering. The king's mastery over nature, however, is only by virtue of God's covenant, which is bestowed upon him as a gift. Many scholars have emphasized the unconditional character of the Davidic covenant, but this can be misleading. The king is not given absolute power over the creation, nor is the king's rule without qualification. Rather, the king's rule is dependent upon God and should be characterized by God's righteousness. The king is merely the representative of God. To assume otherwise is hubris. The king should act as God's agent of righteousness on the earth. Through righteousness he should dispense justice to the people and secure the fertility of the earth. Therefore, the king's deeds should also conform to the order of creation. The royal ideology of the basic Israelite worldview, which is not independent, also reflects the harmony-with-nature solution.

COVENANT AND THE ISRAELITE WORLDVIEW

Through our investigation of the covenant, we have detected all three solutions to the human-relationship-to-nature problem. God's covenants with creation and with Israel at Sinai reflect the harmony-with-nature solution. The book of Job presents Job's preference for the subjugation-to-nature solution as a critique of the covenant theology. The royal ideology gives preference to the mastery-over-nature solution, but also reflects the harmony-with-nature solution. The appearance of these diverse solutions in the biblical texts is to be expected, for the value orientation preference model presupposes that all alternative solutions are present in every society. These solutions might simply demonstrate the preferences of diverse subgroups within the Israelite society (the royal establishment, wisdom circles, the masses). Or the different solutions might be the result of varying circumstances and thus second or third order preferences of the same basic value orientation (this interpretation was suggested for the character of Job). In any case, these alternative value orientations pose a problem for understanding the ancient Israelite worldview. As discussed in chapter 1, there is a direct correlation between the solutions to the human-relationship-to-nature problem and the assumptions of the Relationship universal. Do the diverse value orientations indicate diverse worldviews, or can these value orientations be integrated into a single worldview?

Because the assumptions of the Relationship universal are contingent upon the Classification universal, the latter might serve as a key to understanding the relationship of these value orientations. A primary Classification assumption of the ancient Israelites, as a collectivist society, was the distinction between ingroup and outgroup. This assumption takes precedence even over the threefold division between God, humans, and nature, but it is subordinate to the fundamental distinction

between the creator and the creation.[7] The Israelites' classification domains can be diagrammed as in figure 13. A distinction thus needs to be made between a person's value
orientation toward ingroup nature and outgroup nature (which
will tend to replicate a person's attitude toward other ingroup
members in contrast to outgroup members).

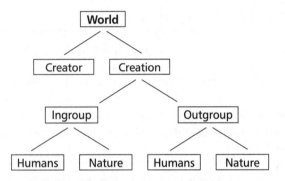

Figure 13. Ingroup/Outgroup Domains

The distinction between ingroup and outgroup explains
why two different value orientations are detected in the royal
ideology. The texts that reflect the mastery-over-nature orientation also emphasize the king's ability to defeat all his enemies, whereas the texts that imply a harmony-with-nature
orientation emphasize the king's role in maintaining the created order by administering justice for the people. These texts

---

[7] The classification of god along ingroup/outgroup lines is problematic. The biblical texts clearly differentiate between Yahweh, who
is the God of Israel, and the gods of the nations. Yet the Israelites are
repeatedly condemned by the prophets for worshipping "foreign" or
"Canaanite" gods. Many of the Israelites simply did not recognize the
ingroup/outgroup boundaries in relation to the gods. The boundaries
between creator and creation served to demarcate a more fundamental
distinction. Those gods that the Israelites associated with the powers
of creation—Yahweh, Baal, and Asherah were the more popular of
these—were worshipped by the people. Monolatry (worship of one
god) among the Israelites can be tied to their recognition of Yahweh as
the sole creator.

reflect the king's orientation toward outgroup and ingroup members respectively. He will demonstrate his mastery over all those outside of his group (Israel), just as God displayed mastery over the agents of chaos in the battle of creation. By defeating his enemies, the king secures the order of creation. In relation to Israel, however, the king will act according to righteousness, that is, the order of creation, and thereby guarantee the blessings of creation.

The Sinai covenant reflects only ingroup relations. The faithfulness of the Israelites to the covenant affects their own experiences of the natural world. Their land will be either fertile or sterile; their land will experience either plenty of rain or drought; their animals either will give birth to offspring or will miscarry; they will either live or die. The relationship between the Israelites and their land is characteristic of the relationship among ingroup members—the harmony-with-nature orientation.

People do not always experience nature as belonging to their ingroup. Like an invincible foreign army that wantonly invades and devastates a society, nature can be encountered as an overpowering enemy from which there is no retreat. The natural world can be viewed as a subjugating outgroup. This was the circumstance with Job. This was also the situation of the peasants, the populace of ancient Israel. With no land, they were under the control of the land owners (outgroup). They were similarly powerless before nature, unable to effect any real change in the natural world. Subjugation-to-nature, like mastery-over-nature, is an orientation toward the natural world of the outgroup, but unlike the mastery-over-nature orientation, this orientation experiences the natural world as dominant and overwhelming.

Each solution to the human-relationship-to-nature problem replicates different societal relations according to ingroup/outgroup boundaries. The harmony-with-nature solution replicates internal ingroup relations. The mastery-over-nature solution replicates ingroup-outgroup relations from the perspective of a dominant ingroup. The subjugation-to-nature solution replicates ingroup-outgroup relations from the perspective of a dominated ingroup. These alternative value orientations are thus complementary and can be integrated into a single model of the Israelite worldview, illustrated in figure 14.

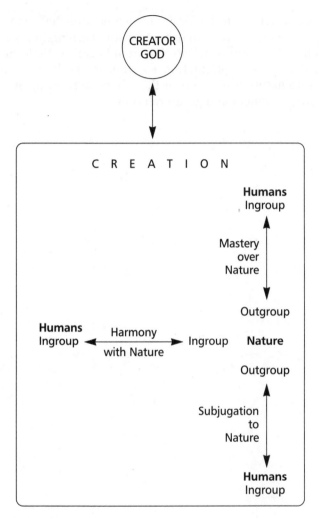

Figure 14. Israel's Worldview and Values Toward Nature

This model of the Israelite worldview is essentially
an expansion of our basic Israelite worldview model. The
mastery-over-nature and the subjugation-to-nature orientations replicate the (positive-negative) relationship between
God the creator and the creation, the ingroup replicates the role
of the creator or the creation respectively. The harmony-with-
nature orientation simply defines the relationship between

humans and nature to be between members of the same in-group. This worldview, with its three distinct orientations, was shared by all ancient Israelites, but each Israelite would have preferred one value orientation solution to the human-relationship-to-nature problem over the others, depending on external circumstances and group relations.

5
IN THE BEGINNING:
THE CREATION MYTHS

THE PRESENT IN THE BEGINNING AND THE END

The ancient Israelites' values toward nature are made most explicit through their myths of the beginning and the end. These myths specifically address the triangular relationship between God, humans, and the natural world. Thus they provide a final yet necessary resource for our investigation of the Israelites' values toward nature and the worldview in which they are rooted.

Although myths of the beginning and the end are ostensibly placed on a temporal continuum, referring to the past and the future respectively, the significance of these myths is focused on the present (van der Leeuw 1957; Pettazzoni 1967:29; Westermann 1972). In other words, these myths are about the present values and conditions of the people who generated them rather than the obscure past or the unknown future. Not all readers of these myths, however, have recognized their present orientation. In part, this is due to a failure by many readers to recognize the mythic character of the Bible's stories and descriptions of the beginning and the end. But more importantly, many if not most readers of the Bible—scholars and laity alike—have failed to distinguish between their own temporal orientation and the temporal orientation of traditional societies, including ancient Israel.

All cross-cultural studies, which of course includes the study of the Bible by twentieth-century Westerners, must take into account cultural differences concerning the perception of time in order to avoid ethnocentrism and misunderstanding

(Maines 1987). Some biblical scholars have therefore attempted to distinguish between the ancient Israelites' view of time and the modern view of time inherited from the Greeks. Based primarily on linguistic evidence, numerous scholars have argued that the Israelites emphasized the *content* of time, whereas the Greeks emphasized the *chronological sequence* of time (Boman 1960). According to this distinction, time for the ancient Israelites was infused with substance and identical to that substance. Time was thought to be simply an empty frame of reference that was filled with events. For example, there were times of harvesting, times of planting, times of war, times of raising children, times of death, times of sorrow, times of joy, and times of peace. In each case, time was characterized by the events that filled it (Pedersen 1926:487–88; Černy 1948:4–7; Rust 1953).

This characterization of the Israelite perception of time, however, does not stand up to close examination. On the one hand, the linguistic arguments marshaled to distinguish Israelite from Greek views of time are fallacious (Barr 1961, 1969; Momigliano 1982). On the other hand, detailed studies of biblical words for time have demonstrated that they do in fact denote chronological sequence (Wilch 1969; DeVries 1975); Hebrew words for time signify both quantitative (chronological sequence) and qualitative (content) aspects with little variance from Greek vocabulary.

A more promising approach for distinguishing between ancient Israelite and modern Western views of time is available through Kluckhohn and Strodtbeck's model of value orientation preferences (Malina 1989a). As with the human-relationship-to-nature problem, this model enables us to categorize possible cultural solutions to the common human problem regarding the temporal-focus-of-human-life; what temporal focus—past, present, or future—forms the framework for solutions to the vital problems of human life? Although this model does not enable us to discern what is unique about Israelite or Western perceptions of time (with no informants to question, the peculiar features of Israel's view of time have probably been lost to history), it does differentiate between the fundamental temporal values of each culture.

In the United States and other Western countries the overwhelming first order preference to this problem is the future-orientation solution. For the majority of Westerners, all human problems can be solved through appropriate future actions. Human goals are placed in the future, and the activity in the present is merely the means by which those goals will be achieved. The future is neither random nor determined, but as the continuation of the present it can be affected by personal choices. An American axiom is that each person has control over his or her own future. The future for Americans is the motivation for all that happens in the present. We act in the present in order to shape our future. The present, in contrast, is limited to a single moment facing an unlimited future and is itself instantaneously becoming the past. Now is an ever changing moment in time's relentless march into the future.

Although future-orientation is the dominant value preference of Westerners, it is a minority preference in the global community. This is primarily because, according to the analysis of James M. Jones, a future orientation depends upon two cultural factors: the belief that if a specific act is performed in the present, then the probability of some future goal will be greater; and the tendency to value goals whose attainment can only occur in the future. A necessary prerequisite for these cultural factors is that the survival needs of the present—food, water, shelter, clothing, protection—must be assured. People are unlikely to be concerned about the future until their own survival in the present is secured. It is therefore not surprising that the future-orientation solution is the dominant preference of U. S. Americans. Our high level of technology and affluent standard of living afford us the luxury of striving for goals in the future. But equally important, we have the means by which to achieve those goals and, by so doing, reinforce our future orientation.

In contrast to the United States, many societies in the world today and most traditional societies prefer the present-orientation solution to the temporal-focus-of-human-life problem. In a present-oriented society, a person's current activity is aimed at achieving proximate goals. The present is the duration of everyday experiences. It is made up of all forthcoming and recent events; it is not only a single moment in the course of time. "The immediate future bound up with present as well as previous activity still resonating in the present are all part of that present, still experienced and all actually present" (Malina 1989a:12). According to the present-orientation solution, the present is like a line segment rather than a point. The present encompasses a range of human experiences: all that one has encountered in the past relative to what one is currently encountering and what one is about to encounter as a result of the past and the present. Together, this range of experience forms a single ongoing context of meaning known as the present.

If the present, according to this orientation, is *experienced* time, then the remote past and the distant future are *imaginary* time (Bourdieu 1963:60–61; Malina 1989a:11–17). Imaginary time is outside the scope of current human experience and, as such, is not subject to the constraints of experienced time. Stories and accounts that take place during experienced time are judged to be true according to their correlation with actual human experiences. In an imaginary world, however, all things are possible; truth is not limited to human experience. Imaginary time is the time of monsters and mythological creatures, heroes and heroic exploits, miracles and disruptions of the rhythms of nature. From the perspective of the Israelites, imaginary time was the exclusive domain of God. The possible world of the past and the future is made possible by God, but because it belongs to the domain of God, the past and the future as possible worlds "cannot belong and never will belong to human beings" (Malina 1989a:15). In other words, humans live and must live in the present. To do otherwise would be tantamount to assuming divine prerogatives.

Experienced time and imaginary time differ not only in their criteria of truthfulness but also in their function (Malina 1989a:24–28). Experienced time is similar to operational time. It is repetitive time, marked by regular intervals, during which the tasks of life—working, eating, sleeping, playing—are carried out. As a result, operational time is primarily subject to environmental constraints. The times of planting and harvesting, for example, are determined by the ecological conditions of a region. Times of eating and defecating are necessitated by the biological demands of the human body. For the cultures surrounding the Mediterranean Sea, warfare and other extended outside activities were conducted only during the dry summer months. The rainy winter months were typically a period of reduced outside activity (Boissevain 1982/3).

Imaginary time, on the other hand, is similar to historical time. It is "concerned with the ordering of events or periods in the life of an individual or a society, which are of contemporary significance" (Rayner 1982:256). Historical time gives warrant to the present society by projecting present concerns and aspirations onto the past and the future. Historical time is the world of the possible; it is subject to social rather than environmental constraints. Traditional cultures turn to historical time in order to explain certain customs, such as Israel's redemption of the first born child from sacrifice (Gen 22:1–18; Exod 13:11–16), or to justify social demands, such as that Israel should follow the laws of the covenant (cf. the numerous examples of God's past benevolence on behalf of Israel and the prophetic warnings of God's coming judgment when Israel transgresses the laws).

Ancient Israel was predominantly a present-oriented society, and the Bible's myths of the beginning and the end reflect imaginary-historical time. They present an imaginative world that is out of sync with human experience. They describe a world in which humans and animals issue from the ground, fruit endows one with life and knowledge, snakes talk, mountains flow with milk and wine, the desert is watered and blossoms, and the lamb and the lion lie down together. Although these myths do not describe the concrete world of Israel's experience, they do present a picture of the social fabric of ancient Israel. Israel's remote past and future were constructed in order to explain, justify, and reinforce Israel's own present social values, customs, and demands. In this way, the biblical myths of the beginning and the end (the latter to be discussed in chapter 6) inform us about ancient Israel's values concerning the natural world and the role of humans in relationship to it and so further illustrate the Israelite worldview.

THE YAHWIST CREATION MYTH

The two biblical creation myths are rich in tradition and symbolism and lend themselves to multifaceted interpretations, as the voluminous secondary literature on these myths attests. For our purposes, the interpretation of these myths will focus on how they function *as myths*, that is, as vehicles for communicating the fundamental values of ancient Israelite society. We are less concerned with, for instance, how these myths might have served political ideologies (Wyatt 1981;

Holter) or religious polemics (Hasel 1972, 1974; Kapelrud 1974; Soggin 1975:88–111). Therefore, our analysis will accentuate the interrelationship between God, humans, and the natural world that is disclosed through the metaphors and structure of the myths.

CREATION INSIDE THE GARDEN: GENESIS 2:4b–25

Creation in the Bible is never creation *ex nihilo,* "from nothing." This doctrine was not formulated until the Hellenistic Age, to which the first reference is 2 Maccabees 7:28. In the biblical tradition, and in the ancient Near East in general, God always works with some material that is either primordial or already there when God begins to create, though the ancient Israelites would not have made this distinction (Andersen 1987:140–41). As discussed in chapters 2 and 3, God creates either through establishing order and fixing boundaries, usually by separating a primordial substance, or through the natural physical processes of birth and growth. In the Yahwist creation myth the earth itself is primordial. God never creates the earth, but the earth without God's creative activity is barren and lifeless.

In typical ancient Near Eastern fashion, the Yahwist creation myth begins by describing that which is absent at the beginning of creation (cf. the beginning of the *Enuma Elish* and the myth of *Enki and Ninhursag*): The earth exists as a dry, sterile desert, with no plants or vegetation because God has not yet created rain and because there is no human to till the ground (2:5). This outlines the purpose of God's creative activity—to create rain and humans to till the ground so that the earth will produce life. In response to the negative aspects of creation, the text states positively that there is a spring that swells up from the earth to water the ground (2:6).[1] From this spring flows a river that branches into four rivers, two of which are the great rivers of Mesopotamia, the Tigris and the Euphrates (2:10–14). The setting of creation that is being described is the Mesopotamian plain (Batto 1992:49; contra

---

[1] On the debated interpretation of this spring, see the linguistic analysis of Albright (1939:102–3), Speiser (1955), Westermann (1984: 200–201), and Andersen (1987:137–40). Cf. the interpretation of Tsumura (1989:93–116).

Meyers 1988:83), which is dependent upon irrigation in order to sustain life. The earth has the potential for life; the subterranean waters can be harnessed in order to make the ground fertile. Yet without humans to till the ground and channel the water into irrigation ditches, the Mesopotamian plain remains lifeless (Wenham 1987:59).

After describing the setting of creation through an elaborate set of temporal clauses, the narrative emphasizes God's first act of creation; God formed the human creature (*'adam*) from the dust (in the sense of dry earth, dirt) of the ground (*'adama*), breathed into its nostrils the breath of life, and the human creature became a living being (2:7).[2] Scholars have frequently noted that God's creation of the human creature evokes the image of a potter who "forms" a vessel on the wheel. In particular, a number of scholars have compared Yahweh in this context with the Egyptian creator god Khnum who fashions humans on his potter's wheel (Gordon 1982:203–4; Hoffmeier 1983:47; Westermann 1984:203). Indeed, this comparison is correct. But just as Khnum's work as a potter should be understood within the context of the birth process—the potter's fashioning of a clay vessel is analogous to the creator god's fashioning of the fetus in the womb (see the discussion in chapter 2)—so also Yahweh's forming of the human creature from the dirt of the ground is a metaphor for humankind's birth out of the earth (contra Wolff 1974a:93). The potter metaphor is simply an abstraction of the birth metaphor. Yahweh acts as a potter who forms the human fetus in the womb of the earth, and then Yahweh acts as a midwife by delivering the human creature out of the earth (cf. Benjamin 1989:119). Yahweh's role in animating the human creature by breathing into its nostrils can be compared to the birth goddess Heket, who is frequently pictured inserting the *ankh*, the sign of life, into the nostrils of those whom Khnum fashioned on the wheel

---

[2] The Hebrew term *'adam* can refer to the human species or the gendered human man. In the first half of the myth (2:4b–24), *'adam* refers to the undifferentiated human species and so has been translated as "human creature." In the second half of the myth (2:25–3:24), *'adam* refers to the individual who results from the human creature after differentiation is introduced and so in this case *'adam* has been translated as "man." Of course, *'adam* also becomes the personal name of the first man, Adam.

(Gordon 1982:204). With the crucial aid of Yahweh, the earth at last is able to produce life.

The creation of the human creature emphasizes the connection between humankind and the earth. Humans have their origin in the ground, and, as Genesis 3:19 makes explicit, humans will return to the ground at death. The Yahwist further accentuates this connection through the pun *'adam - 'adama;* the human creature is characterized by the ground from which it came. In connecting the human creature with the earth, however, the Yahwist is not making a statement about biological origins. The significance of the correlation between the human creature and the earth is metaphorical and not biological. By connecting humans to the earth, the Yahwist counters all attempts by humans to transcend their creaturely status. Humans are of earth, not of heaven, and so their fate is bound to the earth.

The primordial earth remained barren because it lacked two ingredients necessary to sustain life: rain and human labor. Therefore, God first forms a human creature from the dust of the ground. Oddly, God does not proceed to create rain. No rain will fall on the earth until God creates the flood rains in Genesis 7:4. Nor does the human creature, who was created to till the ground, cultivate the barren landscape. Rather, God plants a garden in Eden, which is located in the east (from Israel, that is, in Mesopotamia). Just as God brought the human creature out of the earth, so God causes the earth to produce every kind of fruit tree (2:9). The water for sustaining the garden is undoubtedly supplied by the river that flows out of the garden. The human creature is placed in Yahweh's garden assigned the task of tending and preserving it.

The fact that God, rather than the human creature, planted the garden suggests that the garden was not intended to be the dwelling place of humans. After all, the garden of Eden is the garden of *God.* Humans were created to till the ground and in this manner bring life to the sterile desert. This is their destiny, and the earth outside the garden will be their dwelling. But just as children must remain in the house of their parents until they reach maturity so also the human creature is placed temporarily in the garden of God.

Although the human creature is never specifically described as a king, a few scholars have identified a number of royal attributes that the Yahwist ascribes to the human crea-

ture. The garden, for example, might indicate the human creature's royal status. The garden of Eden is presented as a formal
pleasure garden, characteristic of the royal gardens of ancient
Near Eastern kings (Wyatt 1981:14–15; Hutter 1986; Coote and
Ord 1989:50–54). The human creature's task in the garden is
the work (one might even say "hobby") of kings. It is not the
backbreaking, sweating toil of farming but rather the leisurely
pruning and manicuring of a self-sustaining perennial garden.
The garden of Eden is a paradise in the original use of the term
("paradise" was first used by Xenophon to refer to the pleasure
gardens of Persian kings and nobles).

Similarly, Walter Brueggemann has identified the creation formula, "the LORD God formed the human creature from
the dust of the ground" (2:7), as a royal formula of enthronement. The parade example of the royal formula is found in
1 Kings 16:2: "Since I exalted you [Baasha] out of the dust and
made you leader over my people Israel . . . " Dust serves as a
metaphor in this text for Baasha's preroyal status, which apparently was the status of a commoner with nonroyal lineage.
Dust stands in direct antithesis to royal status in 1 Samuel
2:6–8 and Psalm 113:7, and this relationship is implied in
numerous other passages. Applying this metaphorical interpretation to Genesis 2, Brueggemann concludes:

> Adam, in Gen 2, is really being crowned king over the garden
> with all the power and authority which it implies. This is the
> fundamental statement about man made by J. He is willed by
> God to occupy a royal office. . . . *Thus creation of man is in fact
> enthronement of man.* (1972:12)

Even though a garden paradise does have royal connotations, and dust may metaphorically function as an enthronement formula, neither of these interpretations fits the
Yahwist's narrative. The human creature does not function as
a king in his garden. Rather, the garden belongs to God who
assigns the human creature a task in the garden and sets limits
on the creature's enjoyment of the garden. It is God who
functions as the king in the Yahwist's myth.

A comparison between Genesis 2 and Ezekiel 28:12–19
is appropriate in this context. In contrast to Genesis 2, the latter
text describes the creation of a primordial king in the garden
of Eden. He is specifically identified as a king, and there are
references to his wisdom and beauty and his regalia that are

characteristic of kings. The similarities between these two texts have frequently been observed, but the relationship between them is problematic. In both passages the created being is placed in the garden of Eden and then expelled after claiming divine prerogatives. Even if one text is not directly dependent upon the other, there is at least a common tradition underlying both texts. In any case, the explicit references to the royal attributes of the king in Ezekiel 28 suggest that the royal ideology belonged to the tradition. The Yahwist has simply transformed the creation of the primordial king into the creation of the primordial human (cf. van Seters 1989; 1992:120–21). The royal attributes identified in Genesis 2 are remnants of traditional material from which the Yahwist constructed his narrative.

In the garden of Eden God plants two trees of note, the tree of life and the tree of the knowledge of good and evil (2:9). The former tree is only mentioned twice in the narrative, at the beginning and the end (3:22), and thus scholars have commonly assumed that it was a remnant from an earlier myth or the Yahwist's source material. There have been some scholars, however, who have observed the thematically important role of immortality in this myth, suggesting that the tree of life is integral to the narrative (Hutton 1986; Barr 1992). The presence of the tree of life in the garden assumes that the human creature is mortal, for the tree offers the creature the opportunity of immortality. Whether the human creature is aware of its mortality is a different issue that depends upon the interpretation of the tree of knowledge. Although the human creature can eat from every other tree in the garden, including the tree of life, the fruit of the tree of knowledge is specifically off-limits. God prohibits the human creature from eating its fruit with the threat that "in the day that you eat of it you shall die" (2:17).

Initially, the human creature is the only living being in the garden. Recognizing that it is not good for humans to be alone, Yahweh attempts to create, literally, "a helper corresponding to it" (2:18). So just as God formed the human creature out of the ground, God forms all the animals and the birds in similar fashion. The Yahwist myth emphasizes that humans are similar to the animals and the birds in both substance and method of their creation. All living beings, regardless of species, make up the genus of creature; none are divine. For this reason, when God brings each newly formed creature to the human to be named, God hopes to find a suitable helper for the human from among the other creatures. But God fails in this task; no companion for the human can be formed out of the ground (2:19–20).

A great deal of discussion has centered around the human creature's role in naming all the animals and birds. For some interpreters, naming becomes a symbol of human dominance and control over the creation. Naming, it is claimed, demonstrates the superiority of humans over other creatures (Wenham 1987:68) and is comparable to the Priestly writer's statement that humans should exercise dominion over all the creatures of the earth (von Rad 1972a:82–83; Westermann 1984:228–29). Thus Lynn White suggested that the positive value ascribed to the human creature's naming of the animals justified human exploitation of nature (1967:1205). Although White has been accused of being critically illiterate because he has blurred together the P and the J creation myths, connecting naming with dominion and thus obscuring both P and J (Hiers 1984:45), White has merely drawn out the implications of what biblical scholars had already stated. But scholars have misinterpreted the significance of name-giving. It does not signal human superiority or human dominance over animals. Both of these attributes are lacking in the Yahwist's narrative. Rather, in the myth name-giving is placed in the context of finding a *suitable* helper for the human creature. The significance of name-giving must be understood in this context. "If the act of naming signifies anything about the name-giver, it is the quality of *discernment*" (Ramsey 1988:34). By naming the animals and birds the human creature distinguishes between those creatures that are suitable for a human helper and those that are not (Magonet 1992:40–41). But no creature is found that corresponds to the human.

Because God is unable to form a suitable helper for the human creature from the ground, God splits the human creature (*'adam*) in order to create two complementary individuals (Trible 1978:94–105): man (*'ish*) and woman (*'ishsha*). God puts the human creature into a comatose state (Meyers 1988: 84), takes one of its ribs, and from the rib builds a woman (2:21–22). Prior to this new creation, the human creature was undifferentiated with regard to gender, being either asexual (neither male nor female) or androgynous (both male and female). By splitting the human creature, God introduces differentiation into the human species, but the terms used to describe this differentiation are explicitly social in orientation rather than sexual (Coote and Ord 1989:57). The man is identified foremost as a husband, the woman as a wife. The specific social roles of each individual, however, are not outlined until the second half of the myth. At this point in the myth the Yahwist simply notes that their complementary social roles find fulfillment in the institution of marriage (Hutton 1986: 129); by uniting in marriage, the man and the woman restore the one flesh from which they originated (2:24).

The statement that the man and the woman are naked yet they do not shame each other (2:25; Sasson 1985) acts as a point of transition between the first part of the myth, dealing with creation inside the garden, and the second, depicting creation outside the garden. On one level, it describes the continuing status of the human couple in the garden of Eden. The implication of this statement is that the human couple is sexually unaware. In other words, they do not know that the union of their bodies has the potential to produce new life. They are like children unacquainted with the biological and cultural significance of their bodies, and so their nakedness means nothing to them. On another level, this statement introduces those characteristics of the human couple that become the focus of the second half of the myth.

CREATION OUTSIDE THE GARDEN: GENESIS 3

The second half of the Yahwist creation myth has traditionally been termed the "Fall," with attention given to the human acts of disobedience against God (the foremost example of this is Paul's own interpretation of the story in Romans 5, 1 Corinthians 15, and 1 Timothy 2). Recent scholars, however, have begun to question this theological interpretation of the myth for a variety of reasons. First, although the human couple disregards God's command by eating the forbidden fruit, this act is never called "sin" (Scullion 1974:6–7). "Interpreters may label this act as disobedient; exegetes may consider it sinful. But *God* does not provide such a judgment within either the narration or the discourse of Genesis 3" (Meyers 1988:87). The first reference to sin in the Bible is in Genesis 4:7, in the context of Cain's murder of Abel. Second, the Old Testament itself never characterizes this story as a "Fall." For this reason, the Jewish tradition has preferred to characterize this narrative as the human expulsion from the garden rather than as the "Fall" (Barr 1992:4–20). Third, and most important, this theological interpretation fails to account adequately for the change of status of the human couple.

According to the first part of the Yahwist's myth, the human couple lives in an unreal world (Carmichael 1992:47–54; Amit 1990): humans, animals, and birds alike are born out of the earth; there is no differentiation between humans and other creatures; the woman is created out of the "man"; the human couple is naked like the animals and has no awareness of sexual differentiation; and the human couple live a leisurely life in a pleasure garden planted by God with the possibility of immortality. This is not the world of human experience! As appealing as paradise might be, this is not the world in which humans live, nor is it the world in which humans prefer to live. In the first part of the myth the archetypal man and woman[3] are analogous to children engaging in a rite of passage (Niditch 1985:31–34). They are presented in the unreal world of liminality—the stage of transition between childhood and adulthood (V. Turner 1969:95–97). All humans must eventually mature into adults. To remain in childhood indefinitely is tantamount to denying one's own humanity, for only in adulthood do humans find their fulfillment. For this reason, the human couple does not stay content with the status quo world of the unreal garden of Eden. The man and woman go through a rite of passage in the liminal setting of the garden of Eden (Hutton 1986:136–37) and are transformed into real humans living in a real world. The second half of the Yahwist creation myth is all about this transformation.

In the second half of the myth a new character is introduced: the serpent. Just as this part of the myth is not about the "Fall" of humankind, so also the snake is not the Devil or Satan. This common interpretation is the result of later Christian readings of this story as a foreshadowing of the Christ event, but such an interpretation is foreign to the Old Testament itself. The serpent is only one of the creatures that God

---

[3] The man and woman are archetypes in that they represent the essential features of human life that all ancient Israelites experienced (Meyers 1988:80–81).

formed out of the ground. Specifically, the serpent is identified as the most "crafty" (a Hebrew pun on the word "naked") of all the creatures that God had made (3:1). In the ancient Near East, the serpent was a symbol of both immortality and wisdom (Joines 1974:16–41). The serpent thus stands in contrast to the human couple, who are also "naked," but who are neither immortal nor wise.

Through a dialogue with the woman, the serpent challenges the human couple's childlike obedience to God (3:1–5). God prohibited the humans from eating the fruit of the tree of knowledge with the threat of death, but God offered no rationale for the prohibition. Like children, the human couple followed God's command without question. But for the wise serpent, who knows God's rationale, the prohibition makes little sense. Therefore, the serpent discloses God's rationale to the human couple: God does not want the human couple to be like the gods, knowing good and evil (3:5). Moreover, the serpent recognizes God's threat of death as empty. The humans are already mortal; they will eventually die regardless of the prohibition. (The serpent might have reasoned that once the human couple had knowledge of their own mortality, they would eat the fruit of the tree of life and gain immortality. It should be noted that in the dialogue with the woman, the serpent tells the truth. The humans become like the gods, and they do not die.) The serpent's case against God's prohibition is persuasive to the human couple. They eat the fruit of the tree of knowledge (3:6) and become aware of their nakedness. But because their nakedness is now shameful to them, they cover their genitals with fig leaves (3:7).

Much of the interpretation of Genesis 3 hinges on the meaning of the tree of the knowledge of good and evil and what its fruit provides for the human couple. Unfortunately, the number of proposed interpretations of this tree and its significance is roughly equivalent to the number of scholars who have studied it (a good summary and critique of most of the proposals is given by Westermann 1984:242–45; Wallace 1985:115–32). The context suggests that the knowledge of good and evil must have something to do with the human couple's awareness of sexuality; before they eat the fruit the couple is sexually unaware (they are naked yet not ashamed), but after they eat the fruit they are aware of their sexual nature (they know they are naked and thus cover their genitals). The knowledge of good and evil, then, must entail the knowledge of sexuality. Indeed, the Yahwist uses knowledge as a euphemism for sexual intimacy, especially in reference to Adam and his son: "Now the man knew his wife Eve, and she conceived and bore Cain" (Gen 4:1); "Cain knew his wife, and she conceived and bore Enoch" (Gen 4:17); "Adam knew his wife again, and she bore a son and named him Seth" (Gen 4:25). The knowledge of good and evil, however, is not sexual knowledge *in this sense*. The context of Genesis 3 precludes the possibility of previous sexual relations between the man and the woman. They are not aware of their sexuality until *after* they gain the knowledge of good and evil.

Many scholars have correctly argued that the expression "knowledge of good and evil" is a merism[4] for universal knowledge. In other words, this expression is equivalent to "all knowledge from A to Z." More specifically, in the context of the Yahwist myth this knowledge is what distinguishes humans from the rest of the created beings and so can appropriately be termed "cultural knowledge" (Wellhausen [1883]1983: 302; Oden 1981:213). According to the first part of this creation myth, humans are made of the same substance as the animals, birds, and the earth itself. This homology between humans and the rest of creation is expected. The ancient Near Eastern creation model posits a microcosm/macrocosm relationship between humans and the earth. Yet humans in the real world are also distinct from the earth and the rest of creation. They must be differentiated from the earth out of which they came. In many of the Mesopotamian creation myths this is accomplished with divine blood; humans are created from clay that is mixed with the blood of a slain god. For the Yahwist, the knowledge of good and evil serves this purpose. By acquiring knowledge, the man and woman gain the potential for culture; they are now able to distinguish themselves from the rest of creation.

The connection between the cultural knowledge acquired by the human couple and their new sexual awareness is this: Culture is founded upon the human ability to create. The man

---

[4] *Webster's Third New International Dictionary* defines "merism" as a figure of speech in which "a totality is expressed by two constitutive parts." See the discussion and examples in Honeyman.

and woman have become like the gods, which is symbolized by their knowledge of their ability to create new life for themselves. Sexuality is the catalyst for the rite of passage from childhood to adulthood (van Gennep [1909]1960:67). God had previously caused the earth to produce vegetable and animal life—hitherto divine prerogatives. Now the human couple, through eating the forbidden fruit, gain knowledge of their ability to create like God (Oden 1981:213; Coote and Ord 1989:55). The man now knows to sow seed in the woman and by extension in the earth to create new life (Eilberg-Schwartz 1990:161). Cultural knowledge introduces a division of labor into the relationship between the man and the women. The woman will bear children; the man will till the ground and plant crops (Coote and Ord 1989:60). Through eating the fruit of the tree of the knowledge of good and evil, the humans are transformed from creatures of nature into creatures of culture.[5]

The man and the woman ate from the forbidden tree at the serpent's prompting and thereby became creators themselves, and Yahweh describes the consequences of their actions. These have traditionally been labeled "curses," but only the serpent (and by extension the rest of the animal kingdom) and the ground are explicitly cursed. The man and the woman are not cursed, yet they must suffer the consequences of their actions. These negative consequences have sometimes been interpreted as divine punishment, but this understanding does not fully account for their ambiguous nature. On the one hand, the text suggests that God plays an active role in the enactment of these consequences. Specifically, it appears that God intensifies the consequences that the man and the woman must suffer. On the other hand, these consequences inevitably result from the human couple's actions (Naidoff 1978:10). The consequences reflect the occasionally painful reality of adulthood. Only in a qualified sense can these consequences be interpreted as God's punishment.

In contrast to the human couple, who disregarded God's command, the serpent, who committed no sin against God, is

---

[5] A striking parallel to the transformation of the human couple is present in the *Epic of Gilgamesh*. Enkidu is created out of clay and lives like a wild animal. Then he is transformed into a civilized man through a sexual encounter with a harlot. The harlot's response to Enkidu's transformation highlights the parallel: "You have become [wise] Enkidu, you have become like a god" (Dalley 1991:56).

explicitly cursed by God. The serpent only revealed the truth to the human couple, yet because of its actions, it must slither on its belly and eat dust (3:14). This curse undoubtedly functioned as an etiology, an explanation, of the peculiar locomotion and character of snakes. Such creatures could not have "naturally" been so unusual; they must have done something to end up that way (Meyers 1988:88).[6]

Although the curse is directed toward the serpent primarily, the serpent is symbolic of all animals, domestic and wild. Because the serpent persuaded the humans to eat the fruit of knowledge, the harmony between humans and animals is disrupted. Cultural knowledge brings differentiation between humans and animals, and this differentiation results in enmity (3:15). For the serpent this enmity takes the form of a constant battle with the woman, but this represents the enmity between animals and humans that is presumed by culture. Humans will recognize animals no longer as fellow creatures but as sources of food, clothing, and labor. Similarly, animals will not recognize humans as one of their own kind and thus will bolt from them or attack them.

The consequences that affect the woman entail pain in childbirth and subordination to the man (3:16). The man names her Eve because she will be the mother of all living (3:20). With knowledge the woman can give birth to human life, a role previously performed by the earth with the aid of God. The task of giving birth, however, is inherently painful. Moreover, the myth suggests that God will make childbearing even more painful than it naturally would have been. Many female creatures bear their offspring, but only the woman will suffer such great pains in childbirth. In the first part of the Yahwist creation myth, the woman was differentiated from the man in order to be a suitable helper for him. The human couple was presented as a socially complementary unit, but the social role of each was not specified. Having acquired cultural knowledge, however, the woman recognizes her social role as concerned primarily with childbearing. Her cultural activity will be in the domestic sphere; bearing and raising children, preparing food, and managing the household economy—though

---

[6] Propp suggests that this curse implies that the serpent was originally thought to be a lizard (1990:195).

during labor-intensive times such as the harvest, the woman will also need to work in the fields (Meyers 1988:139–64).

With regard to bearing children, the woman will be subject to the "rule" of the man. In other words, the statement, "he shall rule over you" (3:16), must be understood in the context of the woman's task of bearing children (Meyers 1988:113–17; Coote and Ord 1989:63). This statement does not constitute a general assertion of male dominance over women! It is culturally specific. In ancient Israel the husband could demand that his wife bear him children. The bearing of many children was essential in order to overcome the high mortality rate and still provide enough laborers to maintain subsistence. In order to ensure a large enough family despite the woman's possible reluctance to bear children—many women in the ancient world died in childbirth, resulting in a significantly reduced life expectancy from that of a man (Meyers 1988:112–13)—the man could demand sexual relations with his wife. However, because the woman's "desire" will be for her husband, such "rule" by the husband will not be considered oppressive.

Through the acquisition of cultural knowledge, the man recognizes his primary role in subsistence. By tilling the ground and cultivating crops, the man will provide food for his family. No longer will the man be able to gather food leisurely from God's garden; he must sweat and toil in agricultural labor. This is the task for which man was created. But the man's labor will be especially severe because the ground is cursed due to him: The ground will only produce thorns and thistles (3:17–18). Unlike the situation of the woman, the man does not experience intensified pain and suffering. Rather, the man will encounter the hostility of the ground because God has not yet caused rain to fall on the earth (2:5). The ground will remain cursed without rain as a result of the man's actions, but this curse will come to an end with the flood. Since the man has acquired cultural knowledge and now knows how to provide for his own subsistence, he will be forced to leave the garden to eke out an existence in the barren desert that is the earth.

Although the man and the woman differentiated themselves from the rest of God's creatures by gaining the knowledge of good and evil, they nevertheless remain creatures. Their substance is the substance of creation. The human creature was formed from the dust of the ground, and humans will return to dust when they die (3:19). So that the human couple does not further encroach upon divine prerogatives, especially immortality, God drives the humans out of the garden, bars its entrance, and revokes access to the tree of life (3:22–24). However, before God expels the humans from the garden, God clothes them with garments (3:21). Because the garments are made from animal skins, they symbolize the new differentiation between humans and animal, which God endorses by clothing the humans. But more importantly, the garments also represent the differentiation between humans and God. God's message to the human couple is clear: This far, but no further! The man and the woman have become creators like God, but they are not, nor will they ever be, divine. Their garments symbolize their human status (Oden 1987:92–105).

The Yahwist creation myth wrestles with the status of humans. According to the fundamental Classification domains of creator and creation, where do humans fit? Clearly, humans belong to the creation domain. Human existence is not independent, and humans are mortal like the rest of creation. Yet humans are also like the creator. Humans replicate God's creative activity within the creation. The Yahwist's presentation of the status of humans is illustrated in figure 15. The two trees in the Yahwist's narrative differentiate the three domains of the world. Nature and culture are the subdomains of creation. By eating the fruit of the tree of knowledge, humans move from nature to culture. The tree of life demarcates the domain of divinity. Although humans of culture can create like God, they cannot become divine. The tree of life is barred to human access.

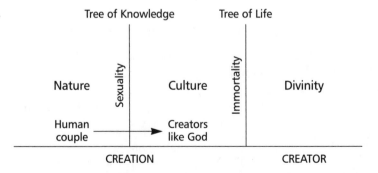

Figure 15. The Status of Humans

If the human acquisition of the knowledge of good and evil in Genesis 3 cannot properly be labeled the "Fall," the same cannot be said for the human use of this knowledge that the Yahwist presents in the subsequent chapters of Genesis. The knowledge of good and evil enables humans to develop culture, and so humans build cities (4:17), create music (4:21), and invent technology (4:22). But humans also murder other humans (4:8, 23) and have sexual relations with divine beings (6:1–4). Cultural knowledge unleashes the evil inclination of humans so that their wickedness becomes abundant on the earth (6:5). Therefore, God regrets the creation of humans, and decides to destroy all the living creatures that God made (6:6–7). According to the Yahwist, God wipes out all living creatures with a flood produced by a torrential rainstorm lasting forty days. Only one family is spared, the family of Noah, because Noah finds favor in God's sight (6:8).

The Yahwist's flood myth completes his creation myth.[7] The creation myth begins by noting that the earth is barren because of two factors: God has not caused rain to fall on the earth, and there is no human to till the ground. By eating the fruit of knowledge, the man is transformed from a caretaker of a pleasure garden into a cultivator of the earth. Yet the ground remains cursed without rain. After the flood, however, the cursing of the ground comes to an end. God institutes a regular seasonal cycle, which is characteristic of the eastern Mediterranean region that includes periodic rainfall (8:22). The ground is now receptive to human cultivation. At last the ground will readily yield its produce so that even humans can plant a garden (9:20). The advent of rain completes the process of creation.

THE YAHWIST'S VALUES TOWARD NATURE

The Yahwist's story, of course, does not end with the flood, but this is a suitable stopping point for our investigation

---

[7] Unlike J and P's creation myths, which remain distinct since they are placed side by side in the biblical text, J and P's flood myths are difficult to discern because they have been mixed together like a shuffled deck of cards. A conventional scholarly division of the text by sources is as follows. The Yahwist flood myth: 6:5–8; 7:1–7, 10, 12, 16b–20, 22–23; 8:2b–3a, 6, 8–12, 13b, 20–22. The Priestly flood myth: 6:9–22; 7:8–9, 11, 13–16a, 21, 24; 8:1–2a, 3b–5, 7, 13a, 14–19; 9:1–17.

of the Israelites' values toward nature. Through the multivalent metaphors of his creation myth the Yahwist was wrestling with the ambiguity of human existence. In origin, in substance, and in death, humans are like the rest of creation. They are born from the earth, sharing the same substance as the ground, and will return to the earth when they die. Humans are fellow beings with the animals and the birds. They are and always will be creatures of nature.

But humans are also like God; they have the knowledge of good and evil. Humans are distinct from the rest of creation in that they have gained cultural knowledge. They have acquired the ability to create like Yahweh; they can bring forth new human life and cause the earth to produce plant life. Outside of the garden, they create other aspects of culture. Being like God, however, has its drawbacks! Although culture frees humans from some of the constraints of nature, culture lacks the tranquillity of the garden. The harmony between humans and animals is disrupted. Their relationship now is characterized by hostility; one will prey upon the other. Moreover, the tasks of creating are inherently painful. The woman experiences the travail of childbirth, and the man must toil and sweat to provide a subsistence for his family. Although human life is difficult as a result of cultural knowledge, this is the inevitable lot of humans in the real world.

In describing this ambiguous human condition, the Yahwist appears to vacillate between the harmony-with-nature and the mastery-over-nature solutions to the human-relationship-to-nature problem, though the latter solution remains subordinate to the former. Ontologically, humans are part of the created world, unable to eradicate their natural being. Humans are bound to the natural world and share the fate of the natural world. The human acquisition of cultural knowledge, however, qualifies the determinism of nature. Although humans are not able to free themselves from nature, they can act upon and transform the natural world to create culture. Nature becomes an outgroup, distinct from human culture. Culture is the sphere of human mastery-over-nature that disrupts the harmony between humans and the rest of the natural world. But this disturbance in the harmony of nature does not have ultimate significance. In the end, humans, like all other natural creatures, will die.

THE PRIESTLY CREATION MYTH

CREATION IN SEVEN DAYS: GENESIS 1:1–2:3

The Priestly creation myth is unlike the Yahwist creation myth in both form and content. Whereas the Yahwist's myth resembles an elaborate tale and employs a wide variety of rich metaphors in order to accentuate the ambiguity of human existence in the world, the Priestly writer's myth is a highly structured, straightforward discourse on the order of creation. One scholar has even characterized this myth as Priestly doctrine—"ancient, sacred knowledge, preserved and handed on by many generations of priests, repeatedly pondered, taught, reformed and expanded most carefully and compactly by new reflections and experiences of faith" (von Rad 1972a:63)—though perhaps this is overstated. In any case, few readers would fail to recognize the striking differences between the Yahwist and the Priestly creation myths.

In contrast to the dry barren earth with which the Yahwist myth begins, the Priestly myth begins by describing a formless world dominated by water: "In the beginning when God created the heavens and the earth, the earth was a formless void and darkness covered the face of the deep, while a wind from God swept over the face of the waters" (1:1–2).[8] These verses give the setting of God's creative activity. They describe a situation closely akin to the opening scene of the *Enuma Elish*. According to this myth the primordial state of the cosmos consists only of the undifferentiated, mingling waters of Tiamat (salt water) and Apsu (sweet water) from which the gods are born. Creation in the *Enuma Elish* entails the establishment of order, classification, and differentiation: Apsu is bound;

---

[8] Genesis 1:1 has traditionally been translated as, "In the beginning God created the heavens and the earth," or in some similar fashion. The term "beginning" is thus understood to be an absolute beginning (Eichrodt 1962). Many other creation myths in the ancient Near East, and the Yahwist creation myth in particular, suggest that "beginning" should be understood as a relative beginning. Moreover, the comparative evidence argues in favor of interpreting vv. 1–2 as temporally subordinate to God's specific acts of creation that follow. In other words, these verses describe the state of the precreated world at the time *when* God began to create (Speiser 1982:11–13).

Tiamat is slain, split, and confined within set boundaries; and the gods are stationed at their appointed positions in the cosmos. Similarly, the Priestly writer begins his creation myth by describing the primordial state of the cosmos as a chaotic, undifferentiated world, symbolized by the waters that cover an empty and unproductive earth (Tsumura 1989:30–43). The "plot" of the remainder of the myth focuses on God's ordering and categorizing of this primordial material into a world suitable for human habitation.

Like the Yahwist creation myth, the Priestly creation myth does not support the doctrine of creation *ex nihilo*. In typical ancient Near Eastern fashion, the Priestly writer has God utilize existing elements in order to create the world. Creation in the ancient Near Eastern cultures entailed not the producing of something from nothing but rather the ordering of a world or the birth of new elements from existing ones. Some critics might argue, however, that in the Priestly myth God does create by divine fiat, suggesting some notion of creation from nothing. But even this widely accepted characterization of the P creation myth must be qualified. The divine fiat is indeed a feature of this myth, but only in the case of light does God create by command alone. In all other cases the myth states that God "made," "separated," or "created" (with no specified method) something or that the earth itself brings forth life. The divine fiat, then, does not indicate creation from nothing.

After describing the setting of creation, the Priestly writer immediately turns to God's creation of the world. In a highly formulaic discourse, the Priestly writer structures God's creative acts into a seven-day scheme—six days of creation and a day of rest. Moreover, the description of each of the six days of creation follows a recurring pattern. The text for each day begins with the declarative formula, "And God said," followed by a command specifying what will be created. The execution of the command is signaled by the formula, "And it was so." Then the actual creation in fulfillment of the command is described. In most cases, God is the actor in creation, but on the third day the earth itself brings forth plants and trees. Upon completion of the divine command, God's approval of the creation is sealed with the statement, "And God saw that it was good." Finally, the text for each day ends with the temporal formula, "And there was evening and there was morning, the [first-sixth] day" (Anderson 1977:151–52; Westermann 1984: 84–85).

Although much of the content of the Priestly creation myth undoubtedly is dependent upon earlier creation traditions (scholars have noted similarities with Mesopotamian, Egyptian, and earlier Israelite myths), the formal structure of the myth reflects the Priestly writer's own contribution. In particular, the Priestly writer conformed the creation traditions he inherited into a seven-day scheme for the purpose of ordering both space and time (Coote and Ord 1991:51). With regard to space, the Priestly writer divided the six days of creation into two parts, each consisting of four acts of creation with two acts on the third and the sixth days (Anderson 1977:154–55). There is a slight anomaly in the Priestly writer's symmetrical scheme because the waters are never created. They are primordial. On the second day, God creates the sky by separating the waters above (which produce rain, snow, and hail) from the waters below (1:6–8). Then on the third day God separates the land from the waters (1:9–10). As a result, the creation of the seas is the by-product of God's second and third act of creation. The structure of creation is illustrated in figure 16.

Environments		Occupants	
Day 1	Light	Day 4	Heavenly Luminaries
Day 2	Sky (Rain/Seas)	Day 5	Sea Monsters, Fish, Birds
Day 3	Land Vegetation	Day 6	Animals Humans

Figure 16. The Six Days of Creation

Although the order of creation initially appears to be arbitrary, the Priestly writer has actually classified the world according to a meaningful spatial pattern. The key to understanding this classification is the fourth day. On that day God creates the sun, the moon, and the stars (1:14–19).[9] But light

---

[9] The text actually states that God created the "*greater light* to rule the day and the *lesser light* to rule the night" (Gen 1:16). Most commentators agree that the Priestly writer is precluding the implica-

was created on the first day! How can light exist without the sources of light? Was the Priestly writer simply ignorant of the causal connection between heavenly luminaries and light, or did he have a specific purpose for this arrangement? Light appears to have been created first, according to the Priestly writer, in order to offset the primordial darkness. Light was created to alternate with darkness, forming day and night (1:3–5). Light and darkness are not a substance but rather an environment or a habitat in which living beings exist. The sun, moon, and stars are thus presented as the "beings" of this environment. The sun is the "being" that inhabits and moves about in the realm of light, and the moon and the stars occupy the realm of darkness. Similarly, in each of the first three days God creates an environment, whereas in the second three days God creates the corresponding inhabitants of each environment; birds are created for the sky, sea monsters and fish for the waters, and animals and humans for the land and vegetation. The Priestly creation myth, therefore, categorizes space into four distinct environments and assigns the appropriate occupants to each domain.

The Priestly creation myth also orders time. By structuring the creation according to a seven-day scheme, the Priestly writer ascribes sacred significance to the seven-day weekly cycle. Thus the week is sacred time (Eliade 1959:68–113) and a symbolic repetition of God's creation of the world.[10] At the climax of this sacred time is the Sabbath itself. Although the observance of the Sabbath in ancient Israel pre-dates the Priestly writer (the origin of the Sabbath is unknown), the Sabbath in the biblical tradition has been shaped overwhelmingly by the work of the Priestly writer (Coote and Ord 1991:86).

Two aspects of the Sabbath are relevant to our discussion here. First, according to the Priestly writer, the Sabbath is foremost a repetition of the rest of God. Upon completion of the tasks of creation, God rested on the seventh day (2:1–3). In the ancient Near Eastern creation myths the creator god's rest

---

tion that God created other gods since the Hebrew words for sun and moon are the names of known deities.

[10] Levenson argues persuasively that the Priestly emphasis on seven days stems from the seven-day New Year festivals during which the creation of the world was celebrated (1988:66–77). Cf. the different conclusion by Coote and Ord (1991:79–84).

is a divine prerogative. The creator god demonstrates divine rule by resting in the temple-palace (Batto 1987b; Wallace 1988:237–41). Similarly, the Priestly writer associates creation and Sabbath rest with the building of the Tabernacle, God's wilderness "temple" (Blenkinsopp 1976:280–81; Wallace 1988: 244–50). By connecting creation with the Sabbath, the Priestly writer has provided a means by which the people of Judah, exiled in a foreign land without king or temple, can proclaim the sovereignty of God.

The Priestly writer also connects the Sabbath with the Sinai covenant. In fact, the Sabbath is described as the symbol of the covenant (Exod 31:12–17). Human observance of the Sabbath is related to one's faithfulness to the stipulations of the covenant in the same way that God's divine rest on the seventh day is related to the acts of creation on the previous six days. This correlation between Sabbath and covenant suggests that humans symbolically participate in the creation of the world by following the stipulations of the covenant. Human actions make a difference in this world! When humans follow the covenant, the order of creation is maintained. The established boundaries remain fixed. If humans neglect or reject the covenant, however, the creation itself suffers. The order of creation disintegrates, and the world reverts to its original chaotic state. By connecting creation, Sabbath, and covenant, the Priestly writer thus ascribes cosmogonic significance to human activities (Levenson 1988:127).

Humans play the focal role in the Priestly creation myth. The six days of creation are oriented toward the creation of humans, the crowning species of creation, and about their creation the Priestly writer makes the most extensive and detailed statements.[11] With regard to the creation of humans,

---

[11] Bergant has argued that the structure of the Priestly creation account suggests that the verses reporting the creation of humans are a literary insertion. With regard to the fish and the birds, God "said . . . made . . . and blessed . . . ," but concerning the animals, God only "said . . . and made. . . . " The creation of humans was then inserted with the original blessing of animals going to the humans along with the commission of dominion (1991:9). This fragmentation of the text, however, is unnecessary. The blessing of the animals is indeed transferred to humans, but this is because humans are classified with the other earth creatures. The creation of humans is presented as "an amplification and specification of the creation of the land animals,"

the Priestly writer draws upon two distinct and unrelated observations about the nature of humankind. The first accentuates how humans are distinct from the rest of the creation. They are "like God" in their status and function within the created order. The second observation underscores how humans are similar to the rest of the creation. The human species is differentiated according to sex and thus has a role in reproducing and sustaining created life (Bird 1987:32–33). Although originally independent, these two observations have been combined by the Priestly writer into a single discourse on the creation of humans:

> [26]Then God said, "Let us make humankind in our image, according to our likeness; and let them have dominion over the fish of the sea, and over the birds of the air, and over the cattle, and over all the wild animals of the earth, and over every creeping thing that creeps upon the earth." [27]So God created humankind in his image, in the image of God he created them; male and female he created them. [28]God blessed them, and God said to them, "Be fruitful and multiply, and fill the earth and subdue it; and have dominion over the fish of the sea and over the birds of the air and over every living thing that moves upon the earth." (Genesis 1:26–28)

It is important for the reader of this passage to recognize that two distinct observations on the nature of humankind have been juxtaposed in this discourse. Otherwise, the reader might be tempted to interpret the "image of God" in light of the sexual differentiation of humans (Trible 1978:15–21) or the procreation of humans as an expression of their subduing the earth. But these interpretations are not adequate. First, they fail to account for the fact that the animals undoubtedly are also differentiated sexually (even though the text itself is silent) and the birds and the fish are also commanded to be fruitful and multiply but they are not created in the image of God (cf. Wolff 1974a:95). As the image of God, humans are distinct from all other creatures. The "image of God" must refer to some aspect of humans in which they are distinct. Second, these interpretations fail to explain why the Priestly writer describes only humans as male and

---

and thus the blessing of the animals has given way to the blessing of humankind (Bird 1981:145).

female. The Priestly creation myth is concerned not only
with the order of creation but also "with the means by which
the orders of life will fill the newly created world and perpet-
uate themselves in it" (Bird 1987:34). Therefore, the Priestly
writer refers to "plants yielding seed" and fruit trees that "bear
fruit with the seed in it" (1:11), and the birds and the fish are
given the command, "Be fruitful and multiply" (1:22). Humans
are also given the command to be fruitful and multiply, but in
their case this command is problematic. The sexuality of the
birds, the fish, and the animals is assumed by the Priestly
writer, but such an assumption cannot be made for humans
because they are in the image of God. For the Priestly writer
God had no form of sexuality, no sexual differentiation. The
Priestly writer thus states explicitly that humans were created
male and female. The differentiation of humans into male and
female distinguishes humans from God; "male and female"
describes how humans are *not* in the image of God (Bird
1987:34–35).

The specific ways in which humans are in the "image of
God" are difficult to assess because the Priestly writer does not
explicitly give content to this expression. The basic thrust of
the expression is that humans are *like* God. It is possible that
the Priestly writer intends to suggest that humans are like God
in appearance or form (J. Miller 1972). In Genesis 5:3, for
example, the Priestly writer states that Adam begat Seth according to his image. It is also possible that the Priestly writer
is deliberately ambiguous in his designation of humans as the
image of God. In other words, the Priestly writer wanted to
state that humans are like God without specifying in what
ways (Barr 1968/9; 1972:19–20). The context of Genesis 1:26–
28, however, suggests that the "image of God" is closely connected to human dominion and rule over the earth (von Rad
1972a:60; Bird 1981:137–44). But even so, the exact connection between humans being in the image of God and having
dominion over the earth is not specified. Humans might be
functionally like God, ruling on the earth as God would rule
(Tigay 1984), or humans might have dominion *because* they
are like God in some unstated way (Barr 1972:20). Perhaps we
can be no more specific. The result appears to be the same in
either case; humans are distinct from all other creatures in that
they are like God and have dominion over the earth.

Ultimately, the "image of God" is comparable to the knowledge of good and evil. It is the attribute of humans by which they are distinguished from the rest of creation. The Yahwist emphasized the significance of human culture; humans have the "knowledge" to create their own environment and to produce life—human and agricultural—like God. Similarly, by connecting the "image of God" with dominion, the Priestly writer emphasized the human ability to exercise its will over creation. Humans are not simply objects of creation, subjected to the fixed orders of creation. Humans have some measure of control over creation like God. The terms that the Priestly writer uses to describe this control are *rada*, "to rule," and *kabash*, "to subdue." These terms derive from the royal and military sphere. They are often used in reference to a king who is able to conquer and control enemy territory. Indeed, Psalm 8 praises God for having created humans like kings:

> [5]Yet you have made them a little lower than God,
>   and crowned them with glory and honor.
> [6]You have given them dominion over the works of your hands;
>   you have put all things under their feet,
> [7]all sheep and oxen,
>   and also the beasts of the field,
> [8]the birds of the air, and the fish of the sea,
>   whatever passes along the paths of the seas.
>   (Psalm 8:5–8)

Although *rada* and *kabash* may carry violent connotations (as one would expect in reference to a conquering king), such connotations are lacking in the Priestly writer's use of these terms. Humans may rule the animals, but they do not eat them (though cf. Dequeker 1977), nor are animals terrified of humans. Humans are commanded to subdue the earth, but this is probably analogous to the Yahwist's emphasis on tilling the ground (Barr 1972:21–22).

Although humans are given dominion over the earth, their rule is not absolute. The Priestly writer's discourse on the creation of humans cannot be divorced from the rest of his creation myth, the focal theme of which is the establishment of order. Human dominion must conform to the order of creation. This is implied from the context of Genesis 1, but it is explicitly stated in later Priestly texts. For example, the Priestly writer condones sexual relations only between a man and a woman. According to the order of creation, humans were created male and female. Thus, homosexual relations or sexual relations between humans and animals are strictly forbidden (Lev 18:22–23; 20:13, 15). Similarly, once animals are declared suitable for food, only certain animals may be eaten (Lev 11). Animals that appear to violate the order of creation (e.g., the catfish which swims in the water but is covered with a skin rather than scales that are appropriate to fish) are considered unclean and are thus unacceptable for food (Douglas 1966:41–57; Carroll 1985; Eilberg-Schwartz 1990:218–21). For the Priestly writer, human rule of the earth is subject to the stipulations of the covenant, for these stipulations outline the order of creation.

FLOOD AND NEW CREATION: GENESIS 6–9

The relationship between human dominion and the order of creation can be stated more emphatically. Human rule of the earth serves either to actively maintain the order of creation, or to cause its disintegration. Human dominion is not neutral! It affects the order of creation. Moreover, the order of creation is given a ritual dimension. When humans violate the order of creation, they not only bring disorder into the world, they ritually defile themselves and often that with which they come into contact. Ritual pollution is not ultimately dangerous to the order of creation. Coming into contact with a corpse, for example, defiles a person, but otherwise the person experiences no onerous consequences. Ritual impurity normally lasts a set period of time or can be cleansed through the appropriate rituals. But some violations of the created order—murder, sexual abominations, idolatry—defile a person permanently. Progressive violations even pollute the earth itself. Such pollution cannot be *ritually* cleansed; the creation itself must be purged. Such pollution undermines the order of creation (Frymer-Kensky 1983). Only when humans rule according to the created order is the world suitable for human habitation.

Humans in the biblical tradition rarely exercise their dominion properly, within the constraints of the created order. Too often they ignore the order of creation or disregard the stipulations of the covenant and thus bring the collapse of creation upon themselves. This characteristic of human dominion serves as the premise for the Priestly writer's flood myth. Like the Yahwist flood myth, this flood myth completes the author's creation myth. The myth begins by emphasizing the wretched state to which human dominion has fallen: "Now the earth was corrupt in God's sight, and the earth was filled with violence" because "all flesh[12] had corrupted its ways upon the earth" (6:11–12). According to the Priestly writer, human violence results in the corruption, or rather, the pollution, of the earth (Frymer-Kensky 1977:153; 1983:409). The text of P itself presents no specific acts of violence. In its canonical context the text of P presupposes the Yahwist's references to the murders by Cain and Lamech, but the evidence from the chronological references in the flood myth suggests that the Priestly flood myth was written independently of J so that it is uncertain what "violence" might have originally referred to (Barré 1988:17; contrary Anderson 1978). Whatever the nature of this violence, the Priestly writer understands it to be an abuse of human dominion. Rather than maintaining the order of creation, humans brought disorder into the world, thereby polluting and destabilizing the creation.

The creation can tolerate only so much disorder. Eventually, it will disintegrate to the chaos that originally characterized the world. The Priestly writer, like the Yahwist, thus presents the flood as the consequence of human actions. But in contrast to the Yahwist who imagined the flood as simply the result of much rain, the Priestly writer attributes the flood to the collapse of the principal boundaries of creation: "all the fountains of the great deep burst forth, and the windows of the heavens were opened" (7:11). The boundaries that separate the waters from the sky and the land break open so that the world returns to its primordial, undifferentiated, watery state.

The flood myth, however, does not end with the world in chaos. On New Year's day—almost one year after the waters broke loose (Barré 1988)—the earth is dry (8:13). The flood is not just the disintegration of creation but also the means of purging the creation. The flood cleanses the creation from the pollution caused by human violence. Noah and his family

---

[12] The reference to "all flesh" could refer to all creatures—birds, fish, animals, and humans alike. Certainly, all creatures are corrupted by the violence and inevitably experience its effects. But in the context of the creation and the flood, "all flesh" refers specifically to the human species. Only humans are the source of violence (Anderson 1984a:161–65).

alone are spared because he is righteous and blameless (6:9).
The result of the flood is a new creation. This is the significance of the flood ending on New Year's day, for on this day
God's creation of the world and victory over chaos is celebrated
(Eliade 1959:77–80).[13] The recreation of the world, necessitated by its pollution, entails first the destruction of the creation. Only through the catastrophic collapse of creation is a
new creation possible.

After the flood, Noah and his family are given the mandate: "Be fruitful and multiply, and fill the earth" (9:1). Like
the first humans, Noah and his family must act to sustain the
creation. Unlike the first humans, however, no mandate is
given for Noah to exercise dominion on the earth. Human
dominion is assumed, and the Priestly writer gives two laws
for regulating this dominion. First, humans may exercise dominion by eating other living creatures, but the blood of the
creatures must be drained (9:2–3). Blood is the symbol of life.
By draining the blood of creatures, humans demonstrate that
life belongs to God's dominion rather than their own. They are
able to eat other creatures only by virtue of God's grant. Second, human blood may not be shed. Whoever, or whatever,
kills a human, will in turn be killed by humans, "for in his own
image God made humankind" (9:6). Human life belongs to God
and is not subject to human dominion. The interpretation of
the explanatory clause in this injunction is ambiguous. The
clause could ascribe special sanctity to human life; human life
is more precious than all other life because humans are in the
image of God (Wenham 1987:193–94). Such an interpretation,
however, does not adequately account for the context of the
flood and the central focus of human dominion. Because humans are made in the image of God, they are given dominion
over the earth. But humans abused their dominion and polluted the earth, bringing about the catastrophic flood. So that
the creation will not again be destroyed by human pollution,
God regulates human dominion; humans may kill animals for
food if they drain the blood, but they may not kill other
humans. Moreover, God imposes the threat of death to ensure

---

[13] On the fourth day of the Babylonian New Year's festival (the
Akitu festival), the priests recited the *Enuma Elish* and celebrated
Marduk's creation of the world.

human compliance with these regulations. But because humans are made in God's image, *humans* rather than God will
impose the death penalty (Tigay 1984:174). Human dominion
will be self-regulating so that God need not destroy the creation
again with a flood.

THE PRIESTLY WRITER'S VALUES TOWARD NATURE

The Priestly creation myth has traditionally been interpreted from the perspective of the mastery-over-nature solution to the human-relationship-to-nature problem, and not
without some merit. Humans are distinguished from the rest
of creation; humans alone are made in the image of God.
Humans receive dominion over the earth, and so can exercise
their wills over creation. Clearly, the Priestly creation account
is at odds with the subjugation-to-nature solution. Yet the
mastery-over-nature solution does not accurately correspond
to the Priestly account either, for it does not account for the
human situation within the context of creation. Human dominion is limited by the order of creation. Humans are part of the
creation and so must conform to the created order. Specifically,
dominion is the means by which humans maintain this
order. When human dominion is exercised according to
the order of creation, it further maintains that order. Otherwise, human dominion corrupts the creation, leading to its
eventual collapse. The mastery-over-nature solution to the
human-relationship-to-nature problem, then, is subordinate to
the harmony-with-nature solution for the Priestly writer. Only
when humans act in accord with the order of creation is their
activity productive rather than destructive.

The Priestly writer and the Yahwist presume similar basic
value orientations toward nature. Ultimately, humans are part
of creation, and therefore subject to the constraints or boundaries of creation. Humans cannot emancipate themselves from
creation, but neither are humans slaves to creation. In relation
to their value orientations, human dominion and the knowledge of good and evil (cultural knowledge) serve the same
purpose: They describe metaphorically the autonomy that humans have *within* the order of creation. Humans can transform
creation! For the Yahwist, such activity is possible because
humans have become creators like God by acquiring cultural
knowledge. For the Priestly writer, humans are created in the

image of God and entrusted with the task of ruling the earth. And as long as humans rule according to the order of creation, they contribute to the process of creation. Both the Priestly writer and the Yahwist root their values toward nature in the ambiguity of the human situation. Humans are part of the creation yet also exceptional in the creation.

6
IN THE END: THE ESCHATOLOGICAL MYTHS

THE BEGINNING IN THE END

Both the J and the P creation myths present the human situation in positive terms. Humans have cultural knowledge, or humans are made in the image of God and are thus given dominion over the earth. Humans are like God. But the reality of the human situation is not so positive. Rarely are humans content simply to be *like* God; rarely have humans lived in dependence upon God their creator. Rather, humans have used cultural knowledge and exercised dominion to achieve their own desires. They have attempted to *become* God. According to the Yahwist, humans have an evil inclination with the result that they murdered other humans and had sexual relations with divine beings. According to the Priestly writer, humans have disregarded the order of creation, and so have corrupted it. In both cases, however, the Yahwist and the Priestly writer are not describing human deeds of the distant past. The creation myths are about the present and so are the tales of human rebellion against God and the created order. Human abuse of cultural knowledge and dominion is the present reality for the Yahwist and the Priestly writer.

The two flood myths are also about the present rather than some primordial catastrophe. They both attest to the inevitable consequences of the present hubris of humans, but differ in their emphasis. For the Yahwist, the flood myth underscores God's preservation of creation despite the evil inclination of humans. This is in accord with the Yahwist's own positive orientation toward human history. Despite human failure and rejection of God, Yahweh repeatedly redeems his people. If the Yahwist wrote during the early years of the Davidic empire, as is traditionally argued, then his epic probably reflects the optimism of the Davidic court. David had united the diverse peasant groups of Palestine and organized them into a powerful kingdom. He had conquered the peoples of Edom, Moab, Ammon, Aram and established diplomatic ties with Phoenicia and Philistia. Trade and tribute brought prosperity to the region. Israel prospered under David despite humankind's propensity for evil. If the Yahwist wrote during the exile, as some recent studies suggest, then his epic witnesses to a confidence in Yahweh's inevitable redemption of his people; just as Yahweh repeatedly redeemed his people in the past, so Yahweh will redeem his people from exile and return them to their land. In either case, the Yahwist stresses the stability of creation. God recognizes that humans are *inherently* inclined toward evil, and so God promises to preserve the creation lest God again regrets having created them.

In contrast to the J flood myth, the Priestly flood myth accentuates the connection between violence—the consequence of the perversion of human dominion—and the corruption of creation. Because humans are part of the order of creation, human actions affect the created order. Humans pollute the creation when they do not exercise dominion within the constraints of creation. Eventually, the order of creation is unable to withstand the continual human assault against it. The creation itself succumbs to the pollution caused by humans and must be recreated or cleansed in order for it to sustain life. The Priestly writer emphasizes this connection between human actions and the collapse of creation because this was the Priestly writer's present experience. The author of P wrote during the Babylonian exile, or shortly thereafter. The people of Judah had just experienced the collapse of creation as they knew it; Jerusalem and the temple were destroyed, King Jehoiachin was stripped of his crown and sent into exile (King Zedekiah was butchered along with his family), and many of the people were forcibly taken from their homes and exiled to Babylon. The Priestly flood myth, then, served as a paradigm of the people's experience of exile. The created order collapsed because the people of Judah rebelled against God and so polluted the land (Frymer-Kensky 1983: 409–10). But like the flood, the exile did not mark the end of creation. Rather, the exile was the means by which God cleansed the people and the land and thereby restored the order of creation. Life was possible beyond exile because God was establishing a new creation that would be guaranteed by covenant.

Despite different emphases, the Yahwist and the Priestly writer present the same essential myth following the pattern of catastrophe and new creation.[1] This mythic pattern is not unique to the biblical tradition, but occurs throughout the ancient Near East and Mediterranean and around the world. This ubiquitous myth attests to a fundamental insight of pre-modern humans that the creation of a new world entails the destruction of the present world. The present world, with its corruption and evil, simply cannot be fixed. The world must be dismantled so that a new, unblemished world can be built in its place (Eliade 1963:54–74). For the Yahwist and the Priestly writer, this myth is projected back to the beginning and is thus combined with a creation myth in order to explain and give meaning to their present situation. For the prophets, on the other hand, this myth is projected into the future. They envision that the present order will be destroyed because of the sins of Israel and the nations. Human rebellion against God has polluted the world beyond restoration. But the creation will not end in destruction. The prophets also envision the creation of a new world, free from human sin and its consequences. The

---

[1] The catastrophe/new-creation myth corresponds in metaphor and structure to the ubiquitous ancient Near Eastern conflict myth. Specifically, the catastrophe/new-creation myth is a development and elaboration of the conflict myth with a distinct emphasis. Whereas the conflict myth focuses on the *emergence* of a world and employs metaphors of order and differentiation, the catastrophe/new-creation myth stresses the *transition* from one age or world to the next and uses metaphors of pollution and cleansing. The conflict myth is generally oriented toward the divine realm and focuses on the status of Yahweh's kingship. The catastrophe/new-creation myth, on the other hand, tends to focus on the state of the creation. It is terrestrially oriented and underscores the effect of humans on the creation. This distinct emphasis of the catastrophe/new-creation myth, however, should not obscure its affinities with the conflict myth.

present order will be destroyed so that the creation can be remade into the world that God intended.

The prophets never articulate this eschatological myth in narrative form comparable to the biblical creation and flood myths. The urgency of their messages precludes such a possibility. Their writings consist primarily of oracles—speeches given in the name of Yahweh—that intend to communicate a divine word to both people and king. Nevertheless, by examining selected metaphors and the underlying structures of the prophetic oracles, we can detect the myth of catastrophe and new creation. This myth becomes the paradigm for many of the prophets' oracles. It forms the fundamental perception of reality from which the prophets are able to discern God's judgment on the present world and to herald the coming of a glorious new world.

Many of the prophets reflect the catastrophe/new-creation myth in varying decrees. This myth itself does not determine the content or the focus of their message but rather provides the metaphors and the structure of their message. The content of the prophetic oracles is determined by the specific social situation of each prophet. On the one hand, the preexilic prophets (Amos, Hosea, Isaiah, Zephaniah, Jeremiah) tend to focus on God's judgment of Israel and Judah. The people of Israel and Judah have rebelled against God. They have rejected the covenant, trusted in their own ways, and, through their corruption, polluted the land. Yet these prophets are not without hope for the people. The people will indeed experience the collapse of creation. But the prophets also offer a vision of a new creation, the corollary to catastrophe—the people and the land will be cleansed from pollution. The exilic prophets (Ezekiel, Second Isaiah), on the other hand, tend to address their oracles to people who have already suffered the consequences of their sins. They have already experienced the collapse of the created order. The exilic prophets, then, prepare the people to experience God's new creation. The message of the postexilic prophets (Obadiah, Joel, and a number of anonymous oracles) tends to be more complex, reflecting both aspects of the myth. God has redeemed the people by returning them to their homeland in Palestine, but the people are not experiencing the effects of God's new creation: the people are still subject to foreign rulers; they suffer from economic depression; and there is bitter strife within the community of

God's people (Hanson 1979). Therefore, the postexilic prophets predict the advent of a new cosmic catastrophe. Although
the catastrophe will be directed toward the nations, Israel itself
will not remain unscathed. Only after the eclipse of this final
catastrophe will God's new creation dawn.

Before we turn to examine the prophets' use of the catas-
trophe/new-creation myth, two notes about the language of the
prophets must be made. First, the prophets consistently mix
historic/realistic language with metaphorical language. For
example, the destruction of Jerusalem by the Babylonians is
described in terms of the collapse of creation itself. Such
metaphorical language is not just hyperbole. Rather, the prophets employ numerous cosmic metaphors to underscore the
significance of the historical events that occasion their oracles.
Through metaphors they give meaning to these events. Second,
the prophets use ingroup/outgroup distinctions to refer to the
creation, and these correspond to the horizontal model of
sacred space discussed in chapter 4. Jerusalem and the land of
Israel are symbolically placed at the center of the world and
the nations at the periphery. The center, the land of the ingroup, is the land of creation. The world was created at the
center. The periphery is the land of the outgroup and remains chaotic and life-threatening. The catastrophe that
results from Israel's sins, then, occurs at the center. Israel's sins
corrupt the creation that is characteristic of the center. The
center reverts to chaos as it is consumed by the periphery. The
new creation that is anticipated by the prophets stems from the
center. It is only the center that will be transformed into the
garden of Eden and only the ingroup people at the center who
will experience the new creation. The nations at the periphery
will benefit from the new creation only as they are related to
the center.

THE PREEXILIC PROPHETS

AMOS

In the book of Amos, the first of the so-called classical
prophets, the catastrophe/new-creation myth is reflected
primarily in the cluster of metaphors associated with the

expression, "the day of Yahweh"—"the day of the LORD" in most
English translations of the Bible. According to Amos's oracle,
the people of Israel long for the day of Yahweh. They think that
the day of Yahweh will bring them prosperity and victory over
all their enemies. But because the people of Israel, specifically
the rich in Israel, have oppressed the poor in the land (2:6–8;
8:4–6), the day of Yahweh will bring only destruction to Israel:

> [18]Alas for you who desire the day of the LORD!
>> Why do you want the day of the LORD?
>> It is darkness, not light;
> [19] as if someone fled from a lion,
>> and was met by a bear;
>> or went into the house and rested a hand against the wall,
>> and was bitten by a snake.
> [20]Is not the day of the LORD darkness, not light,
>> and gloom with no brightness in it? (Amos 5:18–20)

Few topics have generated more discussion and debate
among biblical scholars than the subject of the day of Yahweh.
Yet despite the vast amount of literature on the subject (see the
bibliography in Loretz 1986:77–79), the quest for the origin and
meaning of this expression has failed to produce a consensus.
The day of Yahweh has been interpreted variously as the day of
Yahweh's enthronement (Mowinckel 1922; 1958; [1962]1992:
I.106–92), the day of Yahweh's war (von Rad 1959), the day
of Yahweh's theophany (Weiss 1966; Hoffmann 1981), and the
day of Yahweh's execution of the covenantal curses (Fensham
1966). Although each of these interpretations has accurately
focused on a particular aspect of the day of Yahweh tradition,
none has proved to be sufficient—none can fully account for
the prophetic use of this expression. The day of Yahweh[2]
generally refers to a forthcoming event, though in several
passages it refers to a past event (Everson 1974). It is associated
with metaphors of war, kingship, judgment, and cosmic up-
heaval, and the effects of the day are directed against Israel and

---

[2] In addition to the expression, "the day of Yahweh," the concept
of the day of Yahweh is represented in the Bible by a number of related
locutions such as: "a day of Yahweh," "the day of Yahweh's venge-
ance," "the day of Yahweh's wrath," "the day of Yahweh's anger," "a
day of Yahweh's tumult, trampling, and confusion," "the day of Yahweh's sacrifice," "the day of Yahweh's feast," and "on that day."

on different occasions against the nations. Without addressing the origin of this concept (though see Cross 1973:91–111), the diverse metaphors associated with the day of Yahweh are best explained in reference to the conflict myth. Only the broad background of the conflict myth can adequately account for all the features of the day of Yahweh tradition (Simkins 1991:243–55).[3] In other words, the day of Yahweh refers to the day of Yahweh's cosmogonic battle against chaos. On that day Yahweh will appear to judge and to destroy enemies who threaten his kingship over creation. On that day Yahweh will defeat chaos and be enthroned anew in his temple-palace. On that day Yahweh will restore order to creation and cleanse the earth from the pollution that defiled it. The day of Yahweh encapsulates the catastrophe/new-creation myth.

In the book of Amos, the day of Yahweh is directed against the people of Israel. Through their cultic acts and celebration of Yahweh's victory over chaos, the people hope that God will come and judge the nations around them, that God will increase their prosperity and peace at the expense of the nations. They long for the day when Yahweh will extend the order of creation into the periphery and thereby enlarge Israel's domain. Indeed, the nations are guilty of violent crimes and deserve God's judgment (1:3–2:3), but Israel, for its part, has transgressed God's covenant. Through corruption and oppression of the poor, Israel has polluted the land. Therefore, Amos proclaims that the day of Yahweh will be against Israel. By their own deeds, the people of Israel have hastened the collapse of the created order; they have made the center like the periphery:

> [8]Shall not the land tremble on this account,
>   and everyone mourn who lives in it,
>   and all of it rise like the Nile,
>   and be tossed about and sink again like the Nile of Egypt?
> [9]On that day, says the Lord God,
>   I will make the sun go down at noon,
>   and darken the earth in broad daylight,
> [10]I will turn your feasts into mourning,
>   and all your songs into lamentation;

---

[3] The day of Yahweh tradition includes the variety of themes and images that occur in association with the specific expressions that denote the concept of the day of Yahweh (see n. 2).

> I will bring sackcloth on all loins,
>> and baldness on every head;
> I will make it like the mourning for an only son,
>> and the end of it like a bitter day. (Amos 8:8–10)

This text reflects the basic presupposition that "anyone in Israel who tampers with the just orders of life draws the earth and its inhabitants into perdition at the same time" (Wolff 1977:329). Israel's rejection of God's covenant affects both the terrestrial and celestial realms. All creation will be destroyed because Israel has violated the order of creation. No longer will creation be celebrated through festival and song;[4] only mourning and lamentation are possible because of the coming catastrophe.

According to Amos, the people of Israel stand on the brink of catastrophe. God, who created the earth and established order out of chaos (5:8–9; 9:5–6), will also destroy the world that has been corrupted by God's people. The catastrophe/new-creation myth serves as the paradigm by which Amos proclaims God's judgment on Israel's sins. For this reason, the book of Amos begins with a short oracle heralding the Divine Warrior's march to battle:

> The LORD roars from Zion,
>> and utters his voice from Jerusalem;
> the pastures of the shepherds wither,
>> and the top of Carmel dries up. (Amos 1:2)

Yahweh is the Divine Warrior who must fight in a new cosmogonic battle of creation against his own people. This oracle sets the tone for the entire book, and most of the oracles reinforce this message. Nevertheless, the creation will not end in catastrophe. The book of Amos ends in a salvation oracle that proclaims the dawn of a new creation:

> [13]The time is surely coming, says the LORD,
>> when the one who plows shall overtake the one who reaps,
>> and the treader of grapes the one who sows the seed;
> the mountains shall drip sweet wine,
>> and all the hills shall flow with it.

---

[4] The connection with the day of Yahweh suggests that the feasts refer to the New Year festival, during which God's creation of the world was celebrated.

[14]I will restore the fortunes of my people Israel,
    and they shall rebuild the ruined cites and inhabit them;
they shall plant vineyards and drink their wine,
    and they shall make gardens and eat their fruit.
[15]I will plant them upon their land,
    and they shall never again be plucked up
    out of the land that I have given them. (Amos 9:13–15)

From the perspective of the Yahwist creation myth, the garden of Eden is not the natural habitat of humans. It is the garden of *God*, and so the human couple are driven from it once they gain cultural knowledge lest they eat of the tree of life and become immortal. Humans are created to till the ground and plant their own gardens. Human access to the garden of Eden is barred forever by God. The rest of the biblical tradition, however, found a way past the cherubim and the flaming sword that guard Eden. In the new creation the whole land will be transformed into a garden like Eden. Amos thus proclaims that in the new creation the earth will be a fertile paradise with the result that the land will produce so much abundance that the gathering of one crop will not be completed before it is time to plant the next crop. The earth will be cleansed so that the land will freely bear its produce without toil and sweat (Cornelius 1988:49). Moreover, humans will not be mere exploiters of this garden, demanding of its produce and offering little in return. Rather, the prophet likens Israel itself to a garden. Just as God planted the garden in Eden, so God will plant the people of God in the land. Through agricultural metaphors, Amos emphasizes the essential unity between humans and the natural world. Israel and the natural world will be harmoniously redeemed. The center will flourish in a new creation.

HOSEA

Along with Amos, Hosea prophesies against the northern kingdom of Israel during the reign of Jeroboam II. But whereas Amos prophesies during the height of his reign when the elite in Israel experience unmatched prosperity, Hosea prophesies at the end of his reign and during the years that follow. These are turbulent years. Assyria is on the rise, and Israel's monarchy is subject to repeated coups. The final downfall of Israel is

inevitable. For the prophet Hosea these events signal God's
judgment on Israel. Using a variety of metaphors, Hosea announces God's judgment on the land and the people: The land
of Israel will become desolate (5:9); the people will eat but not
be satisfied (4:10); the women will be unable to conceive and
bear children (9:11–12, 14); and Israel will suffer war and exile
from the land (8:14; 9:3; 10:10, 14–15). These punishments,
however, are not mere local events. They are cosmic in scope
because the sins of Israel are cosmic in their effect:

> [1]Hear the word of the LORD, O people of Israel;
>> for the LORD has an indictment against the inhabitants
>>> of the land.
> There is no faithfulness or loyalty,
>> and no knowledge of God in the land.
> [2]Swearing, lying, and murder,
>> and stealing and adultery break out;
>> bloodshed follows bloodshed.
> [3]Therefore the land [withers],[5]
>> and all who live in it [fade away];
> together with the wild animals
>> and the birds of the air,
>> even the fish of the sea are perishing. (Hosea 4:1–3)

Israel's sins against God have corrupted the creation so that a
drought ravages the land. But this drought is unlike ordinary
droughts, for it affects even the fish of the sea. It is a cosmic
drought that returns the earth to its dry and barren primordial
condition as described in the Yahwist creation myth (cf. De
Roche 1981). The sterile desert of the periphery is consuming
the creation of the center. Moreover, there appears to be an
allusion in this passage to the flood myth. All animals and birds
outside the ark perished during the flood, but the fish for obvious
reasons survived. But in this new catastrophe, even the fish will
be destroyed (Wolff 1974b:68).

It is uncertain whether or not the people of Israel were
actually experiencing a drought during Hosea's time. The language of the text is ambiguous. It could refer to a present or a
forthcoming drought. In any case, we should be cautious about

---

[5] The text of the NRSV has been altered to reflect more accurately
the drought imagery in this verse (Wolff 1974b:65; Andersen and
Freedman 1980:339–40).

lifting historical data from a metaphorical text. Hosea's intention is to communicate to Israel the significance of its sins, and
to this end he employs drought metaphors.

In conjunction with drought metaphors, Hosea also uses
agricultural metaphors to describe Israel. Israel is likened to
both a plant and the one who plants. As a farmer, Israel has
reaped what it has sown; as a plant, Israel suffers from the
drought that consumes the land:

> For they sow the wind,
>   and they shall reap the whirlwind.
> The standing grain has no heads,
>   it shall yield no meal;
> if it were to yield,
>   foreigners would devour it. (Hosea 8:7)

Israel has been plowing wickedness and reaping injustice
(10:13) and suffering desiccation as a result. Israel's own deeds
have corrupted the created order. But Hosea also offers a message of hope. If Israel will follow the commands of God, then life
on the barren earth will become possible. Hosea implores the
people:

> Sow for yourselves righteousness;
>   reap steadfast love;
>   break up your fallow ground;
> for it is time to seek the LORD,
>   that he may come and rain righteousness upon you.
>   (Hosea 10:12)

If the people return to God, God will come "like the spring rains
that water the earth" (6:3). God will provide the water that is
necessary to sustain vegetation so that Israel, like a plant, will
flourish in the land.

> [6]His shoots shall spread out;
>   his beauty shall be like the olive tree,
>   and his fragrance like that of Lebanon.
> [7]They shall again live beneath my shadow,
>   they shall flourish as a garden;
> they shall blossom like the vine,
>   their fragrance shall be like the wine of Lebanon.
>   (Hosea 14:6–7)

According to Hosea, the people are integrally linked to the
natural world. The creation will sustain life only if Israel

follows the ways of God. Otherwise, Israel will wither away with the rest of creation.

The message of Hosea is difficult to interpret. On the one hand, Hosea proclaims God's imminent and inevitable judgment on Israel. Because the people have rejected God's commands, they will suffer the catastrophe that they have initiated. On the other hand, Hosea repeatedly offers hope to the people. The people can prosper and flourish in the land if they return to Yahweh. Even Yahweh appears to vacillate, unable to decide whether to destroy or redeem Israel (11:8–9). Does this suggest that the people's sins do not damage the creation or that such damage is not irreversible? Many scholars have noted the irregularity of Hosea's oracles. Indeed, the Hebrew text of some of the oracles has been corrupted beyond repair. But equally important, the oracles do not appear to be in a finished state. They are more characteristic of preliminary reflections or soliloquies (Andersen and Freedman 1980:45). The exception are the oracles in Hosea 1–3.

In Hosea 1–3 Samaria, the capital and symbol of the people of Israel (Schmitt 1989; 1991: 21), is compared to an adulterous wife, whose relationship to Yahweh is likened to the prophet's relationship with his own wife. In the form of an allegory, Hosea 1 presents God's summons for Hosea to marry a prostitute and to have children of prostitution. Like Hosea's wife, Samaria has forsaken her husband Yahweh to prostitute herself by worshipping other gods and forming political alliances with the nations around her. Although Yahweh loves and cares for Samaria and bestows upon her all the abundance of the earth, Samaria chooses to pursue other lovers. Therefore, just as Hosea pleads with his wife and threatens her with divorce, Yahweh initiates divorce proceedings against Samaria (2:1–13). He will take back all the produce that he has given to her and strip her naked. Samaria and the land of Israel will be devastated.

Following the oracle of divorce, the attitude of Yahweh changes. No mention is made of whether or not the divorce is finalized. Neither is any mention made of whether or not Samaria changes heart and returns to Yahweh. What is described is that Yahweh will approach Samaria like a man who courts a woman. Yahweh will allure her and speak tenderly to her, and she will respond in kind (2:14–15). Yahweh will again be Samaria's husband, and he will take her for his wife forever (2:16, 19–20). The creation itself will celebrate the remarriage of Yahweh to Samaria, for through the redemption of the people of Israel, the natural world is also redeemed (Levenson 1985:77–80):

> [18]I will make for you a covenant on that day with the wild animals, the birds of the air, and the creeping things of the ground; and I will abolish the bow, the sword, and war from the land; and I will make you lie down in safety. . . .
> [21]On that day I will answer, says the LORD,
> I will answer the heavens
> and they shall answer the earth;
> [22]and the earth shall answer the grain, the wine, and the oil,
> and they shall answer Jezreel;
> [23] and I will sow her[6] for myself in the land.
> (Hosea 2:18, 21–23)

This covenant between humans and the animal world—the listing of the animals suggests that they represent all nonhuman living beings (De Roche 1981:404–5)—is unprecedented in the Bible. It can be compared with God's covenant with Noah, which also includes the animals, but that covenant is between God and the animals. Moreover, the Noahic covenant does not reconcile the enmity between humans and animals. This new covenant, however, will bring peace to both humans and animals. The original harmony of Eden will be restored. Bernard Batto has identified this covenant as a covenant of peace, a common ancient Near Eastern motif that signals that a deity's hostility toward humans because of their revolt at creation has ceased (Batto 1987a; Fensham 1965). In the context of Hosea, however, God's hostility does not stem from humankind's revolt at the *dawn* of creation. God will bring destruction on Israel because Israel has transgressed the *present* order of creation by rejecting God's commands. Therefore, God's redemption of Israel must also entail the renewal of creation because Israel's sins have corrupted the created order.

---

[6]Most translations emend the Hebrew text to read "him," referring to God's people, but the feminine pronoun is appropriate in this context, for Samaria, the symbol of the people, has been likened to a wife. Batto suggests that the feminine pronoun refers to the eschatological conditions mentioned in the preceding verses—that is, God will sow peace in the land (1987a:202). This interpretation is possible, though not conclusive.

God's restoration of creation, or new creation, is most clearly articulated in vv. 21–23. God will reestablish the ecological web that unites God's own creative activities with both the natural world and humankind (Koch 1979:47). God is the agent of creation; God is the one who will initiate the creation ("answer" has the connotation of "respond to"), and God is the one who will plant the people of Israel in the land. The creation will respond in like fashion. In contrast to the drought that is consuming Israel, the heavens will water the earth so that it will shoot forth its produce and provide the sustenance for Israel to live in the land.

The repeated references to "on that day" (2:16, 18, 21) give this redemption an eschatological tone. God's redemption of Israel and the land is a new creation, not simply the repair of the existing order of creation. The relationship between Hosea's oracles of judgment and oracles of salvation corresponds to the structure of the catastrophe/new-creation myth. The emphasis of the prophet on the need for the people to return to Yahweh does not qualify the inevitability of the coming catastrophe. Rather, the prophet simply models for Israel the appropriate response to God's promised, though not inevitable, new creation. This interpretation is confirmed by the prophet's allegorical understanding of his own redeeming actions on behalf of his adulterous wife:

> [4]For the Israelites shall remain many days without king or prince, without sacrifice or pillar, without ephod or teraphim. [5]Afterward the Israelites shall return and seek the LORD their God, and David their king; they shall come in awe to the LORD and to his goodness in the latter days. (Hosea 3:4–5)

The Israelites will experience the collapse of creation that their sins have hastened upon them, but then God will redeem them through a new creation.

ISAIAH OF JERUSALEM

Although Isaiah does not explicitly refer to the Sinai covenant, he stands in the same tradition as Amos in condemning the rulers and elite of Judah for oppressing the common people in their quest for wealth and power. The source material for his judgment against Judah is the royal theology, which is the theological reflection of the royal ideology discussed in chapter 4. The royal theology proclaims Zion to be the dwelling of God and the center of creation and thus a city of righteousness, and the Davidic rulers to be God's earthly executors of peace and justice (Gottwald 1985:377–78). But reality did not correspond to this theology. Jerusalem had become a city of injustice, and the king did not walk in the ways of God.

Isaiah's preference for the royal theology rather than the Sinai tradition as the source material of his oracles might reflect his own social standing. He appears to have been from a noble Jerusalem family and was possibly even a temple priest. In any case, he had access to both the king and the chief priests. But Isaiah might also have preferred the royal theology because the people's understanding of this theology served as a catalyst for their sins. In other words, Isaiah might have used the royal theology against the rulers and elite of Judah in order to correct their misappropriation of that theology.

The royal theology was dangerous because it elevated the importance of humans, especially the king. The king was considered to be the adopted son of God. He was supreme over all creatures and able to act like God in this world. Eventually, this unique position of the king was democratized so that all humans were viewed as kings (Ps 8). (Traces of this lofty view of humans can be detected in both the J and the P creation myths.) As long as humans recognize that they are subordinate to God and the order of creation, such a theology is not problematic. However, the rulers and elite of Judah had usurped God's position. In their haughtiness, they viewed the world as their exclusive domain and all its riches as their plunder. The royal theology was distorted to legitimate humankind's basic sin: human self-exaltation over God. Therefore, Isaiah used the same royal theology to condemn Judah and thereby to herald the coming destruction of the people and the land.

In a spectacular vision in which Yahweh is enthroned in his heavenly temple surrounded by seraphs, Isaiah is privy to the deliberations of the divine assembly (6:1–13). The divine assembly has declared judgment on Judah, but the assembly needs a messenger to proclaim God's judgment to the people. Isaiah volunteers. God then gives Isaiah a message of irreversible doom to prophesy. When Isaiah asks how long he should proclaim this message, Yahweh responds:

> [11]Until cities lie waste
>> without inhabitant,
> and houses without people,
>> and the land is utterly desolate;
> [12]until the LORD sends everyone far away,
>> and vast is the emptiness in the midst of the land.
>>   (Isaiah 6:11–12)

Isaiah offers no hope for the people of Judah in this world. Their sins have so corrupted the creation that the present order will inevitably be destroyed.

Some of the specific sins of Judah are listed in an elaborate oracle centering around the day of Yahweh. The people have turned to divination and soothsaying and have bowed down to idols of their own making (2:6, 8). The emphasis here is not on the people's worshipping other gods but is on their exalting themselves above God (Watts 1985:35). They also have hoarded silver and gold and have amassed a large army (2:7). Their hunger for wealth and power is a further indication of their self-exaltation. The rulers and the elite of Judah have exalted themselves over God, but God will humble them. Their pride and arrogance will shrink before the glory and majesty of God. Isaiah then uses the cosmic metaphors of the day of Yahweh to describe the coming catastrophe on Judah:

> [12]For the LORD of hosts has a day
>> against all that is proud and lofty,
>> against all that is lifted up and high;
> [13]against all the cedars of Lebanon,
>> lofty and lifted up;
>> and against all the oaks of Bashan;
> [14]against all the high mountains,
>> and against all the lofty hills;
> [15]against every high tower,
>> and against every fortified wall;
> [16]against all the ships of Tarshish,
>> and against all the beautiful craft.
> [17]The haughtiness of people shall be humbled,
>> and the pride of everyone shall be brought low;
>> and the LORD alone will be exalted on that day.
>>   (Isaiah 2:12–17)

The rulers and elite of Judah have corrupted the order of creation by usurping the position of God. Therefore, the creation itself will be destroyed. Specifically, Isaiah describes the destruction of all that is high and lofty in the creation or that might impress humans with its greatness (Kaiser 1972:36). But this text also speaks of the essential unity of creation. Humans, as created beings, are representative of all creation when they arrogantly assault God's rule of the creation. All creation suffers as a result. In the end, only Yahweh will be exalted.

Most of Isaiah's oracles announce God's judgment on the people of Judah. They detail the crimes of the people and herald the coming catastrophe. Nevertheless, like the prophets before him, Isaiah also presents a beacon of hope. The coming catastrophe is but the prelude to a new creation when the people will live in peace according to justice and righteousness—that is, according to the order of creation (Schmid 1984: 107). Some of these oracles of salvation have been added by later writers wanting to buffer and qualify Isaiah's harsh sentence on the people but some undoubtedly stem from Isaiah himself.[7] Likewise, Isaiah 32:9–20 and 10:33–11:9, two oracles in which the coming catastrophe and the new creation are juxtaposed, are probably from the prophet himself.

In the former oracle, Isaiah addresses the elite women of Jerusalem. He calls them from the complacency of their luxuriant lifestyle to lament, for soon the fruit crops will be destroyed and the fields will be overgrown with thorns and briers. Isaiah states no specific cause for the agricultural catastrophe. Some commentators have assumed, based on v. 14, that the devastation of the crops is caused by war (Kaiser 1974:330), but it could also be the result of natural catastrophes such as drought. Regardless of the cause, such a catastrophe will have severe consequences for the people of Jerusalem. But the catastrophe will not be limited to just the agriculture. Even Jerusalem itself will be devastated.

> For the palace will be forsaken,
>   the populous city deserted;
> the hill and the watchtower
>   will become dens forever,
> the joy of the wild asses,
>   a pasture for flocks. (Isaiah 32:14)

---

[7] Determining which parts of the book of Isaiah preserve the words of Isaiah of Jerusalem is difficult. Throughout the first part of the book (chs. 1–39) his words have been mixed with the words of later prophets and editors. Nevertheless, many of these additions appear to be further expansions and elaborations of Isaiah's own words.

The images that Isaiah marshals recall the Yahwist's creation myth. The land will become a barren wilderness with only thorns and briers like the land outside the garden of Eden that was deprived of rain. Its only inhabitants will be wild animals,[8] demonic and symbolic of chaos (Talmon 1966:43). The center of creation that is the land of Israel will be consumed by the chaos of the periphery.

The collapse of the created order, however, will only be temporary. The world will remain barren only

> [15]until a spirit from on high is poured out on us,
>   and the wilderness becomes a fruitful field,
>   and the fruitful field is deemed a forest.
> [16]Then justice will dwell in the wilderness,
>   and righteousness abide in the fruitful field.
> [17]The effect of righteousness will be peace,
>   and the result of righteousness, quietness and trust forever.
> [18]My people will abide in a peaceful habitation,
>   in secure dwellings, and in quiet resting places.
>   (Isaiah 32:15–18)

The wilderness that results from the catastrophe will be transformed by a new creation. In this new creation the people of God will live securely in peace, and their actions will be characterized by justice and righteousness. Justice and righteousness should not be equated with mere human conduct. They refer to a sphere of activity that emanates from God (Koch 1982:57–60; Berquist 1993:59–61). It is God alone who is just and righteous, and the creation is the manifestation of God's justice and righteousness (see Pss 33:4–7; 89:9–14; and the discussion by Levenson 1988:104–6). Humans are just and righteous only when they live in accord with creation, only when their actions correspond to the ways of God. This will be the mark of the new creation. Because the people of God will live according to God's righteousness and justice, the creation will remain secure. Human faithfulness to God will safeguard the creation forever.

In the second oracle Isaiah likens the coming catastrophe to the deforestation of the august cedar forests of Lebanon:

---

[8] The term translated by the NRSV as "flocks" refers literally to a group of animals. The type of animal in the flock or herd is not specified. In the context of this oracle, it appears to refer to a herd of wild asses.

³³Look, the Sovereign, the LORD of hosts,
    will lop the boughs with terrifying power;
  the tallest trees will be cut down,
    and the lofty will be brought low.
³⁴He will hack down the thickets of the forest with an ax,
    and Lebanon with its majestic trees will fall.
               (Isaiah 10:33–34)

Isaiah's metaphor in this passage is transparent; God will destroy the people because of their haughty pride. Isaiah's focus in this oracle, however, is not on the inevitable catastrophe that is coming upon Judah but on the hope of a new creation. Reference to the coming catastrophe is made in order to set the stage for God's new act of creation.

Although the people will be destroyed like the felling of trees, God will bring new life to the stump that was the lineage of David. God will cause the stump to shoot out new branches; a new king will arise to govern God's people. Unlike the previous kings of Jerusalem who rejected the imperatives of the royal theology, this new David will reign with justice and righteousness. He will truly be a son of God and God's regent over creation (11:1–5).

As in the message proclaimed by Hosea, Isaiah envisions that the new creation will also entail a transformed relationship between humans and animals. Because God's righteousness will prevail on the earth, the whole creation will be reconstituted as God intended it. No longer will there be enmity between humans and animals:

⁶The wolf shall live with the lamb,
    the leopard shall lie down with the kid,
  the calf and the lion and the fatling together,
    and a little child shall lead them.
⁷The cow and the bear shall graze,
    their young shall lie down together;
    and the lion shall eat straw like the ox.
⁸The nursing child shall play over the hole of the asp,
    and the weaned child shall put its hand on the adder's den.
⁹They will not hurt or destroy
    on all my holy mountain;
  for the earth will be full of the knowledge of the LORD
    as the waters cover the sea. (Isaiah 11:6–9)

Isaiah's vision of an idyllic harmony within the animal world is troublesome for many ecologically informed readers. Is not the natural world *inherently* violent? The balance of nature is dependent upon one species' preying off another. Nature is "red in tooth and claw," yet without violence it would cease to sustain itself. Therefore, commentators have commonly acknowledged the utopian character of this vision.

Despite its unrealistic vision, this text can nevertheless offer realistic values. According to one commentator, what concerns Isaiah in this passage "is violence of any kind, even in the animal world, for he cannot accept that as being a rightful part of God's good world, and so he dreams of a day when there will no longer be any need for any living thing to kill another (Gowan 1986:104)." But although human violence is indeed an assault on the order of creation, there is no evidence to suggest that violence among animals was deemed contrary to the created order. For the ancient Israelites, all life belonged to God. Every act of taking life, whether it be human or animal life, was problematic, *but only for humans*. The Bible is not concerned about violence within the animal world. Violence is the concern of this oracle—but only the violence that occurs between the human and the animal world (Kaiser 1972:160–61). Notice that there are two types of animals listed in this oracle: domestic animals raised by humans (lamb, goat, cow), and wild animals (wolf, leopard, lion, bear) that prey on humans and their domestic herds. Domestic animals are part of the human world. They are ingroup members with humans in contrast to wild animals that make up the outgroup; they represent culture rather than nature. They are raised by humans for humans. An attack against them by wild animals is an attack on the human world. Thus, the domestic animals serve as the key for understanding Isaiah's oracle. This oracle is not envisioning the cessation of violence among wild animals but between the animal world and the human world. In the new creation the ingroup/outgroup enmity between humans and wild animals will be reconciled.

In verse 8 Isaiah alludes either to the Yahwist creation myth or to the traditional source material that the Yahwist used to write his myth (the date of both the Yahwist and this oracle is problematic). There he proclaims that the child will not be harmed by the snake, explicitly undoing the enmity that resulted from the human couple's actions in the garden.

According to J, the woman's offspring will strike the head of the serpent's offspring, and the serpent will strike his heel. But in the new creation, the child and the snake will peacefully coexist. The child will play over the snake rather than strike it, and the snake will not attack the child.

One final comment should be made about Isaiah's oracle of the new creation. It is proclaimed from a human point of view. The violence that will be eliminated in the new creation is violence that is directed at the human world. No mention is made about whether, for example, humans will become vegetarians, no longer using animals for food. This might be inferred from the text, but it is not explicitly stated, nor should it be expected. Isaiah was prophesying to humans and so addressed human concerns. Nevertheless, his vision of a new creation has implications beyond its human orientation.

ZEPHANIAH

Isaiah predicts that the Assyrian Empire will be God's agents of judgment against Judah (10:5–6). Indeed, during Isaiah's life the Assyrians, under Sennacherib, invade and devastate much of the land of Judah. Jerusalem survives, according to Isaiah, because of Hezekiah's faithfulness. Roughly a century later, the prophet Zephaniah prophesies the destruction of the Assyrian Empire and its capital Nineveh. But Zephaniah does not focus solely on Assyria. He also proclaims God's judgment on the Phoenicians, the Philistines, the Moabites, the Ammonites, and on the people of Judah. The book of Zephaniah begins with an oracle announcing God's destruction of the whole world:

> [2]I will utterly sweep away everything
> from the face of the earth, says the LORD.
> [3]I will sweep away humans and animals;
> I will sweep away the birds of the air
> and the fish of the sea.
> I will make the wicked stumble.[9]

---

[9] De Roche suggests that this line is an intrusion into the text that was added by a scribe who could not accept the universal scope of Zephaniah's oracle. The oracle was thus reduced to a judgment oracle against the wicked (1980:107–8). This interpretation, however, is not

> I will cut off humanity
> from the face of the earth, says the LORD.
>   (Zephaniah 1:2–3)

This oracle of judgment is universal in scope. The whole world will be destroyed—all human and animal life. The oracle uses language similar to the creation and the flood myths. The listing of humans, animals, birds of the air, and fish of the sea reflects the Priestly writer's enumeration of creatures that God created, but in reverse order (De Roche 1980:106). The repeated reference to the "face of the earth" is reminiscent of the flood myth. This oracle employs the pun *'adam-'adama*—God will cut off *'adam*, "humanity," from the face of the *'adama*, "earth"—in the same manner as the Yahwist creation myth. Whether Zephaniah explicitly refers to the P and the J myths or simply reflects a common creation-flood tradition is uncertain. Nevertheless, these metaphors give cosmic significance to the coming destruction.

Zephaniah identifies the coming catastrophe as the day of Yahweh. It will be a day of sacrifice and a day of wrath. God's fury will be against both Judah and the nations because of the violence done by the peoples and because of their haughtiness. The whole creation will be destroyed so that all the inhabitants of the earth will be annihilated. Yet despite the totality of the day of Yahweh, Zephaniah offers hope to the people of Judah:

> Seek the LORD, all you humble of the land,
>   who do his commands;
> seek righteousness, seek humility;
>   perhaps you may be hidden on the day of the LORD's wrath.
>   (Zephaniah 2:3)

Even though the catastrophe is to be universal, a remnant of Judah may survive. In fact, Zephaniah seems to assume that some will survive, for he claims that to them God will give the land of Philistia, Moab, and Ammon (2:4–10). Moreover, Yahweh will cleanse Jerusalem which he accuses of being a "soiled, defiled, oppressing city" (3:1). Although Yahweh will consume all the earth, he will redeem Jerusalem:

---

necessary. Rather than diminishing the scope of this oracle, this line gives universal scope. All creation is declared to be wicked and subject to God's judgment.

[11]On that day you shall not be put to shame
    because of all the deeds by which you have rebelled
      against me;
for then I will remove from your midst
    your proudly exultant ones,
and you shall no longer be haughty
    in my holy mountain.
[12]For I will leave in the midst of you
    a people humble and lowly.
They shall seek refuge in the name of the LORD—
[13]   the remnant of Israel;
they shall do no wrong
    and utter no lies,
nor shall a deceitful tongue
    be found in their mouths.
Then they will pasture and lie down,
    and no one shall make them afraid. (Zephaniah 3:11–13)

How shall we understand this incongruity in the message of Zephaniah? Does Zephaniah's hope of a remnant undercut his threat of universal catastrophe? Will the day of Yahweh be less destructive than Zephaniah first proclaimed? As we saw with the preceding prophets, the message of Zephaniah should be interpreted in reference to the catastrophe/new-creation myth. Because the earth has been corrupted by human violence and haughtiness, Zephaniah heralds the inevitable destruction of creation. But the world cannot end in catastrophe; the myth also entails a new creation that will emerge out of the destruction of the old. Therefore, Zephaniah also proclaims the survival of a remnant; and although these people are "left over" from the old creation, they are transformed in the new creation. They will become a humble people, doing no wrong, and uttering no lies. The people will be transformed so that their actions will no longer corrupt the earth.

JEREMIAH

Jeremiah prophesies during the final years of the kingdom of Judah. Repeatedly, he condemns the people of Jerusalem and Judah for their continuous and wanton sin. The people have refused to serve God or to follow God's commands and so have polluted the land. In a similar fashion to Hosea,

Jeremiah uses the metaphor of an adulterous wife to describe the people's rejection of Yahweh:

> [1]If a man divorces his wife
>   and she goes from him
> and becomes another man's wife,
>   will he return to her?
> Would not such a land be greatly polluted?
> You have played the whore with many lovers;
>   and would you return to me? says the LORD.
> [2]Look up to the bare heights, and see!
>   Where have you not been lain with?
> By the waysides you have sat waiting for lovers,
>   like a nomad in the wilderness.
> You have polluted the land
>   with your whoring and wickedness.
> [3]Therefore the showers have been withheld,
>   and the spring rain has not come;
> yet you have the forehead of a whore,
>   you refuse to be ashamed. (Jeremiah 3:1–3)

In the surrounding context of this oracle, Jeremiah accuses the people of quickly changing their ways, of claiming to be innocent of infidelity yet seeking other lovers (2:33–37). Behind this text we might image a situation in which the people repeatedly repent of their sins and return to Yahweh, but without a change of heart. Their repentance is superficial, lacking real intent to keep God's covenant (Thompson 1980: 190). In order to illustrate the gravity of the people's situation, Jeremiah draws upon legal material concerning divorce. According to Deuteronomy 24:1–4, if a man divorces his wife and she later marries another, under no circumstances can she return to her first husband as a wife. If she does remarry her first husband, this act is an abomination to God and it pollutes the land. For Jeremiah, the people of God are in a similar situation to the divorced wife. They have prostituted themselves to other lovers, yet repeatedly return to Yahweh. Their actions have thus polluted the land, bringing drought upon them. Here Jeremiah's analogy of Judah's plight with the Deuteronomic law breaks down. From the perspective of the law, the woman's *return* to her first husband pollutes the land. With regard to the people of Judah, however, their *abandonment* of Yahweh in favor of other lovers is the source of the land's pollution.

Although Jeremiah and Hosea share the same metaphors to describe the relationship between Yahweh and his people, they use the metaphors toward different ends. Hosea uses the metaphor to illustrate God's redemption; just as Hosea redeems Gomer out of prostitution and restores her as his wife, God will redeem an unfaithful Israel (Hos 3:1–5). Jeremiah, on the other hand, uses this metaphor to describe the impossibility of the people returning to God. If a remarried women cannot return to her first husband, how much more impossible is it for the people of Judah to return to Yahweh after affairs with other lovers (Holladay 1986:113).

As the prophets that preceded him, Jeremiah presumes a causal connection between the actions of the people and the condition of creation. Human sin corrupts the creation and affects the natural world. Specifically, Jeremiah claims that because the people have turned away from Yahweh, the earth is consumed by a great conflagration. The pastures are dried up (23:10), the grass withers (12:4), and the seasonal rains have not fallen (3:3). The land suffers from a curse (23:10; reflecting a similar tradition as the Yahwist creation myth), and the animals and the birds have disappeared (12:4). For Jeremiah, the natural catastrophe that the people of Judah are experiencing (14:1 explicitly states that the people are experiencing a drought) is a certain indication of God's judgment on them:

> [10]Take up weeping and wailing for the mountains,
>   and a lamentation for the pastures of the wilderness,
> because they are laid waste so that no one passes through,
>   and the lowing of cattle is not heard;
> both the birds of the air and the animals
>   have fled and are gone.
> [11]I will make Jerusalem a heap of ruins,
>   a lair of jackals;
> and I will make the towns of Judah a desolation,
>   without inhabitant. (Jeremiah 9:10–11)

The connection between Judah's sins and the catastrophe is made explicit in the following verses; the life-giving land is being turned into a wilderness because the people have forsaken the law of God and have followed their own desires (9:12–14).

Judah's present natural catastrophe, however, serves also as a harbinger of a catastrophe that is to come. This catastrophe will be cosmic in scope; it will encompass the whole creation.

The people's pollution of the land makes the coming catastrophe inevitable. Jeremiah thus proclaims the approach of the enemy from the north who will bring God's judgment on the people. On a historic level, this cryptic designation undoubtedly refers to the Babylonians (Hyatt 1940; Holladay 1986:42–43). In order to circumvent the vast Syrian desert that spanned the distance between Babylon and Judah, the Babylonian army would travel north along the Euphrates river and then south along the Mediterranean coast, attacking Judah from the north. The historic interpretation of the enemy from the north, however, does not fully account for its meaning, for Jeremiah declares that the Babylonians themselves will be attacked by this enemy (chs. 50–51). This agent of God's judgment also has mythical overtones (Childs 1959; Reimer 1989). In the biblical and Canaanite traditions, "north" does not always refer to a northern geographical location. Often it refers to a mountain peak or pinnacle that is thought to be the dwelling place of a deity (Eissfeldt). The temple on Mount Zion, for example, is located in the "north" (Ps 48:2), though it is in the south of Palestine geographically. Furthermore, the enemy from the north is associated with chaos.[10] Its assault causes the creation itself to quake and crumble. On a mythic level, then, the enemy from the north designates the chaotic foe that is sent by Yahweh from his own dwelling. The enemy from the north signals the return of primordial chaos and the disintegration of the created order. Therefore, when Jeremiah proclaims the coming of the enemy from the north against Judah, he heralds the dawn of a cosmic catastrophe. The people's sins have so polluted the earth that the whole creation must be destroyed. By sending the enemy from the north, Yahweh hastens the collapse of the creation.

The people's refusal to change their ways stirs Jeremiah deeply. Although he is the divinely called envoy of God's

---

[10] Childs first made this connection based on the association of the enemy from the north with the Hebrew term ra'ash, "to tremble, quake," a technical term of the chaos tradition (1959). But for Childs, this term did not denote chaos and was not associated with the enemy from the north tradition until after Jeremiah. More recent studies, however, have shown that ra'ash was always associated with primordial chaos and was used in conjunction with Jeremiah's enemy from the north (Reimer 1989:226).

words of judgment, he agonizes over their repercussions: "My anguish, my anguish! I writhe in pain! Oh, the walls of my heart!" (4:19). He cannot remain indifferent, for he has seen in a vision the devastating effects of the coming catastrophe:

> [23]I looked on the earth, and lo, it was waste and void;
>   and to the heavens, and they had no light.
> [24]I looked on the mountains, and lo, they were quaking,
>   and all the hills moved to and fro.
> [25]I looked, and lo, there was no one at all,
>   and all the birds of the air had fled.
> [26]I looked, and lo, the fruitful land was a desert,
>   and all its cities were laid in ruins
>   before the LORD, before his fierce anger.
>   (Jeremiah 4:23–26)

Jeremiah employs the creation traditions underlying both the Priestly and the Yahwist creation myth to herald the reversal of creation (Fishbane 1971:151–53). Like the unleashed Leviathan, the enemy from the north will dismantle the boundaries of creation. The world will revert to its undifferentiated and empty primordial state. All inhabitants of the earth will perish, and the land will be reduced to a barren desert.

Jeremiah offers little hope to the people of his day. God's judgment on the people is final, the coming catastrophe inevitable. Nevertheless, the book of Jeremiah does contain numerous passages that describe God's redemption of the people. Although many of these passages do not stem from Jeremiah himself (they were likely inserted by later scribes in order to ameliorate Jeremiah's otherwise ominous message), Jeremiah did envision a new creation emerging out of the catastrophe that the people of God would experience.

Jeremiah describes this new creation as a new covenant:

> [31]The days are surely coming, says the LORD, when I will make a new covenant with the house of Israel and the house of Judah. [32]It will not be like the covenant that I made with their ancestors when I took them by the hand to bring them out of the land of Egypt—a covenant that they broke, though I was their husband, says the LORD. [33]But this is the covenant that I will make with the house of Israel after those days, says the LORD: I will put my law within them, and I will write it on their hearts; and I will be their God, and they shall be my people. [34]No longer shall they teach one another, or say to each other, "Know the

LORD," for they shall all know me, from the least of them to the greatest, says the LORD; for I will forgive their iniquity, and remember their sin no more. (Jeremiah 31:31–34)

After the catastrophe, Jeremiah declares, God will make a new covenant with the people. Unlike the old covenant that was written on tablets of stone, this new covenant will be written on the human heart. According to Jeremiah, the old covenant is ineffectual. Despite all that God has done on behalf of Israel, the people continually break the covenant. The failure of the old covenant, however, is due not to the nature of the covenant per se, but to that of humankind. Israel repeatedly rejects God's laws. In the tradition of the Yahwist, Jeremiah recognizes that humans are bent on evil, that they have an evil inclination. In contrast to the old covenant, the new covenant signals not a new set of laws that will be easier to keep, but a new humanity that will be inclined towards following God. Through the coming catastrophe, the evil inclination of humans will be purged. The new creation that ensues from the catastrophe will include a transformed humankind whose very nature will correspond to the law of God (cf. the similar prophecy in Ezek 36:26–28).

THE EXILIC PROPHETS

For the preexilic prophets, God's judgment on the people's sins is experienced through the present disintegration of creation, though the most grievous consequences of God's judgment still lies in the near future. The pollution of the earth caused by human sin makes the total collapse of creation inevitable, but the reality of it is not yet fully known. A coming catastrophe looms on the horizon; the day of Yahweh is at hand. For the prophets of the sixth century, however, the catastrophe has arrived. The destruction of Jerusalem, including Yahweh's temple on Zion and the exile of the people to Babylon, is interpreted by these prophets to be the historical manifestation of God's judgment. The metaphors of cosmic catastrophe serve as appropriate images for understanding the people's experience: the creation has ceased to be life-sustaining; the earth is characterized by chaos rather than order; Yahweh has engaged in a cosmogonic battle against his own people. The people's sins against God and the created order have hastened and brought upon them the destruction of creation itself.

EZEKIEL

Because the people have already experienced God's judgment through war and exile, the prophets of the exile herald the dawn of God's new creation—the redemption of Israel and the natural world. This transition in the prophetic message is best illustrated by the prophecies of Ezekiel. Ezekiel is called to prophesy against Judah during his fifth year in exile (Ezek 1–3). As a temple priest in Jerusalem, Ezekiel was sent into exile in the first deportation in 597 BCE. Jerusalem had just been conquered by Nebuchadnezzar but was not yet destroyed. In Babylon Ezekiel proclaims judgment on Jerusalem and Judah just as Jeremiah continues to do in Jerusalem. The people are still rejecting Yahweh and are consequently going to suffer further at the hands of the Babylonians. After Jerusalem is destroyed in 587 BCE, however, Ezekiel turns from oracles of judgment to salvation oracles. God's judgment has occurred; the order of creation has unraveled. With the catastrophe past, God is about to redeem God's people through a new creation.

Ezekiel describes the coming redemption as a covenant of peace:

> [25]I will make with them a covenant of peace and banish wild animals from the land, so that they may live in the wild and sleep in the woods securely. [26]I will make them and the region around my hill a blessing; and I will send down showers in their season; they shall be showers of blessing. [27]The trees of the field shall yield their fruit, and the earth shall yield its increase. They shall be secure on their soil; and they shall know that I am the LORD, when I break the bars of their yoke, and save them from the hands of those who enslaved them. [28]They shall no more be plunder for the nations, nor shall the animals of the land devour them; they shall live in safety, and no one shall make them afraid. [29]I will provide for them a splendid vegetation so that they shall no more be consumed with hunger in the land, and no longer suffer the insults of the nations. (Ezekiel 34:25–29)

The covenant of peace, as mentioned earlier in this chapter, is the prophetic designation of a common ancient Near Eastern

motif associated with creation (Batto 1987a). At the time of
creation, humans revolted against the gods, disrupting the created order and forcing the gods to destroy humankind through
a cosmic catastrophe. In some traditions the gods destroy humankind with a flood; in other traditions a goddess attempts to
slay humankind in a violent rampage. The hostility of the gods
towards humans in both cases, however, is reconciled by a
covenant. This covenant of peace is established by the head god;
it signals the end of divine hostility and the return of creation to
its original condition.

In applying the covenant of peace to Israel's situation,
Ezekiel declares that the events that culminated in Jerusalem's destruction and the exile of the people marked the end
of God's hostility toward them. The people's sins against
God had brought upon them God's wrath, but now God will
make a covenant of peace with them. As a result, the earth
will be transformed into a new creation so that it will be like
the garden of Eden. In another oracle Ezekiel explicitly
associates the new creation of the land with the garden of
Eden: "And they will say, 'This land that was desolate has
become like the garden of Eden; and the waste and desolate
and ruined towns are now inhabited and fortified' " (36:35).
The creation will be restored to its primordial splendor
before human rebellion against God corrupted it. The land
of Israel, which was polluted by sin and devastated by
invading armies, will become a fertile garden, freely giving
up its produce. The people will be free from the threat of
wild animals and the nations, and will live securely in the
land. The reference to animals in this context probably
includes only those animals, such as the lion, the bear, or
the jackal, that are a threat to humans or domestic animals.
These wild animals are in the same category as the nations;
they are the outgroup in relation to Israel. They are creatures
of the periphery and thus symbolic of chaos.

Although Ezekiel's primary focus is on the redemption of
Israel, his vision of God's redemption also includes the natural
world (limited to the nature of Israel's domain). Because the
land of Israel has been defiled from the people's sins, it too
needs to be redeemed through a new creation. The land needs
to be cleansed from its pollution. Therefore, Ezekiel proclaims
God's coming redemption to the land itself:

> [8]But you, O mountains of Israel, shall shoot out your branches, and yield your fruit to my people Israel; for they shall soon come home. [9]See now, I am for you; I will turn to you, and you shall be tilled and sown; [10]and I will multiply your population, the whole house of Israel, all of it; the towns shall be inhabited and the waste places rebuilt; [11]and I will multiply human beings and animals upon you. They shall increase and be fruitful; and I will cause you to be inhabited as in your former times, and will do more good to you than ever before. Then you shall know that I am the LORD. (Ezekiel 36:8–11)

Clearly, Israel will profit from the restoration of the land, but this new creation is not simply for the benefit of humans (contra Gowan 1986:101–2). The direct address to the land suggests that God will redeem the land for its own sake (DeGuglielmo 1957:308). All God's redeeming actions, described in this oracle, are on behalf of the land. Because the land has a purpose within creation—to bear and sustain life—the redemption of the land will include the increase of humans and animals on the land. Humans in this context benefit the land rather than the reverse. Through the new creation, the land will fulfill its life-giving tasks that the corruption of human sin has undermined.

In a final vision of the recreation of the land, Ezekiel employs metaphors from both the horizontal and vertical models of sacred space in order to describe the transformation of the barren wilderness of Judah into a paradise like the garden of Eden. Out of Mount Zion, below the threshold of the rebuilt temple, Ezekiel sees a mighty river flowing to the east that will be too deep to cross (47:1–6). This river will water the sterile dry desert and bring life to the Dead Sea:

> [7]As I came back, I saw on the bank of the river a great many trees on the one side and on the other. [8]He said to me, "This water flows toward the eastern region and goes down into the Arabah; and when it enters the sea, the sea of stagnant waters, the water will become fresh. [9]Wherever the river goes, every living creature that swarms will live, and there will be very many fish, once these waters reach there. It will become fresh; and everything will live where the river goes. [10]People will stand fishing beside the sea from En-gedi to En-eglaim; it will be a place for the spreading of nets; its fish will be a great many kinds, like the fish of the Great Sea. . . . [12]On the banks, on both sides of the river, there will grow all kinds of trees for food. Their leaves will not wither nor their fruit fail, but they will bear fresh fruit

every month, because the water for them flows from the sanctuary. Their fruit will be for food, and their leaves for healing." (Ezekiel 47:7–10, 12)[11]

In this vision, Mount Zion is both the center of creation and the cosmic mountain from which the divine waters flow. Through the life-giving river that will emanate from the temple and stream into the wilderness, the center, which has been engulfed by the sterile periphery, will again flourish with the fertility of creation. Although the text refers specifically to the land east of Jerusalem—the wilderness of Judah and the Dead Sea—this land is symbolic of the whole land of Israel. The whole land will be turned into a paradise that will be dependent upon the life that issues from Yahweh's dwelling on Zion.

Drawing upon traditions of the old royal theology, which also attest to a life-giving stream flowing out of the temple mount (Pss 36:8–9; 46:4; Isa 8:6), Ezekiel identifies Mount Zion throughout his oracles with the garden of Eden (Levenson 1976:25–36). It is the place from which creation originated, the center of all life. The garden of Eden, however, has been corrupted by human sin. Rather than a life-giving paradise, it has become a polluted wasteland that is unable to support life. The destruction of Jerusalem and the temple by the Babylonians is thus likened to the collapse of creation. But in God's coming redemption Zion will be recreated like the garden of Eden, and the river that will flow from the temple will be like the river of Eden. As the river in Eden sustained the vegetation of the garden, so also the river from Zion will cause the desolate ground to shoot forth abundant fruit trees. Its fertilizing waters will even bring life to the sterile waters of the Dead Sea so that it will teem with fish. Everywhere the river goes will abound with life.

SECOND ISAIAH

The themes of redemption and new creation that are prominent in Ezekiel form the central focus of the anonymous prophet who has come to be known as Second Isaiah.[12] No-

---

[11] Verse 11 is commonly recognized to be a later insertion (Zimmerli 1983:508).

[12] The oracles of Second Isaiah have traditionally been recognized in Isaiah 40–55, but chs. 34–35 should also be included in this corpus.

where in his oracles does this prophet issue a word of judgment against the people of God. He offers only a message of comfort and redemption. According to Second Isaiah, the people of Judah, who were defeated and exiled by the Babylonians, have already suffered sufficiently for their sins (40:2). Therefore, Second Isaiah proclaims Yahweh's imminent redemption of Israel from exile. Yahweh has anointed Cyrus, king of Persia, to conquer Babylon (45:1). By Yahweh's command he will be victorious and will allow the people in exile to return to their homeland and to rebuild Zion. However, Yahweh's coming redemption of his people will not take place solely on the plane of human history. Redemption encompasses also the natural world. Because the destruction of Jerusalem and the exile of the people entailed the collapse of the creation, God's redemption of the people will only be possible through a new creation.

For the people suffering in exile, Yahweh's ability to redeem them is questionable. Did not the Babylonians destroy Yahweh's temple? Are not the people under domination in a foreign land? If Yahweh remains king, over what does he rule? According to Second Isaiah, Yahweh's coming redemption is certain because Yahweh is the creator, the king over the creation.

> [21]Have you not known? Have you not heard?
>   Has it not been told you from the beginning?
>   Have you not understood from the foundations of the earth?
> [22]It is he who sits above the circle of the earth,
>   and its inhabitants are like grasshoppers;
> who stretches out the heavens like a curtain,
>   and spreads them like a tent to live in;
> [23]who brings princes to naught,
>   and makes the rulers of the earth as nothing.
>   (Isaiah 40:21–23)

Yahweh is no mere local god! As the creator, he rules over all creation. Jerusalem was destroyed by his will. The people were sent into exile by his will. Similarly, Yahweh has called Cyrus to redeem his people (Ollenburger 1987:64–66):

> [12]I made the earth,
>   and created humankind upon it;
> it was my hands that stretched out the heavens,
>   and I commanded all their host.

¹³I have aroused Cyrus in righteousness,
>   and I will make all his paths straight;
> he shall build my city
>   and set my exiles free,
> not for price or reward,
>   says the LORD of hosts. (Isaiah 45:12–13)

Because Yahweh is the creator, Yahweh will achieve his purposes for his people and for his creation.

In a message similar to that of Ezekiel, Second Isaiah declares that Zion will be transformed into a fertile paradise like the garden of Eden:

> For the LORD will comfort Zion;
>   he will comfort all her waste places,
> and will make her wilderness like Eden,
>   her desert like the garden of the LORD;
> joy and gladness will be found in her,
>   thanksgiving and the voice of song. (Isaiah 51:3)

At the mundane level, Second Isaiah would merely be claiming that the deserted and fallow environs surrounding Jerusalem would again be tilled and planted in the wake of the devastation caused by the Babylonian army. But God's redemption is never mundane! Because God is the creator, God's redemption is through a new creation. Zion will not merely be replanted. It will be created anew, cleansed from all human pollution. For Second Isaiah, this will be a cosmic event because it will be the creator who will do it.

The goal of Second Isaiah's message to the exiles is not just to comfort them with the certain hope of God's coming redemption but also to encourage them to participate in this redemption by returning to Zion. Despite the fact that the people were forcibly removed from their homeland and settled in a foreign land, the people appear to have been reluctant to leave Babylon. Babylon had become their home, and the many born in Babylon knew no other homeland. Moreover, the return journey to Palestine would be long and arduous. Some would undoubtedly die on the trip; others would suffer attacks from bandits and wild animals. All would make the journey by sacrificing the familiarity and security of Babylon for an uncertain future in Palestine. Therefore, Second Isaiah gives little direct attention to God's redemption of Zion. Rather, he focuses on the incompatibility of Yahweh and Babylon and on the people's triumphal procession back to Zion.

Drawing upon the early epic traditions of Israel, Second Isaiah likens Babylon to Egypt. Just as Egypt was the land of death at the periphery, so also is Babylon. And just as Yahweh delivered the Israelites from bondage in Egypt, so also God is about to deliver God's people from Babylon in a new exodus. However, unlike the old exodus, the people will not have to cross the barren desert to reach Zion, the center of creation. Yahweh is going to transform the periphery. The desert will be watered so that it will flourish like the center. Every mountain will be lowered and every valley will be raised so that no obstacle will block the people's return (40:4). In order to further ease the journey, Yahweh will build a highway through the wilderness on which the people will travel to Zion (35:8).

[16]Thus says the LORD,
> who makes a way in the sea,
> a path in the mighty waters,
[17]who brings out chariot and horse,
> army and warrior;
they lie down, they cannot rise,
> they are extinguished, quenched like a wick:
[18]Do not remember the former things,
> or consider the things of old,
[19]I am about to do a new thing;
> now it springs forth, do you not perceive it?
I will make a way in the wilderness
> and rivers in the desert.
[20]The wild animals will honor me,
> the jackals and the ostriches;
for I give water in the wilderness,
> rivers in the desert,
to give drink to my chosen people,
[21]   the people whom I formed for myself
so that they might declare my praise. (Isaiah 43:16–21)

In this oracle the new exodus is compared and contrasted with the first exodus of God's people. Just as God was victorious in the first exodus by defeating the Egyptians and by making a way for the Israelites to cross the sea (vv. 16–17), God will triumph again by delivering the Israelites from the Babylonians (cf. 51:9–11). The Israelites' exodus out of Egypt had been the central theme of their confession to Yahweh. Yahweh was known as the God who brought Israel "out of the land of Egypt, out of the house of slavery" (Exod 20:2). But no longer. Israel's first exodus will pale in comparison to the new exodus that Yahweh is about to perform for them, for Yahweh will bring life to the wilderness:

> [18]I will open rivers on the bare heights,
>   and fountains in the midst of the valleys;
> I will make the wilderness a pool of water,
>   and the dry land springs of water.
> [19]I will put in the wilderness the cedar,
>   the acacia, the myrtle, and the olive;
> I will set in the desert the cypress,
>   the plane and the pine together. (Isaiah 41:18–19)

The desert in the periphery will experience the fruits of God's new creation. It will be transformed into a garden like the garden of Eden at the center. As a result, the new exodus will not be arduous. The people will not grow faint or weary on the journey. There will an abundance of food and drink so that the people can return to Zion in a triumphal procession:

> And the ransomed of the LORD shall return,
>   and come to Zion with singing;
> everlasting joy shall be upon their heads;
>   they shall obtain joy and gladness,
>   and sorrow and sighing shall flee away. (Isaiah 35:10)

Second Isaiah also likens the coming redemption of the people in exile to God's redemption of Noah:

> [9]This is like the days of Noah to me:
>   Just as I swore that the waters of Noah
>   would never again go over the earth,
> so I have sworn that I will not be angry with you
>   and will not rebuke you.
> [10]For the mountains may depart
>   and the hills be removed,
> but my steadfast love shall not depart from you,
>   and my covenant of peace shall not be removed,
>   says the LORD, who has compassion on you.
>   (Isaiah 54:9–10)

In the same way that Noah was spared in God's destruction of creation and was granted a covenant of peace, now God will grant the entire people a covenant of peace.

God's hostility toward this people has come to an end (cf. 54:7–8), and the earth will be restored through a new creation. Whereas the rainbow was the sign of the Noahic covenant, the new creation itself will attest to God's eternal covenant of peace (cf. 55:13). But even if the new creation crumbles (which, of course, it will not), God's covenant with the people will remain secure.

THE POSTEXILIC PROPHETS

Although both Ezekiel and Second Isaiah placed God's coming redemption in a cosmic perspective, it was tied up with historical events, namely, the release of the exiles from Babylon and the restoration of Zion. These historical events did happen. Freed by Cyrus's edict, many of the people returned to Palestine (though more remained in Babylon). The temple was rebuilt, the priesthood was reestablished, and an heir to the throne of David was appointed governor of the province of Judah. Nevertheless, God's glorious redemption, prophesied by Ezekiel and Second Isaiah, failed to materialize. No new creation had taken place. Rather, the people suffered natural disasters and economic depression. Life in a restored Palestine was worse than in Babylon.

For many of the postexilic prophets (most of whom remain anonymous, for they simply appended their oracles to existing works), the hard times of this period meant that the destruction of Jerusalem had not been the fullness of the cosmic catastrophe predicted by earlier prophets, that the exile had not fully cleansed the creation from pollution, that the total collapse of creation still lay ahead for the people. For example, in a series of oracles that have come to be known as the Isaianic Apocalypse (Isa 24–27), a prophet announces that Yahweh is about to lay waste the whole earth and scatter its inhabitants because the earth remains polluted from human sin:

[4]The earth dries and withers,
  the world languishes and withers;
  the heavens languish together with the earth.
[5]The earth lies polluted
  under its inhabitants;

for they have transgressed laws,
    violated the statues,
    broken the [ancient] covenant.[13]
    ⁶Therefore a curse devours the earth,
    and its inhabitants suffer for their guilt;
    therefore the inhabitants of the earth dwindled,
    and few people are left. (Isaiah 24:4–6)

The destruction of Jerusalem and the exile had only affected Israel; this catastrophe did not bring God's judgment on the nations. Therefore, these postexilic prophets proclaim the dawn of a new cosmic catastrophe foreshadowed by the present calamities. But unlike the earlier catastrophe, this new catastrophe will be directed at and encompass all the nations. The whole creation will be devastated. Although Israel will not remain unscathed in the coming catastrophe, these prophets also herald the final redemption of God's people: the nations will be destroyed, never to oppress Israel again; Israel will live in peace and God will dwell on Zion; and the earth will be recreated as a garden paradise. According to the prophet of the Isaianic Apocalypse, God will take away the shame of God's people (25:8), restore Jerusalem as a city of righteousness (26:1–15), swallow up death (25:7), and finally eliminate chaos by killing Leviathan (27:1).

That the nations too had to be judged through a cosmic catastrophe was already anticipated by both Ezekiel and Second Isaiah. Drawing upon the tradition of the enemy from the north, Ezekiel prophesies that Yahweh will bring Gog and all his allies from the distant north against the land of Israel and the people of God, who have been restored to the land (38:1–16).[14] Numerous attempts have been made to identify the Gog of this prophecy. Gyges of Lydia has been the most popular suggestion. But Gog is not a historical individual. Ezekiel uses the name Gog—derived from the name "Magog," a known

---

[13] The text of the NRSV reads "everlasting covenant," which suggests the Noahic covenant, but it is difficult to understand how this covenant would be broken since the obligation of this covenant is on Yahweh. The Hebrew text can also be rendered "ancient covenant," which leaves unspecified the nature of the covenant (Levenson 1988:28).

[14] Many scholars have attributed Ezekiel 38–39 to a later, postexilic, scribe. This interpretation is plausible, but the style and content of this passage are compatible with the rest of the book of Ezekiel.

northern territory (cf. Gen 10:2)—precisely because it has no historical referent and can easily be associated with the enemy from the north (Ezek 38:17 makes an explicit reference to Jeremiah's prophecies of the enemy from the north). Shrouded in mythic images, Gog is simply a cipher for the eschatological enemy of Yahweh. Moreover, Gog represents the nations. In addition to his northern allies, Ezekiel allies him with Persia, Ethiopia, and Put (Libya)—that is, with a nation from the east, south, and west respectively. Gog's allies include nations from all four corners of the earth and so represent all nations.

Although Yahweh will bring Gog against his own people, Yahweh's purpose will not be to judge Israel but to destroy Gog and the nations:

> [18]On that day, when Gog comes against the land of Israel, says the Lord GOD, my wrath shall be aroused. [19]For in my jealousy and in my blazing wrath I declare: On that day there shall be a great shaking in the land of Israel; [20]the fish of the sea, and the birds of the air, and the animals of the field, and all creeping things that creep on the ground, and all human beings that are on the face of the earth, shall quake at my presence, and the mountains shall be thrown down, and the cliffs shall fall, and every wall shall tumble to the ground. [21]I will summon the sword against Gog in all my mountains, says the Lord GOD; the swords of all will be against their comrades. [22]With pestilence and bloodshed I will enter into judgment with him; and I will pour down torrential rains and hailstones, fire and sulfur, upon him and his troops and the many peoples that are with him. (Ezekiel 38:18–22)

Yahweh's defeat of Gog will entail the collapse of the whole creation. The reference to the "great shaking" signals the return of chaos (Childs 1959:196). The nations in their repeated assaults on the people of God have arrogantly challenged Yahweh's kingship over creation. Yahweh will thus march out to fight Gog in a new cosmogonic battle. With the typical weapons of the storm god, Yahweh will defeat the nations by bringing about the reversal of creation. Their dead bodies will then be the main course for a great sacrificial banquet. The birds and wild animals will eat their flesh and drink their blood (39:17–20). Finally, the land of Israel will be cleansed of the bones and the discarded weapons of war (39:9–16), and Israel will be restored securely in its land (39:21–29).

Second Isaiah similarly prophesies a coming catastrophe on all the nations (Isa 34). Although Second Isaiah singles out Edom because of the violence it carried out against the people of Judah following the destruction of Jerusalem, Edom is representative of all the nations. Because the nations have violated the order of creation by assaulting the people of God, Yahweh will slaughter them in a horrific blood-bath; the land will be strewn with their bodies and the mountains will flow with their blood (34:2–3). The heavens will collapse (34:4); the streams will be turned into pitch and the land into sulfur (34:9); and the land will revert to chaos, bearing only thorns and thistles and inhabited by wild animals (34:11–15). The coming catastrophe against the nations will result in the complete destruction of creation.

Later prophets built upon this tradition of God's judgment on all the nations. Obadiah, for example, condemns the Edomites for their treatment of God's people after the destruction of Jerusalem (vv. 1–14). As in the case of Second Isaiah's prophecy of judgment, Edom is symbolic of all the nations. Although Obadiah lacks many of the cosmic metaphors characteristic of the other prophetic writings, he does claim that the day of Yahweh is coming against the nations (vv. 15–16). We can infer from this metaphor that Obadiah envisioned the destruction of the nations through a cosmogonic battle. Yahweh will fight the nations who pose a threat to his kingship over creation. Through the battle the creation itself will be destroyed, but upon God's inevitable victory the world will be created anew. Then the people of God, who will survive the catastrophe, will inherit and possess the land of the nations (vv. 17–21).

In an anonymous oracle that has been appended to the prophecies of Zechariah, a prophet in the tradition of Ezekiel 38–39 foresees the assault of the nations against Jerusalem: "For I will gather all the nations against Jerusalem to battle, and the city shall be taken and the houses looted and the women raped; half of the city shall go into exile, but the rest of the people shall not be cut off from the city" (14:2). But then Yahweh will march forth to fight and destroy the nations (14:3–5). Upon Yahweh's victory, the creation will be reconstituted. There will no longer be cold or frost that inhibit the earth's ability to produce (14:6). Darkness will never again consume the night (14:7). A river of living waters will flow out

of Jerusalem to bring life to the periphery (14:8). And Yahweh
will establish his kingship over the whole earth (14:9).

The most elaborate of the postexilic prophecies that reflect the catastrophe/new-creation myth is the book of Joel.[15]
Joel is a difficult book to understand. The first part of the book
focuses on the destruction caused by a severe locust plague.
The second part of the book focuses on God's judgment of the
nations. What unites the two parts of the book is the theme of
the day of Yahweh; both the locust plague and the destruction
of the nations are heralded as the day of Yahweh. For Joel, the
locust plague experienced by the people of Judah both serves
as a metaphor of the nations' assault against them and signals
the beginning of a cosmic catastrophe that will culminate in
God's defeat of the nations in a cosmogonic battle.

A locust plague severely devastated the land around
Jerusalem. The locusts have destroyed the crops, defoliated the
trees and vines, devoured the pastures, and caused a shortage
of food so that even the daily temple offerings have ceased.
Their relentless assault on the people and the land is likened
by Joel to an invading army:

> [6]Before them peoples are in anguish,
>   all faces grow pale.
> [7]Like warriors they charge,
>   like soldiers they scale the wall.
>   Each keeps to its own course,
>   they do not swerve from their paths.
> [8]They do not jostle one another,
>   each keeps to its own track;
>   they burst through the weapons
>   and are not halted.
> [9]They leap upon the city,
>   they run upon the walls;
>   they climb up into the houses,
>   they enter through the windows like a thief. (Joel 2:6–9)

This is no ordinary locust plague, for with their advance the
locusts hasten the collapse of creation. At their march the earth
and the heavens tremble, the sun, moon, and stars no longer

---

[15] The interpretation of the book of Joel can only be cursory in
this context. For a detailed analysis of Joel from the perspective of the
catastrophe/new-creation myth, see Simkins (1991:101–241; 1993).

shine (2:10). They transform the land that is like the garden of Eden into a desolate desert like the periphery (2:3). Joel thus recognizes the locust plague to be the day of Yahweh.

Although the people have suffered from the locust plague, their distress will only be temporary. The day of Yahweh is not a day of judgment against them. Joel enumerates no sins of the people. The call to "return to Yahweh" (2:12–17) does not mean "repent of your sins" but rather "honor Yahweh with the appropriate cultic rites of mourning" (Simkins 1991:171–90). Yahweh will remove the locusts from the land and destroy them in the sea (2:20). Yahweh will restore the land so that the threshing floors will be full of grain and the vats will overflow with wine and olive oil (2:21–24).

According to Joel, the day of Yahweh must also include God's destruction of the nations. The nations have to be judged for their corrupt treatment of God's people (3:1–8). Joel thus interprets the locust plague as a metaphor of God's coming judgment on the nations. Just as the locusts invade the land of Judah so also God will gather all the nations to war outside Jerusalem (3:9–12). There Yahweh will judge the nations and defeat them in a cosmogonic battle that includes the collapse of creation, but the people of God will be safe on Mount Zion (3:15–16). After the nations are destroyed Yahweh will recreate the world. Just as Yahweh will restore the agricultural bounty that was devastated by the locust plague, God will recreate the land after the nations and their corruption have been purged from it:

> In that day the mountains shall drip sweet wine,
>   the hills shall flow with milk,
> and all the stream beds of Judah
>   shall flow with water;
> a fountain shall come forth from the house of the LORD
>   and water the Wadi Shittim. (Joel 3:18)

In Joel's vision only the center, the land of Judah, will be recreated. It will be transformed into a garden paradise, and it will remain forever undefiled by the nations (3:17). However, the land of the nations at the periphery will become a desolate wilderness. Because of violence done to the people of God, the land of the nations will remain outside the creation of God (3:19).

THE PROPHETS' VALUES TOWARD NATURE

In the preceding analysis of the prophets, we have used the catastrophe/new-creation myth as a model for fleshing out the structure and the metaphors of the prophets' message. This model does not exhaust or fully explain the writings of the prophets, nor was it intended to. Rather, we have employed this model because it draws attention to the prophets' values toward the natural world. By focusing on the status of the creation, this model makes explicit what the prophets presupposed about the triangular relationship between God, humans, and the natural world, and especially about the interrelationship between humans and nature.

Although each of the prophets that we examined delivers a unique message, determined by a specific historical situation, all the prophets share the same worldview: humans and the rest of nature are united in creation—humans affect the natural world with their actions and are affected by the condition of nature. This integral relationship between humans and nature has been articulated by Frank Cross in an essay aptly entitled, "The Redemption of Nature":

> The creation, created "good," falls into decay, sterility, wilderness, cursed by God. The earth is cursed for the sake of the rebellion of one of its natural creatures. The human spirit corrupts nature, and man is one with nature. Humankind belongs wholly to the realm of nature, mortal. His attempt to become a god, to transcend the insecurity of mortal flesh, is his primal sin. He is not half-god, half-animal. His soul contains no spark of the divine. He is an animal, a stately animal, theomorphic indeed, but he cannot free himself now or in the Beyond from nature. In him nature is an actor in the drama of salvation, and also apart from him nature is an actor, fleeing the divine wrath, transfigured by the divine glory, redeemed insofar as man is redeemed, damned insofar as humanity is damned. (1988:95–96)

The unity of humans and nature in creation, however, should not obscure the fundamental distinction between humans and the rest of the natural world. For the prophets, only humans have sinned against God, and only humans must return to God. Apart from humans, nature might be an actor in the drama of salvation, but only humans are moral actors (causal agents), affecting the whole creation with their actions.

The prophets place little confidence in human actions. Humans have always been inclined towards evil and corruption, and human actions alone are insufficient to redeem the world from humanity's sins. On the other hand, the prophets place great confidence in God. God will redeem what humans have destroyed. God will recreate the world and transform humans so that they will no longer sin against God and creation. Because human sin has corrupted the natural world, nature too stands in need of redemption. But also because humans are united with the rest of nature in creation, humankind cannot be redeemed apart from the redemption of the natural world. The hope of humankind is linked with the natural world in the redemption of all creation.

The writings of the preexilic and postexilic prophets reflect primarily the harmony-with-nature solution to the human-relationship-to-nature problem. Human sin adversely affects the natural world. On a theological level, sin is a human affront against God or the commands of God. But the commands of God are not arbitrary. God is the creator, and thus the commands of God correspond to the order of creation. On a ritual level, sin pollutes the world so that it needs to be cleansed. On a cosmic level, sin deteriorates the order of creation which must be reconstituted. Human sin ultimately destroys the creation itself (cf. Kay 1988). As a result, human redemption depends upon the recreation of the world.

Some of the prophets—passages in Ezekiel and Second Isaiah, but most notably the postexilic prophets[16]—also reflect the subjugation-to-nature and the mastery-over-nature solutions to the human-relationship-to-nature problem. The subjugation-to-nature orientation is the response to oppression from the outgroup. In the book of Joel, for example, the people of Judah were suffering from devastation caused by an unprecedented locust plague. But unlike the preexilic and exilic prophets, Joel does not attribute the plague to the people's sins. The catastrophe is not the inevitable result of the people's

[16] The prophet Haggai, in contrast, reflects the harmony-with-nature orientation by blaming the people's experience of economic and ecological depression on their own failure to rebuild the temple.

actions, but rather is caused by an outgroup (a locust plague personified as an invading army) over which the people have no control. As in the case of Job, the people's only recourse is God.

Hope of redemption is implicit in the catastrophe/new-creation myth. God will redeem the people in the midst of the cosmic catastrophe through a new creation (reflecting the harmony-with-nature orientation), resulting in a reversal of the people's orientation toward the outgroup. No longer will the people be subjugated to the nations or to a hostile natural world. Their land will be restored to a fertile paradise, but the land of the nations (the outgroup) will become desolate and overrun with wild animals. In contrast to the king's mastery-over-nature orientation, this orientation is eschatological. It is actualized solely through the actions of God. God alone is the master over creation, and God alone will destroy the nations and devastate their land.

CONCLUSION

In contrast to the majority of previous studies of the Bible, this book has focused on the role of the natural world in the religion and culture of ancient Israel. Specifically, I have sought to identify the ancient Israelites' worldview and values toward nature, and thereby contribute to the ecology of ancient Israel. To accomplish this task, I have applied a variety of new models to the biblical data and have focused especially on the Bible's creation myths and metaphors. New models were essential to this investigation because the previous models of biblical interpretation did not give attention to the role of nature in the biblical texts. The creation myths and metaphors provided the key to ascertaining the Israelites' worldview and values by making explicit the Israelites' assumptions concerning the triangular relationship between God, humans, and the natural world.

In the preceding chapters I developed and illustrated a model of the Israelites' worldview and values toward nature. This model diagrams the basic assumptions of the Classification, Relationship, and Causality universals (the assumptions of the Space and Time universals were discussed in chapters 4 and 5). The Israelite worldview, illustrated in figure 14, posits two fundamental relations: an unalterable distinction between God the creator and the creation; and the correlation of humans and the rest of the natural world as two distinct yet integrally related parts of creation. Within this worldview, three value orientations toward nature are possible: mastery-

over-nature, harmony-with-nature, and subjugation-to-nature
(figure 5). Under different circumstances each of these value
orientations was preferred by the Israelites. This was in accordance with the ingroup/outgroup classification. In relation
to their own land and the land of members of their ingroup,
the Israelites preferred primarily the harmony-with-nature orientation. In relation to the natural world of the outgroup,
the Israelites preferred either the mastery-over-nature or the
subjugation-to-nature orientation. The former was preferred
under circumstances in which the Israelites were able to dominate the outgroup, the latter when the Israelites were dominated by the outgroup.

Figure 17 illustrates how each of the biblical texts treated
in this book fit in relation to this model of the Israelite worldview. The texts that present Jerusalem's royal ideology or
theology reflect both the mastery-over-nature and the harmony-
with-nature orientation. According to this ideology, the king
stands in relation to the earth as God is related to the whole
creation. As God's earthly regent—the king never is able to
escape his creaturely status—the king's mastery over the earth
is a manifestation of God's own righteousness and justice. By
defeating all his enemies (the outgroup), the king secures the
order of creation. But the king's deeds must also correspond to
the order of creation. By administering justice and righteousness, the king secures the blessing of creation for his people
(ingroup).

Both the Yahwist and the Priestly writer prefer the
harmony-with-nature solution to the human-relationship-
to-nature problem. Humans are creatures, made of the same
substance as the rest of creation. The Yahwist and the Priestly
writer also emphasize that humans are exceptional in the
creation. Humans have cultural knowledge, or humans are
made in the image of God, and thus are distinct from all other
creatures. Nevertheless, humans cannot escape their creaturely
status. Humans must live according to the order of creation,
and their fate is bound to the fate of creation.

The prophets and the biblical texts presenting the covenant theology also reflect the harmony-with-nature orientation. Humans are linked to the natural world with the result
that human actions have ramifications in nature. Human actions that are in accord with the order of creation, that follow
the stipulations of the covenant, result in the flourishing of

creation. But actions that violate the order of creation and transgress God's covenant bring disorder to the creation. They ritually pollute the land and cause the creation to collapse. As a result, God's redemption of humans entails a new creation.

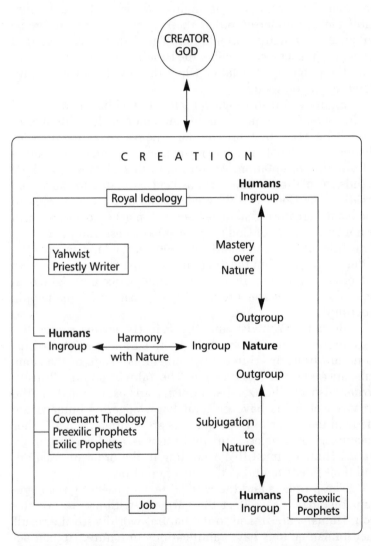

Figure 17. The Biblical Writers' Worldview and Values Toward Nature

The book of Job presents a situation in which the covenant theology's preference for the harmony-with-nature orientation does not correspond to the particular circumstances of Job. The character of Job suffers innocently; his suffering cannot be attributed to transgressions as the covenant theology implies. Job experiences the creation as hostile and overwhelming (outgroup). Therefore, he falls back on his second-order preference, the subjugation-to-nature orientation. Some of the prophets similarly reflect this orientation. The people of Judah had suffered the oppression of the nations (outgroup), which was resulting in the collapse of the creation. But unlike Job, these prophets also envisioned God's new creation when their land will be restored as a new Eden and the land of the nations will be devastated.

As models for biblical interpretation, the ecologically oriented models introduced in this book, including the model of the biblical writer's worldview and values toward nature, provide a viable alternative to the history-versus-nature model that has been dominant in biblical scholarship this century. These models take seriously the Bible's numerous references to the natural world and enable the interpreter to place these references within a meaningful framework. Moreover, these models facilitate a culturally empathic rather than an ethnocentric reading of the Bible. Biblical references to the natural world for instance, can be interpreted in light of ancient Israel's own worldview and values rather than from the perspective of our modern worldview and concerns. These models, therefore, will enable the Bible to be read on its own terms and to be employed authentically in discussions of contemporary issues such as the current environmental crisis.

EPILOGUE:
THE BIBLE AND THE
ENVIRONMENTAL CRISIS

A RELEVANT APPROACH TO THE BIBLE?

Prior to 1970, modern biblical scholars gave little attention to the role of the natural world in the literature of the Bible and in the religious culture of ancient Israel. Too often it was assumed that the religion of Israel was a religion of history, and that the Bible focused exclusively on the relationship between God and humans. The natural world was viewed merely as the stage on which the human drama with God took place. The creation was split into nature and history (the human realm), with God's activity relegated to the latter. This approach is no longer acceptable. It is based on a modern conceptual dichotomy between history and nature that is foreign to the worldview of the ancient Israelites. Moreover, this approach, which was employed to articulate the relevance of Bible for the modern world (this was the agenda of the Biblical Theology Movement), proved to be myopic. In the context of the environmental crisis that began to attract wide public attention in the 1960s, numerous charges were made that the Bible not only fostered anti-environmental attitudes but was actually responsible for the current crisis. Suddenly, the Bible was labeled both irrelevant and dangerous, and biblical scholars scrambled to redeem the Bible from this assault.

That the Bible was regarded as an antagonist to a stable and healthy environment is understandable. References to the natural world in the Bible were either neglected or made subordinate to the Bible's concern for human salvation. How could a human-oriented, biblical religion contribute to the preservation of the natural environment? One theologian recently expressed a common sentiment:

> Does the Bible say anything explicitly about nature that might be ecologically helpful now? The natural world is understood as God's creation, but I know of no biblical passages that urge any special respect. "Love your earthly mother" is not a biblical statement. . . . In sum, nature in the Bible is generally either regarded as a resource, or it fades into the background while, in the foreground, the significant drama of history is played out. (Gulick 1991:183–84)

The problem, however, is not with the Bible itself but with the dominant scholarly interpretation of the Bible. Therefore, a new approach to the Bible, one that takes into consideration the role of the natural world, is needed. This book offers such an approach.

THE MORAL DIMENSION OF THE ENVIRONMENTAL CRISIS

Because concern over the environmental crisis triggered this new focus on the role of the natural world in the religion and culture of ancient Israel, it is appropriate at the end of this study to consider the role that the Bible might play in the discussion of the current crisis. The following presentation can only be cursory at best. I am an expert neither in the intricacy and complexity of the environment nor in ethical theory and application. I leave to qualified others the specific task of applying the Bible to the environmental crisis. Nevertheless, in the remaining pages I will outline some of the basic issues of the current crisis and suggest ways that Israel's worldview and values toward nature can make a positive contribution to discussion of these issues.

Although humans have adversely affected their natural environment throughout every age, the environmental crisis that we are experiencing at the end of the twentieth century is unique in its global scope.[1] No longer can God proclaim that

---

[1] There have, of course, been prior global environmental crises. The catastrophe that resulted in the extinction of the dinosaurs and the more recent ice ages are the most well-known. The distinction of the current crisis is that it is the first global environmental crisis caused by humans.

the creation is good, for humans have polluted the heavens and
the earth. We have poisoned the ground with hazardous chemi-
cals ranging from the toxic wastes that leech out of our landfills
to the pesticides and fertilizers we use in an attempt to make
the earth produce more than it is capable of sustaining. We
have contaminated the oceans and waterways by indiscriminately dumping into them industrial waste and sewage. The
air we breathe, especially in our urban centers, is often un-
healthy due to the smog resulting from the hydrocarbons and
other emissions of our automobiles. In order to avoid low-lying
smog, our coal-burning manufacturers send their pollutants
high into the air, but these pollutants, rich in sulfur dioxides
and nitrous oxides, mix with moisture in the atmosphere and
produce acid rain that kills vegetation, forests, and aquatic life.
Through the use of synthetically derived chlorofluorocarbons
(CFCs), we have even depleted the ozone that protects us from
the harmful ultraviolet radiation of the sun. Pollution, however, is not the only means by which humankind has adversely
affected God's creation. We have become so numerous that we
tax the earth's ability to sustain us. We consume more natural
resources than the earth can reproduce and have threatened
the precarious balance of our ecosystem. Acting as if the earth
were our private domain, we have caused the extinction of
countless animal and plant species.

One could extensively illustrate various facets of the
environmental crisis in which we find ourselves, but this
hardly seems necessary.[2] Is there anyone in our society unaware of the fact that we have polluted and corrupted our
terrestrial home? Ecology and the environment have recently
become hot topics. Everywhere we are reminded about what
we have done to our planet. There has been an explosion of
literature on the subject in bookstores and at newsstands, and
rarely does a week go by without reference to the environmental crisis in the news media. The growing number of environmental groups repeatedly issue warnings of the destruction of
this or that ecosystem and seek to marshal political clout in
order to influence public policy. The environmental crisis has

---

[2] For a presentation of the different aspects of the environmental
crisis, see McDonagh 1986:17–59, McKibben 1989:3–91, Freudenberger 1990:35–83, Nash 1991:23–63, and Gore 1992.

even had an impact on the structures of government, including departments devoted to protecting the natural environment on the state and national level and programs such as mandatory recycling on the local level. Although the extent of the environmental crisis is often debated, few would question its existence.

The environmental crisis is primarily a human problem (Nash 1991:89). Although a number of factors have contributed to the current crisis—including environmental factors such as the climate, topsoil, terrain, and animal species of a given region—the overriding factors can be traced to our use of technology, our social systems and the demands they place on the environment, and our worldview (see the discussion of the human-environment relations model in chapter 1). Humans have been unable or unwilling to live within the natural limits of the environment. Our actions have impacted the environment so that it is unable to sustain our standard of living or our social system without being further altered. Our interrelationship with the environment resembles the trajectory of a downward spiral; developing human social systems place increasing demands on the environment that the environment is increasingly unable to absorb.

As a human problem, the environmental crisis has a moral dimension. Human beings have created the crisis, and it is our actions that "adversely affect the good of humans and otherkind in our relationships" (Nash 1991:23). Humans are morally responsible for alleviating the crisis. Consequently, environmental concern falls within the domain of religion as well as science. Religion can provide us with a symbolic perception of the world. Whereas science can teach us about the diverse ecosystems in which we live, religion can provide us with the moral motivation to live within the constraints of those ecosystems. In a recent statement entitled "Preserving and Cherishing the Earth: An Appeal for Joint Commitment in Science and Religion," a group of prominent scientists, headed by Carl Sagan, emphasized the critical role that needs to be played by both science and religion:

> As scientists, many of us have had profound experiences of awe and reverence before the universe. We understand that what is regarded as sacred is more likely to be treated with care and respect. Our planetary home should be so regarded. Efforts to

safeguard and cherish the environment need to be infused with a vision of the sacred. At the same time, a much wider and deeper understanding of science and technology is needed. If we do not understand the problem, it is unlikely we will be able to fix it. Thus there is a vital role for both religion and science.

The response of world religions to the environmental crisis has been positive. From every corner of the globe religious leaders have emphasized how their faith calls its adherents to revere and care for the natural world. This is equally true for Christianity. Theologians have stressed the intrinsic value that the Christian faith ascribes to the natural world and how humans themselves are called to act in the world as benevolent stewards rather than as despots who exploit nature for their own ends.[3] The Bible, however, is rarely called upon to address the problems of the environmental crisis. The Bible is neglected because many ecologically concerned Christians— especially theologians—believe that either the Bible offers no insights for resolving our present crisis or the Bible is part of the problem, contributing to the environmental crisis. In most cases a few individual passages have been singled out as anthropocentric and thus interpreted as supportive of human exploitation of nature. This is unfortunate; it is "proof-texting of the worst sort" (Nash 1991:75). Our study of ancient Israel's worldview and values toward nature, however, does not support this common interpretation.

THE BIBLICAL WORLDVIEW

If religion is a critical ingredient of any solution to the environmental crisis, then the Bible's contribution must be considered, for it is at the heart of the Christian faith, serving as the foundation for Christian thought and practice. Furthermore, it is our contention that the Bible has a valuable contribution to make, for the Bible presents us with a worldview that recognizes both the intrinsic worth of the natural world and the special position of human beings within the natural world. According to the Israelite worldview, both humans and the rest

---

[3] Admittedly, this is a recent development in Christian theology (Santmire 1985:3–7).

of the natural world share the same status as parts of the creation of God. Both humans and nature are dependent upon God for existence, and both, as the result of God's creative activity, are intrinsically valuable.[4] Nevertheless, humans are exceptional in creation. The Bible uses the metaphors of the "image of God" and the "knowledge of good and evil" to articulate the unique ability of humans to transcend their creaturely status and to act like the creator. Humans can transform the natural world for their own purposes; they can create culture. Yet despite their exceptional character, humans can never escape their natural limits. Humans are ultimately bound to nature; they are affected by the corruption of nature and die like all natural beings.

Appropriating this aspect of the biblical worldview into discussion of the environmental crisis is straightforward. This worldview emphasizes the oneness that we share with the rest of the natural world and thus compels us to care for and preserve our natural environment. Similarly, the recognition that we are exceptional frees us from the bondage of nature. We need not passively accept all that nature hands us—disease, pestilence, drought, flood, and other aspects of nature that threaten human life. We have the power to shape the natural world so that it is more suitable to human habitation. The difficulty, of course, is balancing our development of culture with care and preservation of nature. We must turn to the sciences and other disciplines to establish the limits of each, but the biblical worldview emphasizes that both are essential aspects of any environmental agenda.

Other aspects of the biblical worldview are more difficult to appropriate into the context of the current crisis. An important consequence of this worldview's integral link between humans and the natural world is that human actions have ramifications in nature. This in itself is not problematic, but the Bible gives this connection a moral tone. When the Israelites follow the commands of God's covenant, such as, for example, by worshipping Yahweh alone or by observing the Sabbath, the earth will flourish with life. When they reject

---

[4] Value, of course, is not of one kind. Something can have economic value, scientific value, recreational value, or sacramental value, to name just a few. On the various values of the natural world, see Rolston 1981 and LaBar 1986.

God's commands by following their own desires, the land will
become sterile. The people's sins cause the disintegration of
creation or the ritual pollution of the land. Can such a morally
based dimension of the biblical worldview be relevant to
modern environmentalist issues? The problem with this worldview is summed up by a scholar who is otherwise in favor of
the Bible's contribution to environmentalism:

> A society which explains destruction of pasturage as the result
> of God's anger over idolatry or insincerity in Temple sacrifices
> rather than as the direct outcome of climatic fluctuation or
> overgrazing may have little to offer modern resource manage-
> ment. Few environmentalists today believe that environmental
> deterioration results from oppression of widows and orphans.
> Moreover, the Bible's environmental imagery, blessings, and
> curses refer specifically to one small piece of Middle Eastern
> territory with its own unique ecological geography. Biblical
> environmental messages may be very difficult to translate to
> other places where the climate and agricultural economy are
> quite different. (Kay 1988:327)

In order to translate these aspects of biblical worldview
into an environmentally relevant theology, we must guard
against two similar yet opposite dangers: literalism and anachronism. Literalism would deny the metaphorical and mythic
character of the biblical texts. It would strip the words of their
symbolic referents, reducing them to expressions of mundane
reality. Such a literal understanding of the biblical texts would
prove to be irrelevant to modern environmental issues because
it would presuppose a world that is at odds with the world of
contemporary experience. Human sin as a rejection of the
commands of God does not pollute the land. It does not bring
drought on the land or cause the earth to withhold its produce.
Similarly, human acts of faithfulness to God do not necessarily
correspond to a productive and healthy environment.

Anachronism would deny that our world, our ideas, and
our problems are different from those of the ancient Israelites.
It would read the biblical texts from the perspective of our own
concerns. This approach clearly makes the biblical texts more
attractive for use in contemporary issues, but it lacks consideration for the biblical writers (it denies that they could think
differently from us) and disregards a sense of history (it denies
that things change over time and will continue to do so). Our

understanding of the pollution of the land is not what the biblical writers meant by stating that human sin pollutes the land. Similarly, the environmentalists' warnings of coming ecological catastrophes are not equivalent to the prophets' threats of a cosmic collapse. The biblical writers did not envision our current environmental crisis, nor should we expect them to have addressed it.

The biblical references describing the integral link between humans and the natural world are relevant to modern environmental issues when they are interpreted at the metaphorical and mythic level. The biblical worldview can offer us a symbolic perception of the world. At this level the Bible emphasizes the mutual interdependence that human beings have with the rest of nature. We are dependent upon the natural environment for survival, and although culture enables us to overcome many of the limits of the natural world, it does not free us entirely from the constraints of nature or from our own natural limits. As a result, our fate is integrally linked to the fate of the natural world. By destroying the environment, we are ultimately destroying ourselves. Similarly, nature is dependent upon humankind. The biblical worldview cannot envision a creation without humans (Frymer-Kensky 1987a: 236). Although some environmentalists maintain that the earth does not need humans, the biblical worldview implies that humans are as valuable to the environment as any of the numerous species that face extinction. We are part of nature, and our extinction also would be a loss to the splendor of the natural world.

The Bible places this mutual interdependence of humans and nature within a moral framework; humans adversely affect the natural world when they sin against the commands of God. These commands are not arbitrary. At the symbolic level, they are an expression of God's righteousness and justice manifested in the order of creation. Perhaps the modern environmental discussion could benefit from this aspect of the biblical texts. Is destruction of the environment a moral concern? Are those who actively participate in destroying the creation sinning against God the creator? If so, what abuse of the environment constitutes sin? The current environmental crisis is typically presented in either an anthropocentric (the concern for the future of human life) or biocentric (the concern for all types of life) perspective. Such a discussion could place the current crisis in a theocentric (the concern for God) perspective and symbolically ascribe moral significance to our actions in relation to the environment.

ESCHATOLOGICAL VALUES

An axiom of the environmental movement has been that a society's treatment of the environment is determined by its values toward the natural world. The historical evidence, however, does not support this presumption. Rarely does a society have a homogeneous view of the natural world, and its values toward nature are rarely applicable to all ecological niches. The ancient Israelites, for example, embrace all three value orientations but each in relation to a particular group and under different circumstances. Moreover, societies tend to be inconsistent, even contradictory, in their treatment of the environment in relation to their disposition toward the environment. Societies with benevolent attitudes about the environment have damaged the environment on the same scale as societies with apparently callous attitudes.[5] The causes of the environmental crisis are too complex to be traced to values toward the natural world (Tuan 1970; Dubos 1972:153–61; Kay 1985). This conclusion is confirmed by the model of human-environment relations (figure 1). Human values toward nature (part of the worldview component) cannot be separated

---

[5]Environmentalists and theologians alike have criticized the dominant mastery-over-nature orientation of Westerners as destructive to the ecosystem. Indeed, this orientation can foster exploitation, but it should be noted that other value orientations are equally problematic when misappropriated. Consider the conclusion of an Asian theologian:

> Many of our Asian cultures stress the theme of harmony in nature and the need for man to live in harmony with nature. If, however, along with this emphasis, we do not recover for Asia the biblical emphasis of the special position given to man in creation and the responsibility given to him to maintain order and peace, the idea of harmony in nature would at best be a romantic notion and at worst the basis for a fatalism which allows nature and its laws, as, for example, astrology and the terror manifestations in nature, to control man. (Niles 1978:79—80)

The various value orientations cannot be taken out of their ecological context.

from the social system and the use of technology. A new, benevolent attitude toward nature is insufficient by itself to solve the environmental crisis. It must be accompanied by changes in the social system and the use of technology.

The biblical worldview and values toward nature might serve as a catalyst for transforming our social systems and our use of technology. Their emphasis on the harmony between humans and nature within a moral framework can provide us with a sacred perception of the world. We should live within the constraints and limits of the natural environment because they demarcate the order of creation established by God. Unfortunately, this solution to the environmental crisis is not realistic nor will it be ultimately successful. In an increasingly pluralistic society, a consensus on worldviews and values toward nature is not likely to occur. Moreover, the current environmental crisis exhibits an overall loss of human control in human-environment relations. Our social systems have become semiautonomous; they generate their own needs and values; they place demands on us in addition to the environment. Consequently, our worldview and values toward nature do not readily correspond to our treatment of the environment. The lack of social and moral consensus further contributes to our loss of control (Bennett 1976:68).

The biblical texts place humankind's symbolic corruption of nature in an eschatological context. According to the Bible, all of creation stands in need of God's redemption. This includes not only humankind but also the natural world. Human sin permeates the creation, and humans are inclined towards evil, continually refusing to follow the ways of God. The Bible, therefore, offers a theological explanation for the incongruity between a society's attitude toward nature and their treatment of the environment. The ultimate problem is human nature. The ultimate solution is the redemption of God. The biblical worldview and values toward nature offer an eschatological perspective that symbolically places the environmental crisis in a larger, ultimate context (cf. Schwarz 1974; Muratore 1986).

The Bible stands in judgment over all human efforts to recreate the natural world. Such efforts are valuable, and indeed we are called to them, but such efforts will not be ultimately successful any more than our efforts to free the world from war, poverty, and suffering. These ideals are worth striving for, but the history of humankind demonstrates that they are not human realities. The biblical texts, however, offer hope beyond our human failures. Because it is based on the premise that God is the creator, the Bible includes the hope that God will redeem us and the rest of the world in a new creation. Humans will be transformed so that we are inclined to follow God's commands, and the natural world, which has been polluted through human sin, will be recreated. The eschatological dimension of the biblical worldview thus calls us to care for the natural environment in anticipation of God's coming redemption of creation rather than to restore what has been lost. The biblical worldview generates eschatological values. Our actions on behalf of the environment foreshadow and participate in God's own future redemptive acts on behalf of a new creation.

SELECT BIBLIOGRAPHY

Aharoni, Yohanan
    1979   *The Land of the Bible: A Historical Geography.* Revised Edition. Philadelphia: Westminster.

Albrecht, Don, Gordon Bultena, Eric Hoiberg, and Peter Nowak
    1982   "The New Environmental Paradigm Scale." *Journal of Environmental Education* 13:39–43.

Albrektson, Bertil
    1967   *History and the Gods: An Essay on the Idea of Historical Events as Divine Manifestation in the Ancient Near East and in Israel.* Lund: CWK Gleerup.

Albright, William Foxwell
    1939   "The Babylonian Matter in the Predeuteronomic Primeval History (JE) in Gen 1–11." *Journal of Biblical Literature* 58:91–103.
    1978   *Yahweh and the Gods of Canaan: A Historical Analysis of Two Contrasting Faiths.* Winona Lake, Ind.: Eisenbrauns.

Allen, James P.
    1988   *Genesis in Egypt: The Philosophy of Ancient Egyptian Creation Accounts.* Yale Egyptological Studies 2. New Haven: Yale University Press.

Amit, Yairah
    1990   "Biblical Utopianism: A Mapmaker's Guide to Eden." *Union Seminary Quarterly Review* 44:11–17.

Andersen, Francis I.
　　1987　　　"On reading Gen 1–3." In *Backgrounds for the Bible*.
　　　　　　　Edited by M. O'Connor and D. Freedman. Pages 137–
　　　　　　　50. Winona Lake, Ind.: Eisenbrauns.

Andersen, Francis I., and David N. Freedman
　　1980　　　*Hosea*. The Anchor Bible 24. Garden City: Doubleday.

Anderson, Bernhard W.
　　1975　　　"Human Dominion over Nature." In *Biblical Studies
　　　　　　　in Contemporary Thought*. Edited by M. Ward. Pages
　　　　　　　27–45. Somerville, Mass.: Greeno, Hadden, & Co.
　　1977　　　"A Stylistic Study of the Priestly Creation Story." In
　　　　　　　*Canon and Authority: Essays in Old Testament Reli-
　　　　　　　gion and Theology*. Edited by G. W. Coats and B. O.
　　　　　　　Long. Pages 148–62. Philadelphia: Fortress.
　　1978　　　"From Analysis to Synthesis: The Interpretation of
　　　　　　　Genesis 1–11." *Journal of Biblical Literature* 97:23–
　　　　　　　39.
　　1984a　　 "Creation and Ecology." In *Creation in the Old Testa-
　　　　　　　ment*. Issues in Religion and Theology 6. Edited by
　　　　　　　B. W. Anderson. Pages 152–71. Philadelphia:
　　　　　　　Fortress.
　　1984b　　 "Introduction: Mythopoeic and Theological Dimen-
　　　　　　　sions of Biblical Creation Faith." In *Creation in the
　　　　　　　Old Testament*. Issues in Religion and Theology 6.
　　　　　　　Edited by B. W. Anderson. Pages 1–24. Philadelphia:
　　　　　　　Fortress.
　[1967]1987　*Creation Versus Chaos: The Reinterpretation of
　　　　　　　Mythical Symbolism in the Bible*. New York: Associ-
　　　　　　　ation. Reprint. Philadelphia: Fortress.

Baker, J. A.
　　1975　　　"Biblical Attitudes to Nature." In *Man and Nature*.
　　　　　　　Edited by H. Montefiore. Pages 87–109. London:
　　　　　　　Collins.

Baltzer, Klaus
　　1971　　　*The Covenant Formulary: In Old Testament, Jewish,
　　　　　　　and Early Christian Writings*. Translated by D. E.
　　　　　　　Green. Philadelphia: Fortress.

Baly, Denis
　　1974　　　*The Geography of the Bible*. Revised Edition. New
　　　　　　　York: Harper & Row.

Barbour, Ian G.

1974   *Myths, Models, and Paradigms: A Comparative
         Study in Science and Religion.* San Francisco:
         HarperCollins.

Barr, James

1960   "Theophany and Anthropomorphism in the Old Tes-
         tament." In *Congress Volume, Oxford 1959.* Supple-
         ments to Vetus Testamentum 7. Pages 31–38.
         Leiden: E. J. Brill.

1961   *The Semantics of Biblical Language.* Oxford: Oxford
         University Press.

1968/9   "The Image of God in the Book of Genesis—A Study
         of Terminology." *Bulletin of the John Rylands
         Library* 51:11–26.

1969   *Biblical Words for Time.* Naperville, Ill.: A. R.
         Allenson.

1972   "Man and Nature: The Ecological Controversy and
         the Old Testament." *Bulletin of the John Rylands
         Library* 55:9–32.

1992   *The Garden of Eden and the Hope of Immortality.*
         Minneapolis: Fortress.

Barré, Lloyd M.

1988   "The Riddle of the Flood Chronology." *Journal for
         the Study of the Old Testament* 41:3–20.

Batto, Bernard F.

1983   "The Reed Sea: *Requiescat in Pace.*" *Journal of Bibli-
         cal Literature* 102:27–35.

1987a   "The Covenant of Peace: A Neglected Ancient Near
         Eastern Motif." *Catholic Biblical Quarterly* 49:187–211.

1987b   "The Sleeping God: An Ancient Near Eastern Motif
         of Divine Sovereignty." *Biblica* 68:153–77.

1992   *Slaying the Dragon: Mythmaking in the Biblical Tra-
         dition.* Louisville: Westminster/John Knox.

Beckman, Gary M.

1983   *Hittite Birth Rituals.* Studien zu den Bogazköy-
         Texten 29. Wiesbaden: Otto Harrassowitz.

Benjamin, Don C.

1989   "Israel's God: Mother and Midwife." *Biblical Theol-
         ogy Bulletin* 19:115–20.

Bennett, John W.
1976   *The Ecological Transition: Cultural Anthropology
            and Human Adaptation.* New York: Pergamon.

Ben-Yoseph, Jacob
1985   "The Climate in Eretz Israel during Biblical Times."
            Hebrew Studies 26:225–39.

Bergant, Dianne
1991   "Is the Biblical Worldview Anthropocentric?" *New
            Theology Review* 4, 2:5–14.

Berquist, Jon L.
1993   "The Dangerous Waters of Justice and Righteousness:
            Amos 5:18–27." *Biblical Theology Bulletin* 23:54–63.

Bird, Phyllis A.
1981   "'Male and Female He Created Them': Gen 1:27b in
            the Context of the Priestly Creation Account." *Har-
            vard Theological Review* 74:129–59.
1987   "Genesis 1–3 as a Source for a Contemporary Theol-
            ogy of Sexuality." *Ex Auditu* 3:31–44.

Bjerke, Svein
1979   "Ecology of Religion, Evolutionism and Compara-
            tive Religion." In *Science of Religion: Studies in
            Methodology.* Edited by L. Honko. Pages 237–48.
            The Hague: Mouton.

Blaikie, Norman W. H.
1992   "The Nature and Origins of Ecological World Views:
            An Australian Study." *Social Science Quarterly*
            73:144–65.

Blenkinsopp, Joseph
1976   "Structure of P." *Catholic Biblical Quarterly* 38:275–92.

Boissevain, Jeremy
1982/3   "Seasonal Variations on Some Mediterranean
            Themes." *Ethnologia Europaea* 13:6–12.

Boman, Thorlief
1960   *Hebrew Thought Compared with the Greek.* Lon-
            don: SCM.

Bourdieu, Pierre
1963   "The Attitude of the Algerian Peasant toward
            Time." In *Mediterranean Countrymen: Essays in the
            Social Anthropology of the Mediterranean*. Edited
            by J. Pitt-Rivers. Pages 55–72. Paris: Mouton.

Brueggemann, Walter
1972   "From Dust to Kingship." *Zeitschrift für die alt-
            testamentliche Wissenschaft* 84:1–18.

Carmichael, Calum M.
1992   "The Paradise Myth: Interpreting without Jewish
            and Christian Spectacles." In *A Walk in the Garden:
            Biblical, Iconographical and Literary Images of
            Eden*. Journal for the Study of the Old Testament
            Supplement Series 136. Edited by P. Morris and
            D. Sawyer. Pages 47–63. Sheffield: JSOT.

Carney, Thomas F.
1975   *The Shape of the Past: Models and Antiquity*. Law-
            rence, Kans.: Coronado.

Carroll, Michael P.
1985   "One More Time: Leviticus Revisited." In *Anthropo-
            logical Approaches to the Old Testament*. Issues in
            Religion and Theology 8. Edited by B. Lang. Pages
            117–26. Philadelphia: Fortress.

Catton, William R., and Riley E. Dunlap
1978   "Environmental Sociology: A New Paradigm." *Amer-
            ican Sociologist* 13:41–49.
1980   "A New Ecological Paradigm for Post-Exuberant So-
            ciology." *American Behavioral Scientist* 24:15–47.

Černy, L.
1948   *The Day of Yahweh and Some Related Problems.*
            Prague: Nákladem Filosofické Fakulty University
            Karlovy.

Childs, Brevard S.
1959   "The Enemy from the North and the Chaos Tradi-
            tion." *Journal of Biblical Literature* 78:187–98.
1970   *Biblical Theology in Crisis*. Philadelphia:
            Westminster.

Clifford, Richard J.
  1972   *The Cosmic Mountain in Canaan and the Old Testa-
               ment.* Cambridge: Harvard University Press.
  1980   "Psalm 89: A Lament over the Davidic Ruler's
               Continued Failure." *Harvard Theological Review*
               73:35–47.
  1984a   "Cosmogonies in the Ugaritic Texts and in the
               Bible." *Orientalia* 53:183–201.
  1984b   *Fair Spoken and Persuading: An Interpretation of
               Second Isaiah.* New York: Paulist.
  1985   "The Hebrew Scriptures and the Theology of Cre-
               ation." *Theological Studies* 46:507–23.

Clifford, Richard J., and John J. Collins
  1992   "Introduction: The Theology of Creation Tradi-
               tions." In *Creation in the Biblical Traditions.* The
               Catholic Biblical Quarterly Monograph Series 24.
               Pages 1–15. Washington, D.C.: The Catholic Biblical
               Association of America.

Cohn, Robert L.
  1982   *The Shape of Sacred Space: Four Biblical Studies.*
               AAR Studies in Religion 23. Chico, Calif.: Scholars.

Coogan, Michael D.
  1978   *Stories from Ancient Canaan.* Philadelphia:
               Westminster.

Coote, Robert B.
  1990   *Early Israel: A New Horizon.* Minneapolis: Fortress.

Coote, Robert B., and David R. Ord
  1989   *The Bible's First History.* Philadelphia: Fortress.
  1991   *In the Beginning: Creation and the Priestly History.*
               Minneapolis: Fortress.

Cornelius, Izak
  1988   "Paradise Motifs in the 'Eschatology' of the Minor
               Prophets and the Iconography of the Ancient Near
               East. The Concepts of Fertility, Water, Trees, and
               'Tierfrieden' and Gen 2–3." *Journal of Northwest Se-
               mitic Languages* 14:41–83.

Cox, Harvey
  1965   *The Secular City.* New York: Macmillan.

Crenshaw, James L.
1992   "When Form and Content Clash: The Theology of
            Job 38:1–40:5." In *Creation in the Biblical Tradi-
            tions*. The Catholic Biblical Quarterly Monograph
            Series 24. Edited by R. J. Clifford and J. J. Collins.
            Pages 70–84. Washington, D.C.: The Catholic Bibli-
            cal Association of America.

Cross, Frank M.
1973   *Canaanite Myth and Hebrew Epic: Essays in the His-
            tory of the Religion of Israel*. Cambridge: Harvard
            University Press.
1976   "The 'Olden Gods' in Ancient Near Eastern Creation
            Myths." In *Magnalia Dei: The Mighty Acts of God*.
            Festschrift for G. Ernest Wright. Edited by F. M.
            Cross, et al. Pages 329–38. Garden City: Doubleday.
1988   "The Redemption of Nature." *Princeton Seminary
            Bulletin* 10:94–104.

Dalley, Stephanie
1991   *Myths from Mesopotamia: Creation, the Flood,
            Gilgamesh, and Others*. Oxford: Oxford University
            Press.

Davies, Douglas
1977   "An Interpretation of Sacrifice in Leviticus."
            Zeitschrift für die alttestamentliche Wissenschaft
            89:388–98.

Day, John
1985   *God's Conflict with the Dragon and the Sea: Echoes
            of a Canaanite Myth in the Old Testament*. Cam-
            bridge: Cambridge University Press.

DeGuglielmo, Antonine
1957   "The Fertility of the Land in the Messianic Prophe-
            cies." *Catholic Biblical Quarterly* 19:306–11.

Delaney, Carol
1987   "Seeds of Honor, Fields of Shame." In *Honor and
            Shame and the Unity of the Mediterranean*. Ameri-
            can Anthropological Association Special Publica-
            tion 22. Edited by D. D. Gilmore. Pages 35–48.
            Washington, D.C.: American Anthropological
            Association.

De Moor, Johannes C.
    1980   "El, the Creator." In *The Bible World: Essays in
                Honor of Cyrus H. Gordon.* Edited by G. Rendsburg,
                et al. Pages 171–87. New York: KTAV.

Dequeker, L.
    1974   "Noah and Israel: The Everlasting Divine Covenant
                with Mankind." In *Questions disputées d'Ancien
                Testament: Méthode et Théologie.* Bibliotheca
                Ephemeridum Theologicarum Lovaniensium 33.
                Edited by C. Brekelmans. Pages 115–29. Leuven:
                Leuven University Press.
    1977   "'Green Herbage and Trees Bearing Fruit' (Gen. 1:28–
                30; 9:1–3): Vegetarianism or Predominance of Man
                over the Animals?" *Bijdragen* 38:118–27.

De Roche, Michael
    1980   "Zephaniah I 2–3: The 'Sweeping' of Creation."
                Vetus Testamentum 30:104–9.
    1981   "The Reversal of Creation in Hosea." *Vetus Testa-
                mentum* 31:400–409.

Derr, Thomas S.
    1975   "Religion's Responsibility for the Ecological Crisis:
                An Argument Run Amok." *World View* 18:39–45.

DeVries, Simon J.
    1975   *Yesterday, Today and Tomorrow: Time and History
                in the Old Testament.* Grand Rapids: Wm. B.
                Eerdmans.

Douglas, Mary
    1966   *Purity and Danger: An Analysis of the Concepts of
                Pollution and Taboo.* London: Ark.

Drori, Israel, and Aharon Horowitz
    1988/9   "Tel Lachish: Environment and Subsistence during
                the Middle Bronze, Late Bronze and Iron Ages." *Tel
                Aviv* 15–16:206–11.

Drumbell, W. J.
    1985   "Genesis 1—3, Ecology, and the Dominion of Man."
                Crux 21:16–26.

Dubos, René
1972   *A God Within*. New York: Charles Scribner's Sons.

Eichrodt, Walther
1962   "In the Beginning: A Contribution to the Interpreta-
            tion of the First Word of the Bible." In *Israel's Pro-
            phetic Heritage: Essays in Honor of James
            Muilenburg*. Edited by B. W. Anderson and
            W. Harrelson. Pages 1–10. New York: Harper & Row.
1967   *Theology of the Old Testament*. Volume II. Trans-
            lated by J. A. Baker. Philadelphia: Westminster.

Eilberg-Schwartz, Howard
1990   *The Savage in Judaism: An Anthropology of Israe-
            lite Religion and Ancient Judaism*. Bloomington: In-
            diana University Press.

Eissfeldt, Otto
1932   *Baal Zaphon, Zeus Kasios und der Durchzug der
            Israeliten durchs Meer*. Halle: Max Niemeyer.

Eliade, Mircea
1959   *The Sacred and the Profane: The Nature of Religion*.
            Translated by W. R. Trask. San Diego: Harcourt
            Brace Jovanovich.
1963   *Myth and Reality*. Translated by W. R. Trask. New
            York: Harper & Row.

Ellen, Roy
1982   *Environment, Subsistence and System: The Ecology
            of Small Scale Social Formations*. Cambridge: Cam-
            bridge University Press.

Everson, A. J.
1974   "The Days of Yahweh." *Journal of Biblical Literature*
            93:329–37.

Faulkner, Raymond O.
1969   *The Ancient Egyptian Pyramid Texts*. Oxford:
            Clarendon.

Fensham, F. C.
1965   "The Destruction of Mankind in the Near East." *An-
            nali, Istituto universitario orientale di Napoli* n.s.
            15:31–37.

1966   "A Possible Origin of the Concept of the Day of the
             Lord." In *Biblical Essays*. Die Ou-Testamentiese
             Werkgemeenskap in Suid-Afrika 9. Pages 90–97.
             Potchefstroom.

Ferré, Frederick
1968   "Metaphors, Models, and Religion." *Soundings*
             51:327–45.

Fishbane, Michael
1971   "Jeremiah IV 23–26 and Job III 3–13. A Recovered
             Use of the Creation Pattern." *Vetus Testamentum*
             21:151–62.

Fisher, Loren R.
1965   "Creation at Ugarit and in the Old Testament."
             Vetus Testamentum 15:313–24.

Frankfort, Henri
1948   *Kingship and the Gods: A Study of Ancient Near
             Eastern Religion as the Integration of Society and
             Nature*. Chicago: University of Chicago Press.

Fretheim, Terrence E.
1984   *The Suffering of God: An Old Testament Perspec-
             tive*. Overtures to Biblical Theology. Philadelphia:
             Fortress.
1987   "Nature's Praise of God in the Psalms." *Ex Auditu*
             3:16–30.
1991a   *Exodus*. Interpretation. Louisville: John Knox.
1991b   "The Reclamation of Creation: Redemption and Law
             in Exodus." *Interpretation* 45:354–65.

Freudenberger, C. Dean
1990   *Global Dust Bowl: Can We Stop the Destruction of
             the Land Before It's Too Late?* Minneapolis:
             Augsburg.

Frick, Frank S.
1985   *The Formation of the State in Ancient Israel*. The So-
             cial World of Biblical Antiquity 3. Sheffield: Almond.

Friedman, Richard E.
1987   *Who Wrote the Bible?* New York: Harper & Row.

Frymer-Kensky, Tikva

1977   "Atrahasis Epic and its Significance for Our Under-
     standing of Genesis 1–9." *Biblical Archaeologist*
     40:147–55.

1983   "Pollution, Purification, and Purgation in Biblical Is-
     rael." In *The Word of the Lord Shall Go Forth: Es-
     says in Honor of David Noel Freedman.* Edited by
     C. L. Meyers and M. O'Connor. Pages 399–414. Wi-
     nona Lake, Ind.: Eisenbrauns.

1987a   "Biblical Cosmology." In *Backgrounds for the Bible.*
     Edited by M. O'Connor and D. Freedman. Pages 231–
     40. Winona Lake, Ind.: Eisenbrauns.

1987b   "The Planting of Man: A Study in Biblical Imagery."
     In *Love and Death in the Ancient Near East.* Edited
     by J. H. Marks and R. M. Good. Pages 129–36.
     Guildford, Conn.: Four Quarters.

Geertz, Clifford

1976   "'From a Native's Point of View': On the Nature of
     Anthropological Understanding." In *Meaning in An-
     thropology.* Edited by K. H. Basso and H. A. Selby.
     Pages 221–37. Albuquerque: University of New Mex-
     ico Press.

Geller, Jack M., and Paul Lasley

1985   "The New Environmental Paradigm Scale: A Reex-
     amination." *Journal of Environmental Education*
     17:9–12.

Gnuse, Robert

1989   *Heilsgeschichte as a Model for Biblical Theology:
     The Debate Concerning the Uniqueness and Signifi-
     cance of Israel's Worldview.* College Theology Soci-
     ety Studies in Religion 4. Lanham: University Press
     of America.

1991   "Israelite Settlement of Canaan: A Peaceful Internal
     Process." *Biblical Theology Bulletin* 21:56–66, 109–17.

Gordis, Robert

1985   "Job and Ecology." *Hebrew Annual Review* 9:189–202.

Gordon, B. L.

1971   "Sacred Directions, Orientation, and the Top of the
     Map." *History of Religions* 10:211–27.

Gordon, Cyrus H.
    1977   "Paternity at Two Levels." *Journal of Biblical Litera-*
                ture 96:101.
    1982   "Khnum and El." *Scripta Hiersolymitana* 28:203–14.

Gore, Albert
    1992   *Earth in the Balance: Ecology and the Human Spirit.*
                Boston: Houghton Mifflin.

Gottwald, Norman K.
    1985   *The Hebrew Bible: A Socio-Literary Introduction.*
                Philadelphia: Fortress.

Gowan, Donald E.
    1986   *Eschatology in the Old Testament.* Philadelphia:
                Fortress.

Grønbæk, Jakob H.
    1985   "Baal's Battle with Yam—A Canaanite Creation
                Fight." *Journal for the Study of the Old Testament*
                33:27–44.

Gulick, Walter B.
    1991   "The Bible and Ecological Spirituality." *Theology*
                Today 48:182–94.

Gunkel, Hermann
    [1895]1984 "The Influence of Babylonian Mythology Upon the
                Biblical Creation Story." In *Creation in the Old Tes-*
                tament. Issues in Religion and Theology 6. Edited
                by B. W. Anderson. Pages 25–52. Philadelphia:
                Fortress.

Haldar, Alfred
    1950   *The Notion of the Desert in Sumero-Accadian and*
                West-Semitic Religions. Uppsala Universitets
                Årsskrift 1950:3. Uppsala: B. B. Lundequistska.

Hall, Edward T.
    1976   *Beyond Culture.* Garden City: Anchor/Doubleday.

Halpern, Baruch
    1981   *The Constitution of the Monarchy of Israel.* Harvard
                Semitic Monographs 25. Chico, Calif.: Scholars.

Hanson, Paul D.
  1979   *The Dawn of Apocalyptic: The Historical and Socio-
           logical Roots of Jewish Apocalyptic Eschatology.*
           Philadelphia: Fortress.

Harner, Philip B.
  1967   "Creation Faith in Deutero–Isaiah." *Vetus Testamen-
           tum* 17:298–306.

Harrelson, Walter
  1970   "The Significance of Cosmology in the Ancient Near
           East." In *Translating and Understanding the Old
           Testament: Essays in Honor of Herbert Gordon May.*
           Edited by H. T. Frank and W. L. Reed. Pages 237–52.
           Nashville: Abingdon.

Hasel, Gerhard F.
  1972   "Significance of the Cosmology in Genesis 1 in rela-
           tion to Ancient Near Eastern Parallels." *Andrews
           University Seminary Studies* 10:1–20.
  1974   "The Polemical Nature of the Genesis Cosmology."
           Evangelical Quarterly 46:81–102.

Heidel, Alexander
  1951   *The Babylonian Genesis.* Chicago: University of Chi-
           cago Press.

Hiebert, Theodore
  1992a   "Theophany in the OT." In *The Anchor Bible Dictio-
           nary*, Vol. VI. Edited by D. N. Freedman. Pages 505–
           11. New York: Doubleday.
  1992b   "Warrior, Divine." In *The Anchor Bible Dictionary*,
           Vol. VI. Edited by D. N. Freedman. Pages 876–80.
           New York: Doubleday.

Hiers, Richard H.
  1984   "Ecology, Biblical Theology, and Methodology: Bibli-
           cal Perspectives on the Environment." *Zygon* 19:43–59.

Hillers, Delbert
  1969   *Covenant: The History of a Biblical Idea.* Baltimore:
           Johns Hopkins Press.
  1978   "Study of Psalm 148." *Catholic Biblical Quarterly*
           40:323–34.

1985   "Analyzing the Abominable: Our Understanding of
               Canaanite Religion." *Jewish Quarterly Review*
               75:253–69.

Hobbs, T. Raymond
1989   *A Time For War: A Study of Warfare in the Old Tes-
               tament.* Old Testament Studies 3. Wilmington: Mi-
               chael Glazier.

Hoffmann, Y.
1981   "The Day of the Lord as a Concept and a Term in the
               Prophetic Literature." *Zeitschrift für die alttesta-
               mentliche Wissenschaft* 93:37–50.

Hoffmeier, James K.
1983   "Some Thoughts on Genesis 1 and 2 and Egyptian
               Cosmology." *Journal of the Ancient Near Eastern So-
               ciety* 15:39–49.

Holladay, William L.
1986   *Jeremiah 1.* Hermeneia. Philadelphia: Fortress.

Holter, Knut
1990   "The Serpent in Eden as a Symbol of Israel's Politi-
               cal Enemies: A Yahwistic Criticism of the Solomo-
               nic Foreign Policy?" *Scandinavian Journal of the
               Old Testament* 1:106–12.

Honeyman, Alexander M.
1952   "Merismus in Biblical Hebrew." *Journal of Biblical
               Literature* 70:11–18.

Honko, Lauri
1984   "The Problem of Defining Myth." In *Sacred Narrative:
               Readings in the Theory of Myth.* Edited by A. Dundes.
               Pages 41–52. Berkeley: University of California Press.

Hopkins, David C.
1985   *The Highlands of Canaan: Agricultural Life in the
               Early Iron Age.* The Social World of Biblical Antiq-
               uity 3. Sheffield: Almond.
1987   "Life on the Land: The Subsistence Struggles of
               Early Israel." *Biblical Archaeologist* 50:178–91.

Hughes, J. Donald
1975 *Ecology in Ancient Civilizations*. Albuquerque: University of New Mexico Press.

Hultkrantz, Åke
1979 "Ecology of Religion: Its Scope and Methodology." In *Science of Religion: Studies in Methodology*. Edited by L. Honko. Pages 221–36. The Hague: Mouton.

Hutter, Manfred
1986 "Adam als Gärtner und König (Gen. 2, 8.15)." *Biblische Zeitschrift* 30:258–62.

Hutton, Rodney R.
1986 "God or Beast? Human Self-Understanding in Genesis 2–3." *Proceedings of the Eastern Great Lakes and Midwest Biblical Societies* 6:128–41.

Hyatt, J. Philip
1940 "The Peril from the North in Jeremiah." *Journal of Biblical Literature* 59:499–513.

Jacobsen, Thorkild
1946 "Mesopotamia: The Cosmos as a State." In *The Intellectual Adventure of Ancient Man: An Essay on Speculative Thought in the Ancient Near East*. Pages 125–84. Chicago: University of Chicago Press.
1968 "The Battle Between Marduk and Tiamat." *Journal of the American Oriental Society* 88:104–8.
1970 *Toward the Image of Tammuz and Other Essays on Mesopotamian History and Culture*. Edited by W. L. Moran. Cambridge: Harvard University Press.
1973 "Notes on Nintur." *Orientalia* n.s. 42:274–98.
1976 *The Treasures of Darkness: A History of Mesopotamian Religion*. New Haven: Yale University Press.
1984 *The Harab Myth*. Sources from the Ancient Near East 2/3. Malibu: Undena Publications.
1987a "The Graven Image." In *Ancient Israelite Religion: Essays in Honor of Frank Moore Cross*. Edited by P. D. Miller, et al. Pages 15–32. Philadelphia: Fortress.
1987b *The Harps that Once . . . : Sumerian Poetry in Translation*. New Haven: Yale University Press.

Jenson, Philip Peter
1992   *Graded Holiness: A Key to the Priestly Conception of the World.* Journal for the Study of the Old Testament Supplement Series 106. Sheffield: JSOT.

Jeremias, Jörg
1965   *Theophanie: Die Geschichte einer alttestamentlichen Gattung.* Wissenschaftlich Monographien zum Alten und Neuen Testament 10. Neukirchen-Vluyn: Neukirchen.
1976   "Theophany in the OT." In *The Interpreter's Dictionary of the Bible.* Supplementary Volume. Edited by K. Crim. Pages 896–98. Nashville: Abingdon.

Joines, Karen R.
1974   *Serpent Symbolism in the Old Testament: A Linguistic, Archaeological, and Literary Study.* Haddonfield, N.J.: Haddonfield House.

Jones, James M.
1988   "Cultural Differences in Temporal Perspective: Instrumental and Expressive." In *The Social Psychology of Time: New Perspectives.* Edited by J. E. McGrath. Pages 21–38. Newbury Park: Sage.

Kaiser, Otto
1972   *Isaiah 1–12.* Old Testament Library. Translated by R. A. Wilson. Philadelphia: Westminster.
1974   *Isaiah 13–39.* Old Testament Library. Translated by R. A. Wilson. Philadelphia: Westminster.

Kákosy, L.
1964   "Ideas about the Fallen State of the World in Egyptian Religion: Decline of the Golden Age." *Acta Orientalia Academiae Scientiarum Hungaricae* 17:205–16.

Kapelrud, Arvid S.
1963   "Temple Building, a Task for Gods and Kings." *Orientalia* 32:56–62.
1974   "Mythological Features in Genesis I and the Author's Intentions." *Vetus Testamentum* 24:178–86.
1980   "Creation in the Ras Shamra Texts." *Studia Theologica* 34:1–11.

Kaufman, Gordon D.
1972   "Problem for Theology: The Concept of Nature."
            Harvard Theological Review 65:337–66.

Kaufmann, Yehezkel
1960   *The Religion of Israel: From its Beginnings to the
            Babylonian Exile.* Translated and abridged by
            M. Greenberg. Chicago: University of Chicago Press.

Kay, Jeanne
1985   "Preconditions of Natural Resource Conservation."
            Agricultural History 59:124–35.
1988   "Concepts of Nature in the Hebrew Bible." *Environ-
            mental Ethics* 10:309–27.

Kearney, Michael
1984   *World View.* Novato, Calif.: Chandler & Sharp.

Kikawada, Isaac M.
1983   "The Double Creation of Mankind in Enki and
            Ninmah, Atrahasis I 1–351, and Genesis 1–2." *Iraq*
            45:43–5.

Klimkeit, Hans J.
1975   "Spatial Orientation in Mythical Thinking as Exem-
            plified in Ancient Egypt: Considerations toward a
            Geography of Religions." *History of Religions*
            14:266–81.

Kluckhohn, Florence R., and Fred L. Strodtbeck
[1961]1973 *Variations in Value Orientations.* Evanston, Ill.: Row,
            Peterson. Reprint. Westport, Conn.: Greenwood.

Knierim, Rolf
1981   "Cosmos and History in Israel's Theology." *Horizons
            in Biblical Theology* 3:59–123.

Knight, Douglas A.
1985   "Cosmogony and Order in the Hebrew Tradition." In
            *Cosmogony and Ethical Order: New Studies in Com-
            parative Ethics.* Edited by R. W. Lovin and F. E.
            Reynolds. Pages 133–57. Chicago: University of Chi-
            cago Press.

Koch, Klaus
1979 "The Old Testament View of Nature." *Anticipation* 25, January:47–52.
1982 *The Prophets. Volume I: The Assyrian Period.* Philadelphia: Fortress.
1983 "Is There a Doctrine of Retribution in the Old Testament?" In *Theodicy in the Old Testament.* Issues in Religion and Theology 4. Edited by J. L. Crenshaw. Pages 57–87. Philadelphia: Fortress.

Komoróczy, G.
1973 "The Separation of Sky and Earth: The Cycle of Kumarbi and the Myths of Cosmogony in Mesopotamia." *Acta Antiqua Academiae Scientiarum Hungaricae* 21:21–45.

Kramer, Samuel N.
1972 *Sumerian Mythology: A Study of Spiritual and Literary Achievement in the Third Millennium B.C.* Revised Edition. Philadelphia: University of Pennsylvania Press.

Kuntz, J. Kenneth
1967 *The Self-Revelation of God.* Philadelphia: Westminster.

LaBar, Martin
1986 "A Biblical Perspective on Non–Human Organisms: Values, Moral Considerability, and Moral Agency." In *Religion and Environmental Crisis.* Edited by E. C. Hargrove. Pages 76–93. Athens: University of Georgia Press.

Lakoff, George, and Mark Johnson
1980 *Metaphors We Live By.* Chicago: University of Chicago Press.

Lambert, Wilfred G.
1965 "A New Look at the Babylonian Background of Genesis." *Journal of Theological Studies* 16:287–300.

Lambert, Wilfred G., and A. R. Millard
1969 *Atra-ḫasīs: The Babylonian Story of the Flood.* Oxford: Clarendon.

Leach, Edmund
  1976   *Culture and Communication.* Cambridge: Cambridge
            University Press.

Leeuw, Gerardus van der
  1957   "Primordial Time and Final Time." In *Man and
            Time: Papers from the Eranos Yearbooks.* Edited by
            J. Campbell. Pages 324–50. New York: Pantheon.

Lesko, Leonard H.
  1991   "Ancient Egyptian Cosmogonies and Cosmology." In
            *Religion in Ancient Egypt: Gods, Myths, and Per-
            sonal Practice.* Edited by B. E. Shafer. Pages 88–122.
            Ithaca, N.Y.: Cornell University Press.

Levenson, Jon D.
  1976   *Theology of the Program of Restoration of Ezekiel
            40–48.* Harvard Semitic Monograph 10. Missoula,
            Mont.: Scholars.
  1985   *Sinai and Zion: An Entry into the Jewish Bible.* San
            Francisco: Harper & Row.
  1988   *Creation and the Persistence of Evil: The Jewish
            Drama of Divine Omnipotence.* San Francisco:
            Harper & Row.

Lichtheim, Miriam
  1973   *Ancient Egyptian Literature. Volume I: The Old and
            Middle Kingdoms.* Berkeley: University of California
            Press.
  1976   *Ancient Egyptian Literature. Volume II: The New
            Kingdom.* Berkeley: University of California Press.
  1980   *Ancient Egyptian Literature. Volume III: The Late
            Period.* Berkeley: University of California Press.

Lipshitz, Nili, and Yoav Waisel
  1980   "Dendroarchaeological Investigations in Israel
            (Taanach)." *Israel Exploration Journal* 30:132–36.

Loewenstamm, S. E.
  1980   "The Trembling of Nature during the Theophany."
            In *Comparative Studies in Biblical and Ancient Ori-
            ental Literatures.* Alter Orient und Altes Testament
            204. Pages 173–89. Neukirchen-Vluyn: Neukirchen.

Loretz, Oswald
1986   *Regenritual and Jahwetag un Joelbuch.* Ugaritisch-
            Biblische Literatur 4. Altenberg: CIS.

Lovin, Robin W., and Frank E. Reynolds
1985   "In the Beginning." In *Cosmogony and Ethical
            Order: New Studies in Comparative Ethics.* Edited
            by R. W. Lovin and F. E. Reynolds. Pages 1–35. Chi-
            cago: University of Chicago Press.

Ludwig, Theodore M.
1973   "The Traditions of the Establishing of the Earth in
            Deutero-Isaiah." *Journal of Biblical Literature*
            92:345–57.

Luyster, Robert
1981   "Wind and Water: Cosmological Symbolism in the
            Old Testament." *Zeitschrift für die alttestamentliche
            Wissenschaft* 93:1–10.

Magonet, Jonathan
1992   "The Themes of Genesis 2–3." In *A Walk in the Gar-
            den: Biblical, Iconographical and Literary Images of
            Eden.* Journal for the Study of the Old Testament
            Supplement Series 136. Edited by P. Morris and
            D. Sawyer. Pages 39–46. Sheffield: JSOT.

Maines, David R.
1987   "The Significance of Temporality for the Develop-
            ment of Sociological Theory." *Sociological Quar-
            terly* 28:303–11.

Malchow, Bruce V.
1987   "Contrasting Views of Nature in the Hebrew Bible."
            Dialog 26:40–43.

Malina, Bruce J.
1986   *Christian Origins and Cultural Anthropology: Practi-
            cal Models for Biblical Interpretation.* Atlanta: John
            Knox.
1989a   "Christ and Time: Swiss or Mediterranean?" *Catho-
            lic Biblical Quarterly* 51:1–31.
1989b   "Dealing with Biblical (Mediterranean) Characters:
            A Guide for U.S. Consumers." *Biblical Theology Bul-
            letin* 19:127–41.

1991   "Reading Theory Perspective: Reading Luke-Acts."
            In *The Social World of Luke-Acts: Models for Inter-*
            pretation. Edited by J. H. Neyrey. Pages 3–23. Pea-
            body, Mass.: Hendrickson.
1993   *The New Testament World: Insights from Cultural*
            Anthropology. Revised Edition. Atlanta: John Knox.

Malina, Bruce J., and Jerome H. Neyrey
1991   "First Century Personality: Dyadic, Not Individualis-
            tic." In *The Social World of Luke-Acts: Models for*
            Interpretation. Edited by J. H. Neyrey. Pages 67–96.
            Peabody, Mass.: Hendrickson.

Mann, Thomas W.
1971   "The Pillar of Cloud in the Reed Sea Narrative."
            Journal of Biblical Literature 90:15–30.

Margalit, Baruch
1981   "The Ugaritic Creation Myth: Fact or Fiction?"
            Ugarit-Forschungen 13:137–45.

May, Herbert G.
1955   "Some Cosmic Connotations of *Mayim Rabbîm,*
            'Many Waters.'" *Journal of Biblical Literature* 74:9–
            21.

McCarthy, Dennis J.
1963   *Treaty and Covenant: A Study in Form in the An-*
            cient Oriental Documents and in the Old Testament.
            Rome: Pontifical Biblical Institute.
1967   "'Creation' Motifs in Ancient Hebrew Poetry." *Catho-*
            lic Biblical Quarterly 29:87–100.

McDonagh, Sean
1986   *To Care for the Earth: A Call to a New Theology.*
            Santa Fe: Bear.

McKibben, William
1989   *The End of Nature.* New York: Random House.

Meyers, Carol
1988   *Discovering Eve: Ancient Israelite Women in Con-*
            text. Oxford: Oxford University Press.

Miller, J. Maxwell
1972 "In the 'Image' and 'Likeness' of God." *Journal of Biblical Literature* 91:289–304.

Miller, Patrick D.
1973 *The Divine Warrior in Early Israel*. Harvard Semitic Monographs 5. Cambridge: Harvard University Press.

Mitchell, Christopher W.
1987 *The Meaning of BRK "To Bless" in the Old Testament*. SBL Dissertation Series 95. Atlanta: Scholars.

Momigliano, Arnaldo
1982 "Time in Ancient Historiography." In *Essays in Ancient and Modern Historiography*. Pages 179–204. Middletown, Conn.: Wesleyan University Press.

Moran, William L.
1970 "The Creation of Man in Atrahasis I 192–248." *Bulletin of the American Schools of Oriental Research* 200:48–56.

Morenz, Siegfried
1973 *Egyptian Religion*. Translated by A. E. Keep. Ithaca, N.Y.: Cornell University Press.

Mowinckel, Sigmund
1922 *Psalmenstudien II: Das Thronbesteigungsfest Jahwäs und der Ursprung der Eschatologie.* Videnskapsselskapets Skrifter II. Hist.-Filos. Klass (1921), 6. Kristiania: Jacob Dybwad.
1958 "Jahves Dag." *Norsk Teologisk Tidsskrift* 59:1–56, 209–29.
[1962]1992 *The Psalms in Israel's Worship*. Translated by D. R. Ap-Thomas. Oxford: Blackwell. Reprint. Sheffield: JSOT.

Muratore, Stephen
1986 "The Earth's End: Eschatology and the Perception of Nature." *Epiphany* 6:40–49.

Murphy, Roland E.
1985 "Wisdom and Creation." *Journal of Biblical Literature* 104:3–11.

1990   *The Tree of Life: An Exploration of Biblical Wisdom Literature*. The Anchor Bible Reference Library. New York: Doubleday.

Naidoff, Bruce D.
1978   "A Man to Work the Soil: A New Interpretation of Genesis 2–3." *Journal for the Study of the Old Testament* 5:2–14.

Nash, James A.
1991   *Loving Nature: Ecological Integrity and Christian Responsibility*. Nashville: Abingdon.

Naville, Edouard
1896   *The Temple of Deir El Bahari*. London: Egypt Exploration Fund.

Niditch, Susan
1985   *Chaos to Cosmos: Studies in Biblical Patterns of Creation*. Studies in the Humanities 6. Chico, Calif.: Scholars.

Niebuhr, H. Richard
1951   *Christ and Culture*. New York: Harper & Row.

Niles, D. Preman
1978   "Old Testament: Man and Nature." In *The Human and the Holy: Asian Perspectives in Christian Theology*. Edited by E. P. Nacpil and D. J. Elwood. Pages 71–81. Maryknoll, N.Y.: Orbis.

Oden, Robert A.
1981   "Divine aspirations in Atrahasis and in Genesis 1–11." *Zeitschrift für Alttestamentliche Wissenschaft* 93:197–216.
1987   *The Bible Without Theology: The Theological Tradition and Alternatives to It*. San Francisco: Harper & Row.

O'Flaherty, Wendy Doniger
1988   *Other People's Myths*. New York: Macmillan.

Ollenburger, Ben C.
1987   "Isaiah's Creation Theology." *Ex Auditu* 3:54–71.

Otto, Rudolf
   [1917]1950   *The Idea of the Holy: An Inquiry into the Non-Ratio-
                 nal Factor in the Idea of the Divine and Its Relation
                 to the Rational.* Translated by John W. Harvey. Lon-
                 don: Oxford University Press.

Parker, Simon B.
   1989   *The Pre-Biblical Narrative Tradition: Essays on the
                 Ugaritic Poems Keret and Aqhat.* Resources for Bibli-
                 cal Studies 24. Atlanta: Scholars.

Pedersen, J.
   1926   *Israel: Its Life and Culture I–II.* London: Oxford Uni-
                 versity Press.

Pennington, Nancy, and Reid Hastie
   1991   "A Cognitive Theory of Juror Decision Making: The
                 Story Model." *Cardozo Law Review* 13:519–57.

Petersen, David L.
   1976   "The Yahwist on the Flood." *Vetus Testamentum*
                 26:438–46.

Petersen, David L., and Mark Woodward
   1977   "Northwest Semitic Religion: A Study in Relational
                 Structures." *Ugarit-Forschungen* 9:233–48.

Pettazzoni, Raffaele
   1967   "Myths of Beginnings and Creation-Myths." In *Es-
                 says on the History of Religions.* Pages 24–36.
                 Leiden: E. J. Brill.

Pope, Marvin H.
   1955   *El in the Ugaritic Texts.* Supplements to Vetus Testa-
                 mentum 2. Leiden: E. J. Brill.

Pritchard, James B., ed.
   1969   *Ancient Near Eastern Texts Relating to the Old Tes-
                 tament.* Third Edition with Supplement. Princeton:
                 Princeton University Press.

Propp, William H.
   1987   *Water in the Wilderness: A Biblical Motif and Its
                 Mythological Background.* Harvard Semitic Mono-
                 graphs 40. Atlanta: Scholars.

1990 "Eden Sketches." In *The Hebrew Bible and Its Interpreters*. Edited by W. H. Propp, et al. Pages 189–203. Winona Lake, Ind.: Eisenbrauns.

Quinn, Naomi
1991 "The Cultural Basis of Metaphor." In *Beyond Metaphor: The Theory of Tropes in Anthropology*. Edited by J. W. Fernandez. Pages 56–93. Stanford: Stanford University Press.

Rad, Gerhard von
1959 "The Origin of the Concept of the Day of Yahweh." *Journal of Semitic Studies* 4:97–108.
1972a *Genesis*. Translated by J. H. Marks. Revised Edition. Old Testament Library. Philadelphia: Westminster.
1972b *Wisdom in Israel*. Translated by J. D. Marton. Nashville: Abingdon.
[1955]1984 "Job XXXVIII and Ancient Egyptian Wisdom." In *The Problem of the Hexateuch and Other Essays*. Pages 281–91. London: SCM.
[1964]1984 "Some Aspects of the Old Testament World-View." In *The Problem of the Hexateuch and Other Essays*. Pages 144–65. London: SCM.
[1936]1984 "The Theological Problem of the Old Testament Doctrine of Creation." In *The Problem of the Hexateuch and Other Essays*. Pages 131–43. London: SCM.

Ramsey, George W.
1988 "Is Name-Giving an Act of Domination in Genesis 2:23 and Elsewhere?" *Catholic Biblical Quarterly* 50:24–35.

Rayner, Steve
1982 "The Perception of Time and Space in Egalitarian Sects: A Millenarian Cosmology." In *Essays in the Sociology of Perception*. Edited by M. Douglas. Pages 247–74. London: Routledge & Kegan Paul.

Redfield, Robert
1953 *The Primitive World and Its Transformations*. Ithaca: Cornell University Press.

Reimer, David J.
1989 "The 'Foe' and the 'North' in Jeremiah." *Zeitschrift für die alttestamentlich Wissenschaft* 101:223–32.

Rendtorff, Rolf
1993   "The Paradigm is Changing: Hopes—and Fears." *Bib-lical Interpretation* 1:34–53.

Ringgren, Helmer
1966   *Israelite Religion*. Philadelphia: Fortress.

Roberts, J. J. M.
1976   "Myth *Versus* History." *Catholic Biblical Quarterly* 38:1–13.

Robinson, H. Wheeler
1936   "The Hebrew Conception of Corporate Personality." In *Werden und Wesen des Alten Testaments*. Beiheft zur Zeitschrift für die alttestamentliche Wissenschaft 66. Edited by P. Voltz, et al. Pages 49–62. Berlin: A. Töpelmann.
1946   *Inspiration and Revelation in the Old Testament*. Oxford: Clarendon.

Rogerson, John W.
1974   *Myth in Old Testament Interpretation*. Beiheft zur Zeitschrift für die alttestamentliche Wissenschaft 134. Berlin: Walter de Gruyter.
1977   "The Old Testament View of Nature: Some Prelimi-nary Questions." In *Instruction and Interpretation*. Oudtestamentische Studiën 20. Edited by A. S. van der Woude. Pages 67–84. Leiden: E. J. Brill.
1984   "Slippery Words: Myth." In *Sacred Narrative: Read-ings in the Theory of Myth*. Edited by A. Dundes. Pages 62–71. Berkeley: University of California Press.

Rolston, Holmes
1981   "Values in Nature." *Environmental Ethics* 3:113–28.

Rust, E. C.
1953   "Time and Eternity in Biblical Thought." *Theology Today* 10:327–56.

Sahlins, Marshall D.
1964   "Culture and Environment: The Study of Cultural Ecology." In *Horizons of Anthropology*. Edited by S. Tax. Pages 132–47. Chicago: Aldine.

Santmire, H. Paul
1985   The Travail of Nature: The Ambiguous Ecological
        Promise of Christian Theology. Philadelphia: Fortress.

Sasson, Jack M.
1985   "weִlōʾ yitbōāû (Gen 2.25) and Its Implications."
        Biblica 66:418–21.

Sauneron, Serge, and Jean Yoyotte
1959   "La naissance du monde selon l'Égypte ancienne."
        In La Naissance du Monde. Sources Orientales 1.
        Pages 17–91. Paris: Seuil.

Schmid, Hans H.
1968   Gerechtigkeit als Weltordnung: Hintergrund und
        Geschichte des Alttestamentlichen
        Gerechtigkeitsbegriffes. Beiträge zur Historischen
        Theologie 40. Tübingen: J. C. B. Mohr [Paul Siebeck].
1984   "Creation, Righteousness, and Salvation: 'Creation
        Theology' as the Broad Horizon of Biblical Theol-
        ogy." In Creation in the Old Testament. Issues in Re-
        ligion and Theology 6. Edited by B. W. Anderson.
        Pages 102–17. Philadelphia: Fortress.

Schmitt, John J.
1989   "The Wife of God in Hosea 2." Biblical Research
        34:5–18.
1991   "Israel and Zion—Two Gendered Images: Biblical
        Speech Traditions and their Contemporary Neglect."
        Horizons 18:18–32.

Schwartz, Shalom H.
1990   "Individualism-Collectivism: Critique and Propose
        Refinements." Journal of Cross-Cultural Psychology
        21:139–57.

Schwarz, Hans
1974   "The Eschatological Dimension of Ecology." Zygon
        9:323–38.

Scullion, John J.
1971   "Ṣedeq - Ṣedaqah in Isaiah cc. 40–66." Ugarit-
        Forschungen 3:335–48.
1974   "New Thinking on Creation and Sin in Genesis I–
        XI." Australian Biblical Review 22:1–10.

Sessions, George S.
1974   "Anthropocentrism and the Environmental Crisis."
            Humboldt Journal of Social Relations 2:71–81.

Simkins, Ronald A.
1991   *Yahweh's Activity in History and Nature in the
            Book of Joel*. Ancient Near Eastern Texts and Stud-
            ies 10. Lewiston, N.Y.: Edwin Mellen.
1993   "God, History, and the Natural World in the Book of
            Joel." *Catholic Biblical Quarterly* 55:435–52.

Smith, Jonathan Z.
1993   *Map is not Territory: Studies in the History of Reli-
            gion*. Chicago: University of Chicago Press.

Snaith, Norman H.
1965   "The Sea of Reeds: The Red Sea." *Vetus Testamen-
            tum* 15:395–98.

Soggin, J. Alberto
1975   *Old Testament and Oriental Studies*. Biblica et Ori-
            entalia 29. Rome: Biblical Institute.

Speiser, Ephraim A.
1955   "'ed in the Story of Creation." *Bulletin of the Ameri-
            can Schools of Oriental Research* 140:9–11.
1982   *Genesis*. The Anchor Bible 1. Third Edition. Garden
            City: Doubleday.

Sproul, Barbara C.
1979   *Primal Myths: Creating the World*. San Francisco:
            Harper & Row.

Stager, Lawrence E.
1985   "The Archaeology of the Family in Ancient Israel."
            *Bulletin of the American Schools of Oriental Re-
            search* 260:1–35.

Steward, Julian H.
1955   *Theory of Cultural Change: The Methodology of Multi-
            linear Evolution*. Urbana: University of Illinois Press.

Stuhlmueller, Carroll
1959   "The Theology of Creation in Second Isaiah." *Catho-
            lic Biblical Quarterly* 21:429–67.

Talmon, Shemaryahu
1966   "The 'Desert Motif' in the Bible and in Qumran Lit-
            erature." In *Biblical Motifs: Origins and Transforma-
            tions*. Edited by A. Altmann. Pages 31–63.
            Cambridge: Harvard University Press.

Thompson, John A.
1980   *The Book of Jeremiah*. The New International Com-
            mentary on the Old Testament. Grand Rapids:
            Eerdmans.

Tigay, Jeffrey H.
1984   "The Image of God and the Flood: Some New Devel-
            opments." In *Studies in Jewish Education and Juda-
            ica in Honor of Louis Newman*. Edited by A. M.
            Shapiro and B. I. Cohen. Pages 169–82. New York:
            KTAV.

Tillich, Paul
1957   *Dynamics of Faith*. New York: Harper & Row.

Triandis, Harry C.
1990   "Cross-Cultural Studies of Individualism and Collec-
            tivism." In *Cross-Cultural Perspectives*. Nebraska
            Symposium on Motivation, 1989. Edited by J. J. Ber-
            man. Pages 41–133. Lincoln: University of Nebraska
            Press.

Triandis, Harry C. et al.
1993   "An Etic-Emic Analysis of Individualism and Collec-
            tivism." *Journal of Cross-Cultural Psychology*
            24:336–83.

Trible, Phyllis
1971   "Ancient Priests and Modern Polluters." *Andover
            Newton Quarterly* 12:74–79.
1978   *God and the Rhetoric of Sexuality*. Overtures to Bib-
            lical Theology. Philadelphia: Fortress.

Tsumura, David T.
1989   *The Earth and the Waters in Genesis 1 and 2: A Lin-
            guistic Investigation*. Journal for the Study of the
            Old Testament Supplement Series 83. Sheffield: JSOT.

Tuan, Yi-Fu
 1970   "Our Treatment of the Environment in Ideal and Ac-
               tuality." *American Scientist* 58:244–49.

Turner, Laurence A.
 1993   "The Rainbow as the Sign of the Covenant in Gene-
               sis IX 11–13." *Vetus Testamentum* 43:119–24.

Turner, Victor
 1969   *The Ritual Process: Structure and Anti-Structure.*
               Ithaca: Cornell University Press.

Van Gennep, Arnold
 [1909]1960   *The Rites of Passage.* Translated by M. B. Vizedom
               and G. L. Caffee. Chicago: University of Chicago
               Press.

Van Seters, John
 1989   "The Creation of Man and the Creation of the King."
               Zeitschrift für die alttestamentliche Wissenschaft
               101:333–42.
 1992   *Prologue to History: The Yahwist as Historian in
               Genesis.* Louisville: Westminster/John Knox.

Verheij, Arian
 1991   "Paradise Retried: On Qohelet 2.4–6." *Journal for
               the Study of the Old Testament* 50:113–15.

Wallace, Howard N.
 1985   *The Eden Narrative.* Harvard Semitic Monographs
               32. Atlanta: Scholars.
 1988   "Genesis 2.1–3: Creation and Sabbath." *Pacifica*
               1:235–50.

Watts, John D. W.
 1985   *Isaiah 1–33.* Word Biblical Commentary 24. Waco:
               Word.

Wehemeier, Gerhard
 1970   "Deliverance and Blessing in the Old and New Testa-
               ment." *Indian Journal of Theology* 20:30–42.

Weiser, Artur
 1950   "Zur Frage nach den Beziehungen der Psalmen zum
               Kult: Die Darstellung der Theophanie in dem Psal-

men und im Festkult." In *Festschrift Alfred Bertho-let zum 80. Geburtstag.* Edited by W. Baumgartner, et al. Pages 513–31. Tübingen: J. C. B. Mohr [Paul Siebeck].

Weiss, M.
1966   "The Origin of the 'Day of the Lord' Reconsidered." *Hebrew Union College Annual* 37:29–72.

Wellhausen, Julius
[1883]1983 *Prolegomena to the History of Ancient Israel.* Re-print. Gloucester, Mass.: Peter Smith.

Wenham, Gordon J.
1987   *Genesis 1–15.* Word Biblical Commentary 1. Waco: Word.

Westermann, Claus
1965   *The Praise of God in the Psalms.* Translated by K. Crim. Richmond: John Knox.
1971   "Creation and History in the Old Testament." In *The Gospel and Human Destiny.* Edited by V. Vajta. Pages 11–38. Minneapolis: Augsburg.
1972   *Beginning and End in the Bible.* Biblical Series 31. Philadelphia: Fortress.
1978   *Blessing in the Bible and the Life of the Church.* Overtures to Biblical Theology. Translated by K. Crim. Philadelphia: Fortress.
1984   *Genesis 1–11.* Translated by J. J. Scullion. Minneapo-lis: Augsburg.

White, Lynn
1967   "The Historical Roots of Our Ecologic Crisis." *Science* 155:1203–7.

Wilch, John R.
1969   *Time and Event.* Leiden: E. J. Brill.

Williamson, H. G. M.
1985   "The Old Testament and the Material World." *Evangelical Quarterly* 57:5–22.

Wolff, Hans Walter
1974a   *Anthropology of the Old Testament.* Translated by M. Kohl. Philadelphia: Fortress.

1974b   *Hosea.* Hermeneia. Translated by G. Stansell. Phila-
          delphia: Fortress.
1977   *Joel and Amos.* Hermeneia. Translated by W. Janzen,
          et al. Philadelphia: Fortress.

Wright, G. Ernest
1952   *God Who Acts.* London: SCM.
1957   *The Old Testament Against Its Environment.* Lon-
          don: SCM.

Wyatt, N.
1981   "Interpreting the Creation and Fall Story in Genesis
          2–3." *Zeitschrift für alttestamentliche Wissenschaft*
          93:10–21.
1985   "Killing and Cosmogony in Canaanite and Biblical
          Thought." *Ugarit-Forschungen* 17:375–81.
1987a   "Sea and Desert: Symbolic Geography in West Se-
          mitic Religious Thought." *Ugarit-Forschungen*
          19:375–89.
1987b   "Who Killed the Dragon?" *Aula Orientalis* 5:185–98.

Yee, Gale A.
1992   "The Theology of Creation in Proverbs 8:22–31." In
          Creation in the Biblical Traditions. The Catholic Bib-
          lical Quarterly Monograph Series 24. Edited by R. J.
          Clifford and J. J. Collins. Pages 85–96. Washington,
          D.C.: The Catholic Biblical Association of America.

Zimmerli, Walther
1983   *Ezekiel.* 2 Vols. Hermeneia. Edited by F. M. Cross.
          Translated by R. E. Clements. Philadelphia: Fortress.

Zohary, Michael
1982   *Plants of the Bible.* Cambridge: Cambridge Univer-
          sity Press.

INDEX OF MODERN
AUTHORS

Aharoni, Yohanan, 13
Albrecht, Don, 39
Albrektson, Bertil, 88
Albright, William Foxwell, 90,
    178
Allen, James P., 66–67, 68
Amit, Yairah, 185
Andersen, Francis I., 178, 216,
    218
Anderson, Bernhard W., 3, 6,
    10, 85–86, 90, 110, 195, 196,
    203

Baker, J. A., 3
Baltzer, Klaus, 152
Baly, Denis, 13, 154
Barbour, Ian G., 16, 42, 44
Barr, James, 3, 6, 144, 145, 174,
    182, 185, 200, 201
Barré, Lloyd M., 203
Batto, Bernard F., 114, 135, 136,
    178, 198, 219, 236
Beckman, Gary M., 62
Ben-Yoseph, Jacob, 13
Benjamin, Don C., 179
Bennett, John W., 3, 19–21, 265
Bergant, Dianne, 3, 198
Berquist, Jon L., 224
Bird, Phyllis A., 198–99, 200
Bjerke, Svein, 18
Blaikie, Norman W. H., 38

Blenkinsopp, Joseph, 198
Boissevain, Jeremy, 176
Boman, Thorlief, 174
Bourdieu, Pierre, 176
Brueggemann, Walter, 181
Bultena, Gordon, 39

Carmichael, Calum M., 185
Carney, Thomas F., 16, 17, 117
Carroll, Michael P., 202
Catton, William R., 38
Childs, Brevard S., 8, 232, 245
Clifford, Richard J., 48, 53, 75,
    107, 140
Černy, L., 174
Cohn, Robert L., 136
Collins, John J., 48
Coogan, Michael D., 73–74
Coote, Robert B., 3, 89, 181,
    184, 188, 190, 196, 197
Cornelius, Izak, 215
Cox, Harvey, 7–8
Crenshaw, James L., 161, 163
Cross, Frank M., 72, 87, 90, 108,
    110, 127, 129, 139, 145, 147,
    148, 164, 213, 249

Dalley, Stephanie, 50–52, 54,
    61–63, 188
Davies, Douglas, 133
Day, John, 109

DeGuglielmo, Antonine, 237
Delaney, Carol, 76
De Moor, Johannes C., 72, 80
Dequeker, L., 153, 155, 201
De Roche, Michael, 216, 219,
    227, 228
Derr, Thomas S., 5
DeVries, Simon J., 174
Douglas, Mary, 202
Drori, Israel, 13
Drumbell, W. J., 3
Dubos, René, 6, 264
Dunlap, Riley E., 38

Eichrodt, Walther, 83–84, 194
Eilberg-Schwartz, Howard, 3,
    76, 188, 202
Eissfeldt, Otto, 232
Eliade, Mircea, 132, 140, 197,
    203, 209
Ellen, Roy, 18–19
Everson, A. J., 212

Faulkner, Raymond O., 66
Fensham, F. C., 212, 219
Ferré, Frederick, 44
Fishbane, Michael, 233
Fisher, Loren R., 72
Frankfort, Henri, 39, 165
Freedman, David N., 216, 218
Fretheim, Terrence E., 109, 110,
    127, 129, 130–31, 144–45,
    150, 151
Freudenberger, C. Dean, 258
Frick, Frank S., 3
Friedman, Richard E., 152
Frymer-Kensky, Tikva, 52, 99,
    202, 203, 209, 263

Geertz, Clifford, 28
Geller, Jack M., 39
Gnuse, Robert, 88, 89
Gordis, Robert, 163
Gordon, Cyrus H., 71, 179
Gore, Albert, 258
Gottwald, Norman K., 221
Gowan, Donald E., 226, 237
Grønbæk, Jakob H., 72
Gulick, Walter B., 257
Gunkel, Hermann, 53, 83

Haldar, Alfred, 134
Hall, Edward T., 41
Halpern, Baruch, 165
Hanson, Paul D., 108, 211
Harner, Philip B., 90
Harrelson, Walter, 115
Hasel, Gerhard F., 178
Hastie, Reid, 46
Heidel, Alexander, 53, 64
Hiebert, Theodore, 109, 129–31,
    147, 151–52
Hiers, Richard H., 6, 183
Hillers, Delbert, 87, 90, 152
Hobbs, T. Raymond, 34, 35
Hoffmann, Y., 212
Hoffmeier, James K., 179
Hoiberg, Eric, 39
Holladay, William L., 231, 232
Holter, Knut, 178
Honeyman, Alexander M., 187
Honko, Lauri, 45
Hopkins, David C., 3, 13, 25, 39
Horowitz, Aharon, 13
Hughes, J. Donald, 3, 6
Hultkrantz, Åke, 18
Hutter, Manfred, 181
Hutton, Rodney R., 182, 184, 185
Hyatt, J. Philip, 232

Jacobsen, Thorkild, 44, 49, 53,
    54, 55–59, 87–88
Jenson, Philip Peter, 133
Jeremias, Jörg, 129
Johnson, Mark, 44
Joines, Karen R., 186
Jones, James M., 175

Kaiser, Otto, 223, 226
Kákosy, L., 68
Kapelrud, Arvid S., 72, 164, 178
Kaufman, Gordon D., 5–6
Kaufmann, Yehezkel, 8, 84–85
Kay, Jeanne, 39, 250, 262, 264
Kearney, Michael, 24, 27–31, 122
Kikawada, Isaac M., 61
Klimkeit, Hans J., 133
Kluckhohn, Florence R., 31–33,
    35, 174
Knierim, Rolf, 151
Knight, Douglas A., 53, 160

Koch, Klaus, 3, 141, 160, 220, 224
Komoróczy, G., 54
Kramer, Samuel N., 49
Kuntz, J. Kenneth, 129

LaBar, Martin, 261
Lakoff, George, 44
Lambert, Wilfred G., 54, 62
Lasley, Paul, 39
Leach, Edmund, 133
Leeuw, Gerardus van der, 173
Lesko, Leonard H., 65, 66
Levenson, Jon D., 72, 109, 113,
    141, 152, 158, 166, 197, 198,
    219, 224, 238, 244
Lichtheim, Miriam, 67–71
Lipshitz, Nili, 13
Loewenstamm, S. E., 148
Loretz, Oswald, 212
Lovin, Robin W., 47
Ludwig, Theodore M., 90
Luyster, Robert, 145

Magonet, Jonathan, 183
Maines, David R., 173–74
Malchow, Bruce V., 3
Malina, Bruce J., 28, 31, 34, 42,
    46, 174, 175, 176
Mann, Thomas W., 145
Margalit, Baruch, 72
May, Herbert G., 116
McCarthy, Dennis J., 86, 152
McDonagh, Sean, 258
McKibben, William, 258
Meyers, Carol, 3, 178, 183, 184,
    185, 189, 190
Millard, A. R., 62
Miller, J. Maxwell, 200
Miller, Patrick D., 72
Mitchell, Christopher W., 155
Momigliano, Arnaldo, 174
Moran, William L., 61
Morenz, Siegfried, 66, 67, 69, 71
Mowinckel, Sigmund, 129, 212
Muratore, Stephen, 265
Murphy, Roland E., 144, 151

Naidoff, Bruce D., 188
Nash, James A., 7, 258, 259, 260
Naville, Edouard, 71

Neyrey, Jerome H., 28
Niditch, Susan, 185
Niebuhr, H. Richard, 118
Niles, D. Preman, 264
Nowak, Peter, 39

O'Flaherty, Wendy Doniger, 45
Oden, Robert A., 8, 45, 187,
    188, 191
Ollenburger, Ben C., 239
Ord, David R., 3, 181, 184, 188,
    190, 196, 197
Otto, Rudolf, 134

Parker, Simon B., 87
Pedersen, J., 134, 174
Pennington, Nancy, 46
Petersen, David L., 75, 153–54
Pettazzoni, Raffaele, 173
Pope, Marvin H., 72
Pritchard, James B., 52, 55, 157,
    159, 167
Propp, William H., 136, 189

Quinn, Naomi, 43, 44–45

Rad, Gerhard von, 7–12, 89–90,
    115, 183, 194, 200, 212
Ramsey, George W., 183
Rayner, Steve, 176
Redfield, Robert, 27
Reimer, David J., 232
Rendtorff, Rolf, 17
Reynolds, Frank E., 47
Ringgren, Helmer, 122
Roberts, J. J. M., 88
Robinson, H. Wheeler, 12, 28
Rogerson, John W., 13, 45
Rolston, Holmes, 261
Rust, E. C., 174

Sahlins, Marshall D., 18
Santmire, H. Paul, 8, 260
Sasson, Jack M., 184
Sauneron, Serge, 70
Schmid, Hans H., 166–67, 223
Schmitt, John J., 218
Schwartz, Shalom H., 28
Schwarz, Hans, 265
Scullion, John J., 167, 184

Sessions, George S., 6
Simkins, Ronald A., 8, 122,
    138, 213, 247, 248
Smith, Jonathan Z., 134
Snaith, Norman H., 136
Soggin, J. Alberto, 178
Speiser, Ephraim A., 178, 194
Sproul, Barbara C., 47
Steward, Julian H., 18–19
Strodtbeck, Fred L., 31–33, 35,
    174
Stuhlmueller, Carroll, 115

Talmon, Shemaryahu, 134, 224
Thompson, John A., 230
Tigay, Jeffrey H., 200, 205
Tillich, Paul, 43
Triandis, Harry C., 28, 29
Trible, Phyllis, 3, 6, 97, 183, 199
Tsumura, David T., 178, 195
Tuan, Yi-Fu, 264
Turner, Laurence A., 155
Turner, Victor, 136, 185

Van Gennep, Arnold, 188
Van Seters, John, 182
Verheij, Arian, 39

Waisel, Yoav, 13
Wallace, Howard N., 186, 198
Watts, John D. W., 222
Wehemeier, Gerhard, 155
Weiser, Artur, 129
Weiss, M., 212
Wellhausen, Julius, 187
Wenham, Gordon J., 179, 183,
    204
Westermann, Claus, 48, 78, 127,
    129, 155, 173, 178, 179, 183,
    186, 195
White, Lynn, 4–8, 10, 183
Wilch, John R., 174
Williamson, H. G. M., 3
Wolff, Hans Walter, 179, 199,
    214, 216
Woodward, Mark, 75
Wright, G. Ernest, 8, 123–24
Wyatt, N., 72, 133, 135, 136,
    177, 181

Yee, Gale A., 144
Yoyotte, Jean, 70

Zimmerli, Walther, 238
Zohary, Michael, 104

INDEX OF SCRIPTURE REFERENCES

Genesis
1:1 11
1:1–2 194
1:1–2:3 10, 77–78, 80, 83, 194–202
1:3–5 197
1:6–8 196
1:9–10 196
1:11 80, 200
1:14–19 196
1:16 196
1:20 80
1:21 80
1:22 155, 200
1:24 80
1:25 80
1:26 141
1:26–27 130
1:26–28 199–201
1:28 155
2:1–3 197
2:4b–24 178–84
2:5 178, 190
2:6 178
2:7 179, 181
2:9 180, 182
2:10–14 178
2:17 182
2:18 182
2:19–20 183

2:21–22 183
2:24 184
2:25 184
2:25–3:24 179
3 184–91
3:1 186
3:1–5 186
3:5 186
3:6 186
3:7 186
3:14 189
3:15 189
3:16 189, 190
3:17–18 190
3:19 180, 190
3:20 189
3:21 191
3:22 141, 182
3:22–24 191
4:1 187
4:7 184
4:8 192
4:17 187, 192
4:21 192
4:22 192
4:23 192
4:25 187
5 155
5:3 200
6–9 202–5

6:1–4 192
6:5 192
6:5–7 153
6:6–7 192
6:8 192
6:9 204
6:11–12 203
7:4 180
7:11 203
8:13 203
8:20–22 152–54
8:21 154
8:22 192
9:1 155, 204
9:2–3 204
9:6 204
9:8–16 154–55
9:8–17 152
9:20 192
10–11 155
10:2 245
12:1–3 163
15:5–6 164
15:18–21 164
18 144
20:18 91
21:2 91–92
22:1–18 177
25:21 91–92
28:10–17 144

29:31–35 91
30:2 91
30:22 91
32:22–32 144

Exodus
1–15 158
3:1–5 131
3:2 145
13:11–16 177
14:11 136
15:1–18 109–12
15:3–5 110
15:4 135
15:8–10 111
15:12 111
15:13 111, 136
15:14–16 112
15:17 136
15:17–18 111
19 129
19:1–Num 10:28 158
19:18 145
20:2 242
24:9–11 145
31:12–17 198
34 129

Leviticus
11 202
18:22–23 202
20:13, 15 202

Numbers
11:11–12 98

Deuteronomy 9
11:13–17 160
20:16–18 34
24:1–4 230
30:19 159
32:18 98

Judges
5 129
11:12–28 34

1 Samuel
1 91
2:6–8 181

2 Samuel
7:11b–16 164

1 Kings
16:2 181
22:19–23 141

Job 161–63
1:6–12 141
2:1–6 141
9:22–24 135
10:8–11 93
10:18–19 94
38–42 94
38:4–7 162
38:8–11 77
41:1–4 162
42:2–3 94

Psalms
1:3 100
2 142
2:7–8 165
8 9, 90, 221
8:5–8 201
18:7–15 145–46
19 9
19:1–6 90
22 106
22:1 97
22:9–11 97
24:1 11
33 9
33:4–7 224
33:6–9 90
36:8–9 238
46 142–43
46:1–3 142
46:4 238
46:4–7 143
47 165
48 142
48:2 232
50 142
65 155–56
65:5–8 156
65:9–13 156
72 167
74 9, 112–14
74:1–2 113

74:10–11 113
74:12–17 77, 113
74:13–14 83
74:22–23 114
76 142
76:1–2 140
77 115–17
77:7–9 115–16
77:14–15 116
77:16–20 116
82 141
87:1–3 140
89 9, 166
89:3–4 166
89:9–10 83
89:9–11 166
89:9–14 224
89:22–25 166
90:5–6 100
93 165
93:1–4 165
95 165
96 165
97 165
98 165
99 165
103:15–16 100
104 9, 90
104:7 77
113:7 181
136 9
136:4–9 90
139 99
139:2–3 94
139:13–15 79, 94–95
148 9
148:5–6 150
148:13 150

Isaiah 220–27
1–39 223
2:6 222
2:7 222
2:8 222
2:12–17 222
5:1–2 102
5:5–6 102, 104
6:1–5 141
6:1–13 221

6:8 141
6:11–12 222
8:6 238
10:5–6 227
10:33–34 225
10:33–11:9 223,
  224–27
11:1–5 225
11:6–9 225
11:8 225
14:12–15 139
14:19 140
24–27 243–44
24:4–6 243–44
25:7 244
25:8 244
26:1–15 244
27:1 244
27:2–3 104
27:6 104
29:15–16 95
32:9–20 223–24
32:15–18 224
33:14 223
33:20–22 143
34 246
34–35 148–50, 238
34:2–3 246
34:4 148, 246
34:9 246
34:11–15 246
35:1–2 149
35:5–7 149
35:8 241
35:10 150, 242
40–55 9, 238–43
40:2 239
40:4 241
40:6–8 100
40:21–23 239
41:18–19 242
42:13–16 106–9
43:5–7 137
43:16–21 241
44:2–4 105
45:1 239
45:1–7 96
45:5–7 135
45:8 103
45:9–12 96

45:12–13 239–40
45:13 97
46:3–4 99
49:1 92
49:5 92
49:15 98
51:3 240
51:9–10 83
51:9–11 114–15, 241
51:12–13 115
54:7–8 243
54:9–10 242
55:13 243
66:7–9 105–6
66:13 106

Jeremiah 229–34
1:5 92
2:33–37 230
3:1–3 230
3:3 231
4:19 233
4:23–26 233
9:10–11 231
9:12–14 231
11:16–17 101, 104
12:4 231
14:1 231
17:6 101
17:8 100–101
18:3–6 95–96
18:11b 96
20:13–18 92
20:14–18 92
23:10 231
31:27–28 104
31:31–34 233–34
32:41 104
50–51 232

Ezekiel 235–38
1–3 235
5:5 137
28:12–19 181–82
34:25–29 235
36:8–11 237
36:26–28 234
36:35 236
38–39 244–45, 246
38:1–16 244

38:17 245
38:18–22 245
39:9–16 245
39:17–20 245
39:21–29 245
47 144
47:1–6 237
47:7–10 237–38
47:12 237–38

Hosea 9, 215–20
1–3 218–20
2:1–13 218
2:14–15 218
2:16 218, 220
2:18 219
2:19–20 218
2:21–23 219, 220
3:1–5 231
3:4–5 220
4:1–3 216
4:10 216
5:9 216
6:3 217
8:7 217
8:14 216
9:3 216
9:11–12 216
9:14 216
10:10 216
10:12 217
10:13 217
10:14–15 216
11:1–2 137
11:5 137
11:8–9 218
14:5–7 104–5
14:6–7 217

Joel 247–48
2:3 138, 248
2:6–9 247
2:10 248
2:12–17 248
2:20 248
2:21–24 248
3:1–8 248
3:9–12 248
3:15–16 248
3:17 248

3:18 143–44, 248
3:19 248

Amos 211–15
1:2 214
1:3–2:3 213
2:6–8 212
5:8–9 214
5:18–20 212
8:4–6 212
8:8–10 213–14
9:13–15 214–15
9:5–6 214
9:15 103

Obadiah
1–14 246

15–16 246
17–21 246

Micah
6:1–2 159

Zephaniah 227–29
1:2–3 227–28
2:3 228
2:4–10 228
3:1 228
3:11–13 229

Zechariah
14:2 246
14:3–5 246

14:6 246
14:7 246
14:8 144, 247
14:9 247

2 Maccabees
7:28 178

Romans
5 184

1 Corinthians
15 184

1 Timothy
2 184